HAND BOOK OF ESSENTIAL OILS MANUFACTURING & AROMATIC PLANTS

With Directory of Plant & Machinery Suppliers, International Importers & Exporters and Manufacturers & Exporters of Essential Oils & Aromatic Chemicals

HAND BOOK OF
ESSENTIAL OILS MANUFACTURING & AROMATIC PLANTS

With Directory of Plant & Machinery Suppliers, International Importers & Exporters and Manufacturers & Exporters of Essential Oils & Aromatic Chetnicals

A Complete Hand Book on Essential Oils Mfgs. and Aromatic Plants is a goldmine for new as well as well established entrepreneurs and industrialists. The book covers the invaluable details to produce Essential Oils, Cultivation and ProcessinglExtraction and Aromatic Plants. The book covers machinery suppliers. Project Profiles with profitability have also been included to benefit the new entrants.

Written By
EIRI BOARD OF CONSULTANTS & ENGINEERS

Compiled By
Sudhir Gupta

ENGINEERS INDIA RESEARCH INSTITUTE
4449, Nai Sarak, Main Road, Delhi-110006 (India)
Ph./Fax : 91-011-23918117, 23916431, 23840361
E-Mail : erisidi@bol.net.in Website : www.eiriindia.org

Sole Distributor :
Also : 4/54, Roop Nagar, Opp. Shiv Mandir, Delhi-110007

PRINTED & PUBLISHED BY

ENGINEERS INDIA RESEARCH INSTITUTE

4449, Nai Sarak, Main Road, Delhi-110006 (India)
Ph./Fax : 91-011-23918117, 23916431, 23840361
E-Mail : erisidi@bol.net.in Website : www.eiriindia.org

DISTRIBUTED BY

SMALL INDUSTRY RESEARCH INSTITUTE

New Delhi (INDIA)

ISBN : 81-86732-27-6

Printed in New Delhi (INDIA)

Cost : Rs. 650/–

Printed & Published by Sudhir Gupta for "Engineers India Research Institute", and Laser Type Set by Ismail at Engineers India Research Institute, Nai Sarak, New Delhi and Printed at Archana Printers, East Ram Nagar, Shahadara, Delhi-110032, Phone : 011-22135900, Mobile : 9811357243

Preface

The book named Hand Book of Essential Oils Manufacturing and Aromatic Plants covers latest methods and formulaes to produce various type of Essential Oils and Aromatic Plants. The major chapters of the book are TRENDS IN TRADE OF ESSENTIAL OILS, DAMASK ROSE CULTIVATION AND PROCESSING, ROSE OIL DISTILLATION METHOD, CHEMISTRY OF ROSE OIL, CULTIVATION OF MATRICARIA CHAMOMILLA, CULTIVATION OF DAVANA FOR ESSENTIAL OIL, CULTIVATION AND IMPROVEMENT OF SWEET MARJORAM, EXTRACTION OF ESSENTIAL OILS, ESSENTIAL CHEMICAL CONSTITUENTS PROFILE IN TREE SPICE, FOLK MEDICINAL USES OF INDIGENOUS AROMATIC PLANTS, ESSENTIAL OIL BEARING PLANTS STATUS, PROMISING AROMATIC PLANTS OF INDUSTRIAL VALUE, ESSENTIAL OIL INDUSTRY WASTE UTILIZATION, FRACTIONATION OF ESSENTIAL OIL IN PERFUMERY & TEUPENTINE INDUSTRY, TAGETES MINUTA, ESSENTIAL OIL OF HYPTIS SUAVEOLENS POIT, SUPER CRITICAL FLUID EXTRACTION TECHNOLOGY FOR SPICE EXTRACTION, CITRONELLA OIL, CLOVE OIL, EUCALYPTUS OIL, GINGER OIL, JASMINE ROSE & LILY OIL, JASMINE FLOWER OIL ETC.

The basic object of this book is to furnish a comprehensive treatment on the formulations and processing of diversified Essential Oils and Aromatic Plants. A wide range of process details have been dealt with most obstensibly with special emphasis on the techno-economic and functional aspects of the ingredients. The book covers various Project Profiles on lucrative items. At the end of the book, new addresses of Plant & Equipments suppliers, International importers & exporters and manufacturers & exporters of essential oils & aromatic chemicals are also covered with their present phone/fax/e-mail/websites.

The book has been written for the benefit and to prove an asset and a handy reference guide in the hands of new entrepreneurs & well established industrialists.

Director

ENGINEERS INDIA RESEARCH INSTITUTE

Nai Sarak, New Delhi.(INDIA)
E-Mail : eirisidi@bol.net.in
Website : http://www.startindustry.com

CONTENTS AND SUBJECT INDEX

CHAPTERS *PAGE NO.*

Chapter-1

TRENDS IN TRADE OF ESSENTIAL OILS

Introduction

ESSENTIAL oils remain the basic raw material for perfumery, flavour and cosmetic industries. They are used in a wide range of products like soaps, detergents, cosmetic, agarbattis, disinfectants, deodorants, mosquito repellants, flavouring of food, soft and hard drinks, pharmaceuticals, tobacco, variety of perfumery products, and also used as fixatives and for blending purposes (Fig.). Apart from these know applications in various industrial products the essential oils have become popular in aroma therapy in Japan. The application of essential oil in agriculture as antifeedants, repellants, bioinsecticide, natural herbicide and growth boosters are still open. In this paper an attempt has been made to present an overview of the essential oil industry.

Indian Scenario

India is one of the few countries in the world having varied agroclimatic zones suitable for the cultivation of a host of essential oil bearing plants. Due to increased awareness of health hazards associated with synthetic chemicals coupled with the increased cost of petroleum products, the use of essential oil has been gradually increasing. The consumers are showing increasing preference for natural material over the synthetic. During the last few years with the spurt in the production of essential oils it is emerging as a potential agrobased Industry in India. At present in India about 30 per cent of the fine chemical used annually in perfumes and flavour come from essential oils.

USES OF ESSENTIAL OILS

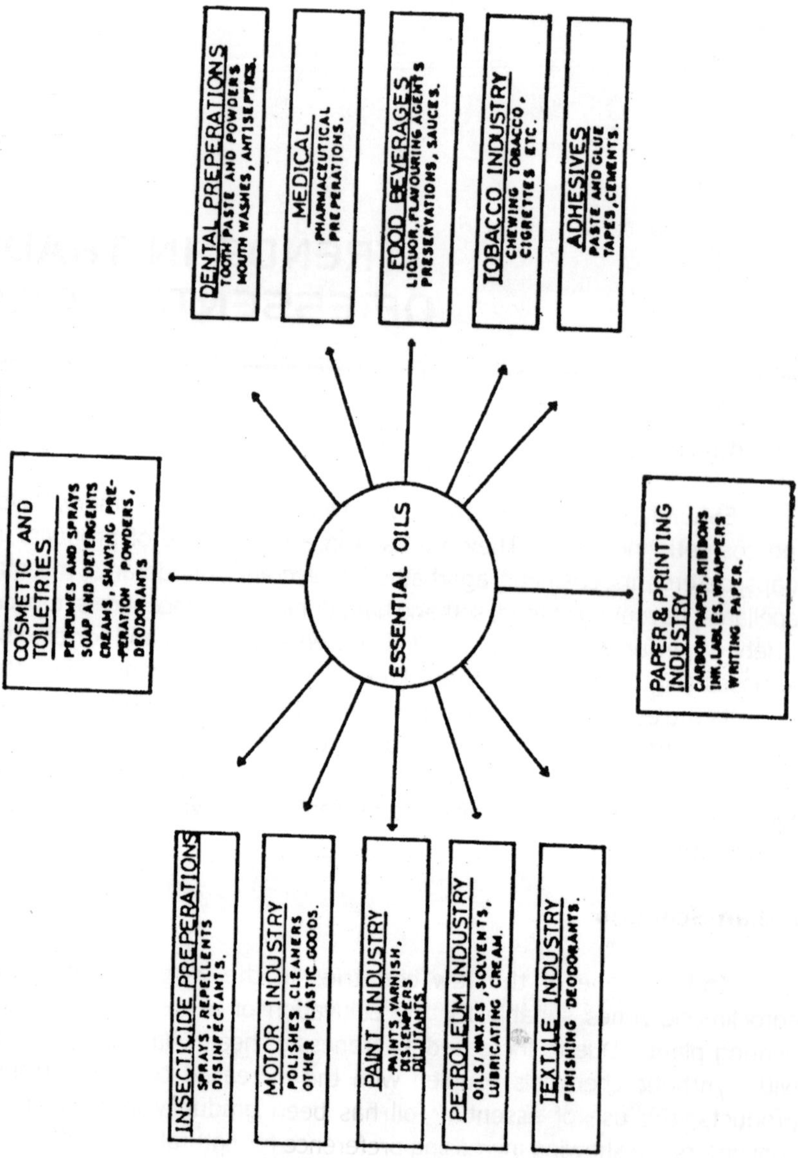

The major items of export are ginger oil, sandalwood oil, lemongrass oil, jasmine, tuberose concrete and the other essential oils. The major buyers of Indian essential oils being U.S.S.R, U.S.A, France, U.K., Netherlands, U.A.E, Saudi Arabia, Spain, Morocco, Germany, Australia, Korea, Taiwan, Pakistan etc. Table 1-5 give the export carning, estimated area production, foreign exchange saved from some selected essential oils, productivity of major tropical essential oils, imports and exports of minor forest products in India. Similarly citronella oil production has reached 500 tonnes when it was totally imported 35 years ago. Also jasmine and tuberose concretes from South India have created a mark in the world market. Thus an interesting scenario in the development of natural essential oils in India has emerged.

Chapter-2

DEMAND FOR ESSENTIAL OIL

In India the demand for essential oil is from few consumer industry products broadly grouped under fragrance, flavours, aromatic chemicals:

Type	**Product**
Fragrance	*Toiletries*
1. Soap	(a) Shampoo
2. personal care products	(b) Tooth paste/powder
or cosmetics	(c) Cream
	(d) Mouth wash
	(e) Talcum powder
Flavour	
1. food stuff	(a) Soft drinks
	(b) processed food
	(c) Chocolates
	(d) Confectoneries, beverages, and ice cream
Aromatic chemical	
Pharmaceutical	(a) Formulations
	(b) Drug other than bulk

There are about 400 blenders in India. They buy natural essential oils from distillers and prepare industrial perfumes and aromatic chemicals by either mixing one variety with the other or blending the essential oils with fine chemicals. Half of the blenders are in the western zone and the rest in the other zones. There are 20 to 25 manufacturing units of large scale, majority of these are classified under the three main groups: fragrance, flavour, and aromatic chemicals.

Chapter-3

Damask Rose (Rosa Damascena mill.) Cultivation and Processing

INTRODUCTION

THE strong and pleasant fragrance attributed to roses is known to mankind since ancient times. Other than ornamental purpose, roses are fragrant flowers. Out of one thousand varieties of roses known to horticulturist only, few exhibit delightful fragrances which are grown in different parts of the world. These are (i) Rosa damascena mill.,(ii) Rosa centifolia Linn.,(iii) Rosa bourboniana Desp.,(iv)Rosa alba Linn., (v) Rosa moschata Hook, and (vi) Rosa gallica linn. In China, Rosa rugosa flowers are used as flavour in China tea called "Mei gui Hua"and other species Rosa davurica know as "Shi Mei" Flowers are used for the preparation of Chinese herbal tea.

Only a few species are grown on commercial scale to produce concentrates of the aromatic principles. Rosa damascena. Mill., commonly known as fasli, chaiti or Damask rose is recognised as the best commercial species of the fragrant roses in many countries as it gives higher yield and better quality of the oil. India, Mughal queen Noorjahan made the first discovery for rose essential oil when she saw the tiny oil droplets on the water used for her bath. She collected the oil which was that time called as"Atri Jahangiri".

ORIGIN, DISTRIBUTION, AREA AND PRODUCTION

Rosa damascena is a temperate plant indigenous to Europe and

Middle East countries of Iran and Turkey. It is believed that the Damask rose has originated from Damascus and introduced in European countries.

Bulgaria, Turkey, France, Italy, Morocco, Russia and India are the main countries where it is cultivated in large scale for the production of oil. Bulgaria,Turkey and Morocco are the largest producers of rose oil in the world producing together 10 tonnes of oil per year while the total world demand is 20 tonnes per year. Over the last 300 years the largest integrated growing area for roses has been developed in Central Bulgaria at the foot of Balkan mountains. Grasse in South France is known for the production of precious Rose "de Mai"Concrete a hybrid of Rosa gallica and Rosa centifolia.

Commercial cultivation of Damask rose in India dates back to Mughal times. Presently its cultivation is restricted in some parts of Uttar Pradesh, Haldighati and Pushkar areas in Rajasthan and in Jammu and Kashmir. In India about 2000 hectares have been brought under its cultivation producing about 10 kg's of the oil annually. Foot hills of Himalayas are suitable for its cultivation.The state of Himachal Pradesh having suitable soil and temperate climatic conditions is best suited for the cultivation of perfumery roses.The mid hill region of this state has similar climate like that of European countries and is best suited for the cultivation of Damask rose.

ROSE PRODUCTS

There are various rose products prepared from fragrant flowers of Damask rose .These are listed as:

ROSE WATER

This is the major product produced in India. Rose water is obtained by water distillation of the flowers. Nowadays, it is a bye -product of rose oil production in modern distillation plants.

ROSE OIL

Rose oil is also obtained from fresh flowers by distillation. Different types of distillation stills and distillation parameters are being employed other than those of our primitive country made "Deg" and "Bhabhka" distillation systems.

ROSE CONCRETE AND ABSOLUTE

Extraction of rose aroma by solvent extraction technique is not common in India. Rose concrete,which is a waxy, semi solid material is produced by solvent extraction (usually with non-polar solvents like hexane and petroleum ether) of fresh flowers. On completion of aroma extraction, the solventis removed by vacuum distillation.

The absolute of rose is prepared from the concrete by extraction with alcohal.This extract is cooled to precipitate the waxes which are removed by filteration.The alcoholic solution is finally distilled under reduced pressure to remove the alcohal leaving behind the highly fragrant absolute.

ROSE ATTAR

This is second most important rose product in Uttar Pradesh. It is a sandal wood oil based product of rose flowers.

GULROGHAN

This is a hair oil prepared from rose petals by enfleurage with wet sesamum seeds.

GULAKAND

Rose petals are conserved in white sugar in the ratio of 1:2 to prepare this product. Gulakand is a very important rose product and large quantities are made in Aligarh (U.P.) and other rose growing areas.

PANKHURI

Dried rose petals are popularly known as Pankhuri. These are used in many Ayurvedic preparations for making cold drinks.

DRIED ROSE BUDS

Fully developed flower buds are plucked and shade dried.These find application in making scented"Pot Pouries" and have good demand for export.

Uses

Rose oil is one of the oldest and most valuable perfumery material. No high grade perfume is compelete that does not contain atleast some quantities of rose oil, which lends beauty and depth to odour blends.The best quality hydrodistilled rose oil imparts characteristic flowering top notes to perfumes, the extracted absolute adds lasting tonalities and increase fixation of odours. A mixture of distilled oil and extracted absolute combines the advantages of the both products. Different rose products are used in cosmetics, beverages, cold drinks, food stuffs, tobacco flavouring like snuff and chewing tobacco, fruits flavours, soft drinks, alcoholic liquors and medicines etc.

CHARACTERISTICS OF ROSA DAMASCENA MILL

According to Tucker and Maciarello, most references to Demask rose cite its origin as being Rosa damascena Miller; however,there is some controursy with regard to this citation, hence, Rosa damascena Auct. indicates that the correct specific citation or Damask rose is presently unkhown. Most authorities believe that the cultivar used to produce the commercial oil is 'trigintipetala" or a selection of it.

It has been confirmed by us that two types of Rosa damascena are grown in Indian plantations. Rose damascena Mill. Var. trigintipetala Dieck (2n=14) is popularly called as kazanlik rose. It flowers once in a year for a period of 25-30 days. It is also known as summer Damask rose and it is considered to be a natural hybrid of Rosa gallica and Rosa phoenicia.

Another variety grown is Rosa damascena Mill. Var. bifera Poir. It is also known as autumm Damask rose which is considered to be a natural hybird of Rosa gallica with rose moschata. It is mostly cultivated in Aligarh, has ayan and Kannauj areas of U.P, and gives a second flush of flowering from Septmber to November. On the basic of studies carried out by CSIR Complex Palampur, the following features of both the types have been established.

CLIMATE

A mild temperate climate is best suited for producing quality grade oil with higher oil yield. Temperature ranging from 0 to 5 C for a period of about 15 days prior to start of blooming enhances the quantity as well as quality of flowers. At the time of flowering, the temperature should be between 25 to 30 C and relative humidity above 60%. High air humidity above 60% and moderate temperature of 15-20 C gives more flower yield. Rosa damascena can be cultivated even in areas with high temperatures but flower yields are very low in comparison to those plants cultivated in temperate climatic conditions.

SITE AND SOIL

Cultivation of rose plantation should be taken up in full sunlight, away from trees or hedges so that it gets sun shine at least during the whole forenoon. It can be cultivated on levelled field, medium to high degree sloppy hills and terraces

The rose flourish well at the foot hills.It withstands wide range of soil pH conditions from 6 to 8 and silty clay loam to sandy soils.

PROPAGATION

Bulgarian rose is propagated through one year old stem cuttings. It can also be propagated through the divisions of old plant, lateral sprouts with roots and seeds.

Stem cuttinga are cillected at the time of pruning in mid October to end of December; 20 cm long,0.75-1.50 cm thick cutting are planted in nursery;2/3 of the stem length is inserted into soil. IBA @ 200-250 ppm is given to induce rooting. These cuttings are ready after one year for transplanting into main field.

FIELD LAYOUT

Soil should be free from weeds and other vegetations. If new land for cultivation, wild bushes and perennial grasses should be cleared. Drainage and irrigation chnnels are to be made at the same time. Proper marking of land at optimum distance is done. 1.5x 1.5 m^2 spacing is sufficient for optimum growth of plants.

TRANSPLANTING

Prior to transplanting in the field, the planting site is cleared of bushes etc. and pits for planting are dug at 1.5 x 1.5 m^2 spacing. Pits of size

45x45x45 cm^3 in good soil or 60x60x60x cm^3. in poor soils are dug and pit soil is allowed to weather at least for one to two months before planting.The soil is refilled in the pit at the time of planting or a few days earlier to planting. Rooted stem cuttings are taken out from nursery and put in the pits.The soil is firmly pressed around the plant. While taken out plants from nursery, the lateral roots should be disturbed as little as possible. It is useful to put 3-4 kg of farm yard manure, 20-25 gm NPK mixture (18:32:16) and 20 gm aldrin powder in the pit at the time of planting.

TIME OF TRANSPLANTING

The best time of transplanting of rooted cutting in the field is mid of November to mid January.The nursery plants are taken out on a cloudy day and planted in the field. Rose plants can also be transplanted in the month of rainy season.

IRRIGATION AND DRAINAGE

Irrigation is necessary in rose plantation at the frequency of 12-15 days during peak periods. However, when plants are established properly after two years, frequency of irrigation may be reduced. Proper drainage in the field is very essential to drain out the excessive rain water from the plantations.

INTER-CULTURE OPERATIONS

It is required to keep the plants free if weeds after planting. Usually two to three times weeding and hoeing are required to be done during the first year. Thorough weeding and circle hoeing around each plant are followed after pruning every year during winter.Two time sickling during rainy season controls the seasonal weeds and grasses in rose plantation.

MANURES AND FERTILIZERS

The quantity of fertilizers and manures should be applied on soil test basis considering various factors like basic fertility of soil, organic content, soil texture, moisture supply, soil pH etc.

Farm yard manure @ 18-20 tonnes/hectare and 100-125 kg NPK_18:32:16) mixed fertilizer should be applied at the time of transplanting of rooted cuttings into the pits. After two years, 160-200 kg nitrogen, 60-

90 kg phosphorus and 40-60 kg potash per hectare per annum are needed in Rose damascena plantation. It is a perennial, moreover soil exhausting crop which remains in the field for more than 10 years.Therefore, split application of fertilizer doses is suggested. Fertilizer application should be completed just after pruning and before the start of monsoon or rainy seasons of each year.

INTER-CROPPING

There is little scope for inter-cropping or other crops in rose plantation. However, in early stage of development of new plantation, suitable inter-crops like pulses and vegetables may be taken during first two years. The rose plantation after two years develop sufficient canopy leaving no space for inter-cropping. Moreover, rose is a sunshine loving plant which prefers neat and clean area and plenty of sunshine.

PRUNING

Pruning is a very important operation in Rosa damascena. It requires a dormant or resting period before flowering. In temperate climate conditions, the dormancy requirement is met naturally due to low winter temperature when plant goes under dormancy and sheds its leaves. In the ensuing springs, new shoots appear which give flower buds. In the region of sub-tropical climate, the rose plants are essentially pruned to induce artifical dormancy. The other purposes of pruning are to train plants into desired form, to keep the desired size, to remove injured and diseased parts, to remove the terminal buds and change the growth habit to encourage bushy roses, to provide more horizontal expansion and finally production of more flower buds.

Time, number and height of pruning are main factors for consideration. Before first flowering season of new plantation, simple tipping off (removal of terminal bud of vegetative shoots) or light pruning is sufficient in the month of December to january. During second year, plants should be pruned twice in a year, once the month of August at 50 cm plant height and again in November-December at 75 cm plant height. Further pruning should be done only once in a year in November to December at one meter plant height. Excessive water shoots be checked to grow, otherwise, size bushes becomes unmanagesble.

FLOWERING

Summer Damask rose (Rosa damascena var.trigintipetala) flowers from early March to mid of April in North Indian plains, from 10th April to 20th May in mid hills of Himachal Pradesh and early May to early June in Kashmir Valley. Exact flowering time depends upon prevailing temperature in the locality. Autumm Damask rose (Rosa damascena var.bifera) also flowers during September to November in sub-tropical plants but yield of flowers is comparatively lower than the main flowering season. Sporadic flowering may continue throughout the year in some cases.The total period of flowering is about 25-35 days but major part of the yield (about 75%) is received within 15 days of peak flowering period.

PLUCKING

The flowers are harvested in the early hours of day when they just open. Plucking starts from 4'o' clock in early morning and continues till all flowers are plucked. Flowers are plucked by hand being nipped of just below the calyx. The works is done on payment by local villagers. On an average 2-3 kg flowers are plucked per hour manually. At the peak of the season production of flowers increase many fold and picking is continued till afternoon in order to gather all the flowers maturing on that day.The pluckers collect the flowers in cotton or polythene bags and transfer to well airy, wooden baskets.

HANDLING OF FRESH FLOWERS

The necessity of proper care begins with the plucking of flowers. At any stage of handling, a big heap of flowers should not be piled. Flowers collected in cotton or poly bags during plucking must be transferred in to well aereated wooden baskets immediately. After harvesting, the flowers should be processed as quickly as possible to prevent fermentation. Fermented flowers loose their oil content and quality. Flowers stored for more than 12 hours loose half of the oil yield.

YIELD

On an average, a well maintained rose plantation yields about 3.5 to 4.5 tonnes of flowers/hectare/year. Agro-climate conditions like foot hills and valleys of Western Himalayas, sloppy hills,having traces of ferrous salt, slightly most, free from acids, well drained and easily permeable soils can yield 4-5 tonnes/ha fresh rose flowers.

Chapter-4

ROSE OIL DISTILLATION METHODS

TRADITIONAL METHODS

In this method, rose attar and rose water are mainly produced. Only a small quantity of rose oil is produced which comes as a bye-product of rose water production.The distillation assembly consist a round Copper Deg in which flowers are charged with water and a long neck copper vessel with immersed in water eich serves as condenser and receiver. A bamboo pipe serves as the vapour connection. It gives only 0.01 to 0.02% oil recovery.

TECHNICAL DRAWBACKS

1. Heat control is difficult so there is possibility of charring.
2. Mud and cloth are used to seal the system.This sealing system is not effective and considerable loss of volatile constituents takes place due to leakage.
3. Due to insufficient heat transfer surface, the use of copper receiver as a condenser is not suitable.
4. Reddish tinge to rose oil and rust coloured sediments are often noticed in rose oil distilled in copper country made stills.

NBRI PROCESS AND DESIGN

A process and field distillation unit was developed by NBRI where 0.03 to 0.04 per cent oil yield was obtained in a single operation.

Special Features

1. Ratio of water in flowers in the still was kept 2:1 which was minimum possible to be taken for distillation.
2. Distillation of flowers and redistillation of distilled rose water was carried out simultaneously in the same still by recycling the distillate.
3. Distillation of flowers was recommended with saline water using common salt instead of ordinary.

DRAW BACKS

1. As direct fire is used to heat the still, ratio of water with respect to flowers gets reduced, so there is possibility of charring.
2. Distillation in saline water alters the top-note of rose oil. The oil gives honey like sweet odour.
3. Being small size field distillation unit, it is not suitable for industrial purpose.

IMPROVED PRODUCTION TECHNOLOGY OF CIMAP, LUCKNOW

Modern technology for large scale production of rose oil has been developed and standardised by CIMAP. The first pilot plant of semi commercial size distillation still based on Bulgarian design was fabricated and installed at Hasayan village located in the heart of rose growing area of Aligarh district and a similar one was installed at CIMAP Regional Centre Pulwama, Kashmir.

SPECIAL FEATURES

1. Suitable for large scale distillations.
2. Considerably higher recovery of rose oil is achieved compared to country made copper stills (0.025-0.30%)
3. Standard quality grade oil is produced.

TECHNICAL FEATURES

1. Removal of volatile rose oil is facilitated by dispersing the flowers in water through mechanical churning/crushing
2. Rose oil is soluble inwater to a great extent and special stripping techniques are used to recover the oil in economical yield i.e.cohobation columm.

DRAWBACKS

It requires comparatively higher investment because production of oil from rose water requires cohobation technique.

PROCESS DEVELOPED BY CSIR COMPLEX, PALAMPUR

1. Cost effective distillation still designed and installed.
2. Suitability of the unit for large scale commercial distillation.
3. Provision for gentle heating to avoid charring for producing quality grade rose oil.
4. To avoid lump formation of flowers for better yields of volatile oil.
5. Redistillation/cohobation/recycling of rose water to recover the oil.

Two types of modifications were considered essential to be incorporated in new type of distillation plant:Structural and Operational.

STRUCTURAL REQUIREMENT FOR PILOT SCALE DISTILLATION OF ROSE OIL

1. Fairly large capacity.
2. Completely stainless steel make.
3. Versatile design, suitable for all the three types of distillations
4. Provision for:
   (a) Electrical heaters and steam jacket for external heating.
   (b) Steam coil for alive steam.
   (c) Recy cling of distilate.
5. Shell and tube type matching capacity horizontal condenser.
6. Bottom round oil receiver kept at an elevated height for recycling purpose.
7. Broad and clear vapour outlet from the top of the lid of still.
8. Proper controlling deviecs such as safety value, pressure and temperature guage, steam controls etc.

OPERATIONAL IMPROVEMENT

1. Direct steam is used through perforated steam coil. It avoids charring, and allows the direct latent heat to the rose petals and wide magnitude of the temperature gradient results in more vaporization of oil.
2. High pressure direct steam evenly distributed through perforated grid gives continuous stirring effects which do not allow the petals to form lumps.

3. The ratio of water to flower in the still is kept 1:1 taking into account the rise of level due to steam condensation. It reduces the distillation effect of water for rose oil.
4. The quantity of distillate is just taken to the equal to flower charge. Most of the oil is recovered in 1:1 ratio of charge and distillate.
5. No need of recycling the distillate but redistillation is required to recover the water oil.
6. No residual water is used repeatedly for enrichment of rose water.

DISTILLATION PROCESS

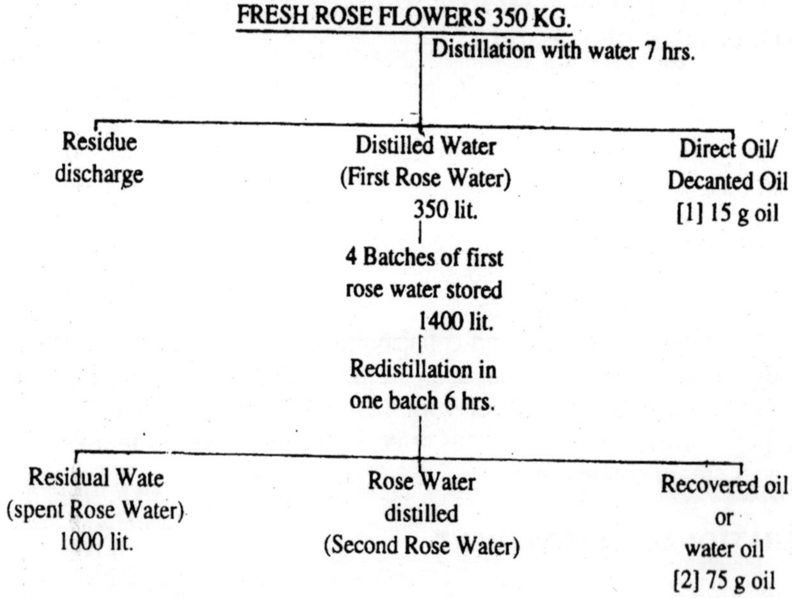

[1] + [2] = Makes commercial Rose Oil 90 gm
Percentage Oil Recovery = 0.0315

Chapter-5

CHEMISTRY OF ROSE OIL

Commercial rose oil is a blend of decanted or direct oil recovered or water oil.Initially rise flowers are hydrodistilled to produce rose water and rose oil.This oil is decanted to Produce 15% of direct oil. Rose water is subjected to steam distillation to give water oil or recovered oil. The direct and water oil are combined to make commercial rose oil.

Rose petals are extracted with non-polar solvents like hexane,petroleum ether. The extract is distilled a low temperature to remove solvent under vacuum to produce waxy,semi solid material known as rose concrete.The absolute of rose is prepared from the concrete by extraction with alcohol.The extract is cooled to precipitate out the waxes.The waxes are removed by filtration.The alcoholic solution is finally distilled under pressure to remove the alcohol leaving behind the absolute. The physico-chemical constituents reported for rose oil are:

(a) Appearance:Transparent pale yellow mobile liquid.
(b) Specific gravity:0.8719 at(30^0)
(c) Refractive index:1.4694 at (25^0)
(d) Optical rotation:(-)2.828
The Observed physico-chemicl constiuents are as:
(a) Appearance:Light greenish liquid
(b) specific gravity :0.867
(c) Refractive index:1.468

A number of reports have appeared on the chemical evaluation of rose concrete, rose absolute and rose oil throughout the world Kahol et al. have given the improved technology for the production of rose oil. Egyptian rose oil composition was reported by Karawya et al..Composition of the absolute of Bulgarian rose was published by Garnero et al. and concrete was found to contain 121 compounds with major esters. In 1978 Mann et al. deteted 174 constutuents in rose oil by GCMS analysis of broad fractions of the oil separated by silica gel column chromatography. Chemical composition of Turkish rose oil using rention times for their identification was published in 1984.Kovats 12 publsihed the result of analysis of 131 compounds from Bulgarian rose oil using a combination of multiple fractional distillation, multiple silica gel column chromatography, extraction and preparative GC for isolation and other spectroscopic methods for their identification.Ohloff and Demole heve discussed the importance of minor constituents like cis rose oxide, nerol oxide oxide, damascnone, 3-hydroxy-damascone in 3-hydroxy B damascenone, and B-damaseane rose oil which are considered to be most important for the beautiful aroma of rose oil.

Omata et al. Have reported sulphur compounds in rose oii using a combination of fractional distilation, column chromatography HPLC GC and GCMS techniques and have characterised number of new sulphur compounds.These sulphur compounds were found to contribute significantly to rose odour and play an important role especially in the middle and base note of rose oil.

In 1989 Akhila at al.used radiotracer studies to examine (E)-(Z) isomerisation of geranial and nerol during the growth cycle of Rose damascena.The results of their study revealed the inter-conversion of geraniol into nerol by reverse isomerisation procedure via redox reaction.The detailed studies by various workers have been reviewed by Lawrence. Besides cultivation techniques, two reports of chemical evaluation on Rosa damascena oil have been published form India. Kahol et al. has evaluated the oil by GLC where only eight major constituents have been identified and reported. Sood et al.have analysed the oil in detail and reported thirty-three constituents uning capillary column in GC.The identification of constituents was carried out by GCMS and other spectral methods as given in Table 1.

Under the plant imporvement porgramme of this institute mass population of Rosa damascena plants were segregated into two dofferent clones of Type-I and Type-II having marked difference in the external morphologicaal characters.The oil produced from these two clones was differen in percentage of various constituents. The details of the constituents identified by GC and GCMS are given in Table 2.

Over the years scientists have tried to identify the odour-impact constituents pf rose oil, however, prior to 1957 no real significant progress was reported.The basic rosaceous character of rose oil is determined by the citronellol content.The key to odour secret of rose oil is hidden among the minor and trace constiuents.The unidentified trace constituents has become the subject of constiderable study. Among those cis-and tras-rose oxide are responsible for the floral green top note of the rose oil.The quality grade rose oil should have the ratio of citronellol/geraniol between 1 to 1.5. Minor constituents of eugenol and methyl eugenol are very important because these impart green and spicy notes to rose oil and are considered to have effect on the total strength of rose oil.

Table 1 - Chemical constituents of Rose oil

Peak No.	Compound	Percentage	Identification
1.	Hexanoal	0.25	GC/MS
2.	Heptanal	0.21	GC/MS
3.	a-pinene	0.65	GC/MS,HNMR
4.	pinence	o.15	GC/MS
5.	Myrcence	0.22	GC/MS
6.	b-phenylethyl alcohol	4.06	GC/MS
7.	Cis rose oxide	0.68	GC/MS, HNMR
8.	Trans-rose oxide	0.29	GC/MS, HNMR
9.	Terpinen-4-ol	0.18	GC/MS
10.	a/hterpineol	0.32	GC/MS, HNMR
11.	Citronellol	40.00	GC/MS
12.	b-phenylethyl acetate	0.35	GC/MS
13.	Geraniol	14.49	GC/MS, HNMR
14.	Citral	0.71	GC/MS
15.	Eugenol	1.57	GC/MS, HNMR
16.	Geranyl acetate	0.94	GC/MS
17.	Methyl eugenon	1.90	GC/MS, HNMR
18.	b-caryophyllene	0.25	GC/MS, HNMR
19.	a-cadinene	0.40	GC/MS, HNMR
20.	Docosane	0.37	GC/MS
21.	Heptadecane	1.83	GC/MS
22.	Farnesol	0.98	GC/MS
23.	Tridecane	0.22	GC/MS
24.	9-eicosene	2.65	GC/MS
25.	Nonadecane	12.30	GC/MS
26.	Heptacosane	2.48	GC/MS
27.	Eicosane	1.35	GC/MS
28.	Tetradecanol	0.29	GC/MS
29.	Henicosane	6.69	GC/MS
30.	Tricosane	1.69	GC/MS
31.	Pentacosane	0.83	GC/MS
32.	Octadecanc	0.53	GC/MS

Table 2 - Chemical constituents of two types

Constituent	Type-I	Type-II
a-pienene	3.5	8.48
Phenylethyl alcohol	11.36	10.83
Cis-rose oxide	0.25	0.09
Trans-rose oxide	0.10 0.04	0.04
4-terpineal	0.68	0.79
Citronellol	15.98	18.65
Geraniol	13..74	20.17
Eugenol	4.69	4.38
Me-Eugenol	6.97	6.28
b-Caryophyllene	0.98	2.45
Docosane	2.27	1.64
Heptadecane	6.74	1.67
9-Eicosene	1.91	0.88
Nonadecane	12.14	3.35
Henicosane	5.82	0.55

Chapter-6

CULTIVATION OF MATRICARIA CHAMOMILLA

INTRODUCTION

CHAMOMILE a well known old time drug is botanically described to three species, viz. Matricaria chamomilla L Syn. M. recutita (L) Raushert (German or Hungarian or small chamomile) Anthemis nobilis L. (English or Roman chamomile Double chamomile) and Ormenis multicaulis Braun Blanquet & Maire (Moroccan camomile). This paper highlights the cultivation and related aspects of Matricaria chamomilla L.

Matricaria chamimilla Syn. M. recutita (Asteraceae) is a diploid species (2n=18) alloogamous in nature exhibiting wide segregation as a commercial crop. M. chamomilla (Persian chamomilla locally Babuna) has been grown in India from the last two hundred years. The drug was introduced in India during the Mughal period and was cultivated in Punjab and Upper Gangetic plains. Three plants viz A. nobilis Linn Corchorus depressus Linn and Matricaria chamomilla Linn are reported under one Unani name Babuna at different places in literature. This created a lot of confusion and misuse of the drug as an adulterant etc. conducted a detailed taxonomic and anatomical study and concluded that Babuna also belongs to the family Compositae and that the correct scientific name of Babuna is M. chamomilla L.

Kashmir Matricaria chamomilla found growing wild over vast areas of waste lands in Kashmir valley has not been explored as a source of bisabolol and its oxides. Comparative studies with Jammu grown German chamomilla has revealed ample scope for developing and utilizing this source. After screening and evaluation it has been found that the wild source is qualitatively and quantitatively conforming to the German standard.

A samll sample of seed of Matricaria chamomilla was obtained from France about 36 years ago by the Regional Research Laboratory Jammu and its experimental cultivation was tried at Jammu (300 m) and Kashmir. Thus was laid the foundation of organized of the crop with improved seed in our country.

USES

Matricaria has a wide domestic use especially among the Germans. The flowers of M. chamomilla contain the essential oil which finds a variety of uses. It is used mainly as an anti inflammatory and antiseptic, also antispasmodic and mildly sudorific. Used internally mainaly as a tisane (infuse 1 table spoonful of drug in 1 litre of cold water do not heat) for disturbances of the stomach associated with pain for sluggish digestion for diarrhoea and nausea more rarely and very effectively for inflammation of the urinary tract and for painful mensuration. Externally the drug in power form may be applied to wounds slow to heal and for skin eruptions and infection such as shingles boils also for haemorrhoids and for inflammation of the month throat and the eyes. Tabulated products from chamomile flower extracts are marketed in Europe and used for various ailments. It is also used as a flavouring agent in fine liquors in perfume compositions. The dried flowers find use in the form of its water extract. Chamomile tea eye washing can induce allergic conjunctivitis. Pollen of Matricaria chamomilla contained in these infusions are the allergens responsible for these reactions. The use of herbal tea preparations eliminated colic in 57% infants.

Ethanolic extracts of Bryonia dioica Anthyllis vulneraria M. chamomilla and M. inodora inhibited the growth of Polio virus, while *A.vulneraria M. chamomilla and M.inodord* in had an anti herpetic effect.

SOIL AND CLIMATIC REQUIEMENTS

It can be grown on any type of soil but avoid growing the crop on rich heavy and damp soils. The crop has been grown very successfully on the poor soils (loamy sand) at the farm of the Regional Research Laboratory Jammu. At Banthra farm of the National Botanical Research Institute Lucknow the crop has been grown successfully on soil with a pH of 9.

In Yugoslavia large areas of saline soda steppes are under this crop. Soils with pH 9 to 9.2 are reported to support its growth. In Hungary it grows extensively on clayey lime soils which are barren lands and considered to be too poor for any other crop. Temperature and light conditions (sunshine hours) have greater effect on essential oils and azulene content than soil type. Chamomilla possesses a high degree of tolerance to soil alkalinity. The plants accumulate fairly large quantiy of sodium (66me/100gm of dry material) which helps in reducing the salt concentration in the top soil.

No substantial differences were found in the characteristic of the plant grown 1500 km apart (Hungary - Finland). Under the cooler conditions in Finland the quantity of the oxide type in the essential oil was lower the in Hungary.

CULTIVATION

Matricaria crop grew successfully in Jammu and Srinagar. It is a winter season crop in the plains of India and in the hills grows successfully from April onwards. The crop was later grown by Chandra on the alkaline soils at Banthra farm.

During the last fifteen years or so seeds of the crop from other countries like Poland Hungary have been cultivated on trial basis. Some pharmaceutical firms have brought seeds from several countries and have grown the crop to meet their internal requirements. The area under the crop in the country is not known but there is a rising demand of dry flowers. It is a truism that commercial cultivation of the crop is economically viable where cheap labour is available.

BOTANICAL CHARACTERS

The crop is an annual with an erect or spreading habit and attains a height of 60 to 90 cm. The stem is glaborous branched, leaves alternate very green and smooth 2-3 pinnatisect with segments short and very linear giving the leaf a finely dissected appearance. Flower head solitary 1.3 -2.5 cm diameter ray florets whitish or yellowish disc florets numerous yellow tubular long peduncles receptacle conic elongated during flowering. Infloresence is a capitulum borne singly on long terminal peduncle with ray old disc florets fruit is a small achene seeds are fine.

PROPOGATION

The seeds of the crop are very minute in size a thousand seeds weigh 0.088 to 0.153 gm. About 0.3 to 0.5 kg of clean seed with a high germination percentage sown in an area of 200 to 250 sq.m. gives enough seedlings for stocking a hectare of land. The crop can be grown by (1) direct sowing of the seed and (ii) transplanting. Moisture conditions in the field for direct sowing of seeds must be very good otherwise a patchy and poor germination id obtained. The transplanting method is generally followed mortality of the seedlings is almost negligible.

The most appropriate time for raising seedlings in the nursery is soon after the cessation of monsoons in North India i.e. during the month of September. Seed germination starts within 4-5 days of sowing and the seedlings are ready for transplanting within 4 to 5 days of sowing and the seedlings are ready for transplanting within 4 to 5 weeks. Seedlings older than 5 weeks should not be transplanted it results in a poor and indifferent crop. Based on thermal model appropriate time and method of sowing was studied the study revealted that transplanting the crop was better than direct sowing the best time to transplant the crop was 10th to 18th October for getting higher yields transplanting should not be delayed beyond the end of October.

The work on crop geometry shows that transplanting the crop at narrow spacings of 15cm 20cm and 30cm gave the highst yields of flowers. In case of varieties with a spreading habit of growth a wider spacing of $40cm^2$ is desirable.

CROP GROWTH

The crop growth is slow till mid January and picks up gradually till early February. As the season warms up there is high activity in crop growth (increase in height branching bud formation) and stray flowers may be seen in the crop. Bud formation is profuse in March there is all round growth in plants the early formed buds open into flowers hence the plucking of flowers has to be also selective althrough the crop cycle. With sudden rise in temperature from 33 C to 39 C within a few days heavy seed setting and plant maturity will be observed in the crop. There is seedshedding and in the next year a self germinated crop is observed.

IRRIGATION

The crop is flood irrigated after transplanting and 2 to 3 additional irrigations during the crop cycle meet the water requirements of the crop. Irrigation during the bloom period is helpful in increasing the flower yield one additional flush of flowers is obtained and seed formation is delayed. Kreches observed that irrigation at the rosette stage increased yield substantially.

On alkaline soils the crop is irrigation more frequently and about 6 to 8 irrigations are required during the crop cycle.

MANURES AND FERTILIZERS

Dutta and Singh observed that application of nitrogen in the form of Ammonium Sulphate at 40 kg/ha significantly increased fresh flower and oil yeild while the oil content decreased from 0.64 to 0.59%. El Hamidi advocates the ratio of 2.2 for N and P for obtaining the highest yield. Application of N at a higher level caused a notable decrease in the chamazuler percentage. Paun and Mihalea found that application of P & K at 50 kg/ha each in autumn before sowing and application of nitrogen at 50 kg/ha spring was responsible for satisfactory crop growth the volatile oil and chamazulene content was not affected. On saline alkaline soils plants showing good response to N & P fertilizers. Application of 20-25 tonnes/ha of FYM was useful before transplanting the crop. In the experience of the author the entire dose of P & K and half the dose of N should be applied as a basal dose, the rest of the nitrogen being applied towards the end of January or just before the crop starts active growth. A dose of 40:40:50/ha is sufficient to obtain very good yield of flowers. Misra & Kapoor found the optimum dose of N and P to lie between 50 60 kg N/ha and 50 kg P O/ha. Emonger and Chweya reported that nitrogen significantly increased the contents of alpha bisobolol and cbamazulene but significantly decreased the contents of bisabolol oxides A and B in the essential oil. Nitrogen signigicantly increased essential oil yield per unit dry flower weight in both Bohemia and Tisane varieties. The quantity of essential oil in chamomile was inversely related to its quality in terms of alpha bisbolol and chamazulenes.

No deficiency symptoms of trace elements have been observed on the crop in the country so far. Peskova has reported the good effect of the sulphates of manganese and cobalt and borax on line borax on lime soils while Koeurik and Dovjak indicated that combined application of boron and molybdenum increased dry matter significantly.

WEED CONTROL

Various harbicides have been used for the control of weede in M. chamomilla. Application of 1 to 1.5 kg/ha of sodium salt of 2,4 D 4 weeks after transplanting gave good control of weeds for 4 weeks chamomille plants showed slight bending of the stems crop growth was supressed but the plants recovered within 3 to 4 weeks of weedicide application. The experimental results of workers abroad suggests that herbicides atrazine prometryne propyzamide chloropropham mecoprop trifluralin linurones give satisfactory control of weeds but these should be used with caution. Herbicde treated crop had lower chamazulene content bisabolol content was lower in the second harvest there was interference in the metabolism of secondary products had little influence on total essential oil content but greater difference were found in quantitiative composition of useful substances.

Singh and Shahi reported that weed removal during 5 to 11 weeks after planting the crop was necessary to obtain higher yield of flower and oil. Hand weeding operation before 5 weeks or extended beyond 11 weeks after planting the crop did not give any additional advantage. Singh et al that uncontrolled weed growth caused 34.4% reduction in dry flower yield as compared to weed free condition. Application of Oxyflourfen 0.6 kg/ha gave higher return.

HARVESTING

The success of Matricaria chamomilla cultivation as a commercial venture lies in how efficiently and efficiently one can collect the flowers at the right stage during the peak flowering season extending over a period of 3 to 6 weeks during the month of March April. Flowering is so profuse that practically every alternate day atleast 30 to 40 units of labour will be required to be emloyed to pluck flowers from an area of 0.25 to 0.3 hectares. As such this crop has an intensive requirement of labour and if this major input is met timely profits are assured.

Flower plucking is a selective process as flowers in all stages viz buds semi opened buds flowers in all stages of bloom appear on the plants. Flowers at the near full bloom stage give the best quality of the product hence care has to be exercised to see that as little as possible buds stems leaves and extraneous material is plumed. Flowering will be observed onplants here there all over the filed from the later half of February these and flowers are plucked at the appropriate stage.

Flowers are produced in flushes and four to five flushes are obtained. The 2nd 3rd and 4th flushes are the major contributors to flower yield. The peak period of plucking lies in between the 2nd week of March to the 3rd week of April in North India. Temperature effects the number of flowers per kg the weight of 1000 flowers is reduced from 130 gm to 80 gm by the second week of April.

On an average a worker can pluck about 2.5 to 3.5 kg of fresh flowers while the more efficient ones can pluck upto 6 kg of fresh flowers.

Trials undertaken with the scoop a hand tool developed by the Germans showed that (i) during collection of flowers extraneous matter (leaves and stems) is also collected and it lowers the qunlity of the flowers (ii) buds semi opened buds and very small flowers are also collected along with the bigger flowers resulting in about 15% reduction in flower yield (iii) used when plants are near about maturity results in more dried stems being collected (iv) the best time to use the scoop is in the 3rd and 4th flushes as larger number of flowers are in the right stage of harvest (v) with a little practice about 20 to 25 kg of fresh flowers are easily collected.

FRESH FLOWER AND OIL YIELD

The averge fresh flower yield is 4000 to 4500 kg/ha. 100 of fresh flowers yields 20 to 25 kg of dry flowers. A maximum fresh flower yield of 7637 kg/ha was reported by Dutta and Singh. On saline alkaline soils Chandra et al reported a maximum fresh flower yield of 4500 kg/ha. The number of flowers per kg is about 7500 to 8000 with increase in temperature from 33 C to 39 C the flower size is further reduced so that there are about 12000 number of flowers in one kg.

The average oil content of dry flowers is 0.5 to 0.88% which compares favourbly with oil obtained in other coumntries Donalisio reported the average essential oil content of Brazilian Matricaria chmomila flowers to be 0.421 %. Average oil yield of 10.8 kg/ha was obtained in our trial.

SEED COLLECTION AND STORAGE

After obtaining 4 plucking the crop is allowed to stand the remaining flowers mature set seeds and are ready for harvest by mid May. Another method is to select out healthy plants in the field take three pluckings of flowers then allow the flowers to mature and collect the flowers from time to time as they keep on maturing. The seed is stored in tightly closed glass containers in linen bags polyvinyl foll bags (0.2 mm thick). After three years the viability of the seed is reduced to fifty per cent.

The deep blue colour of the oil on storage gradually changes to green and finally turns brown under the influence of light and air. These changes take place within 6-12 months of storage.

DRYING FRESH FLOWERS

Flowers of Matricaria chamomilla are delicate and should be dried in the shade with care by poreading them in thin layers. Avoid turning the flowers as far as possible. Over a floor area of 50 sq m about 80 to '100 kg of fresh flowers can be dried at a time. The flowers take about 5-7 days to dry and with a rise in outside temperature (37^0 C and above) it takes about 3 to 5 days.

The best method is to dry the flowers artificially with a blast of air. Mush observed that blowing dry air at a rate which removed 0.07% moisture per minute stimulated hudrolysis and increased evolution of etherial oils in Matricaria chamomilla. Konovalova opined that drying the flowers in a stationary dryer at 40 to 45^0 C preserved best the essential oil and prochamaz ulene content of cham milla that freezing chamomilla. Carle et al observed that freezing chamomilla flowers resulted in higher yields of essential oils and its compounds than any of the various drying procedures tested. The cost of producing one kg of dry flower of Matricaria chamomilla is estimated to vary between 28 to 32 Rs/kg. More than 80% of the cost goes towards the cost of plucking flowers manually.

DISTILLATION

A viscous oil of deep blue colour with a strong characteristic odour and bitter aromatic flavour is obtained from air dry flowers either by steam distillation or solvent extraction. Due to the viscous nature of the oil a lot of oil sticks in the condensor during the process of steam distillation and this results in a low recovery of oil. Alternate heating and cooling of the condensor by steam and water during the distillation proccess help in increasing the oil recovery. The oil consists of high boiling constituents including paraffins hence steam at a relatively high pressure (7 atm per sq. cm) needs to be used for the distillation process.

Depasquale and Selvestri showed that the composition of the oil obtained by solvent extraction differed qualitatively from that of the oil obtained by continuous steam distillation thus 7 methoxy conumarin was present in the former but not in the latter. Reinhold and Gomae have described the production of essential oil using continuous steam distillation system and the effect of harvest technology on the quality of dried chamomilla flowers.

EFFECT OF GROWTH REGULATORS

Application of gibberellic acid (GA) on Matricaria chamomilla at the rate of 50 ppm increased flower yield. This was more marked on well manured plots. Abou Zied et al. observed that application of cycocel to chamomille shortened plant height and spreading area but markedly increased the flower yield with a rise of volatile oil percent and chamazulene content. Higher doses of cycocel used showed greater effect.

DISEASES AND PESTS

In recent years when the crop was cultivatied in the Regional Research Laboratory Jammu no incidence of disease was noticed. However 20 years later in February about two dozen plant were observed to produce symptoms resembling those of plant viruses. These were burnt to prevent further spread of the disease. In early March incidence of leaf blight caused by Alternaria spp. was observed in the crop. A spray of Benlate (0.1%) controlled the disease.

Fluster reported that black been aphid were feeding on M. chamomilla. The insect Nysius minor caused shedding of M. chamomilla flowers (Mathur & Sharma) while Autographa chryson causes defoliation of the plant. Brejcha et al reported that one spray with Fosfothion 0.2% semi systemic insecticide controlled successfully aphid infestation (Doralis fabae Scop) on chamomile in the field in Czechoslovakia methyl bromide (3 kg/100m) proved satisfactory as a fumigant against pest infestation of Ephestia elutella Hb. in the dessicated herb of chamomille. El Bagoury and Monen (found

Metalydacolus longistriatus no sp in the Giza region Egypt to be associated with roots of chnmomille. The drug bettles (I) Lasioderma servicorne and (2) Stegobium paniceum (Anobidae Coleop) are known to cause extensive damage to dry flowers of M. chamomilla under storage conditions.

Aykema reported that Eonostethus venustus occurs at a varirty of waste places in the Dutch provinces of Zealand Utrecht Gelderland and Limburg and is associated with Matricaria and Anthemis. The closely related C. roseus has been captured in the Netherlands since after not having been observed for almost a century.

CHEMICAL COMPOSITION

The deep blue colour of the oil is due to chamazulene which is an important constituent of the sticky oil (average 6%) determines its quality. The chamazulene content of the various chamomiles depends upon the origin and age of the materia. It decreases during the storage of the flowers. Sharma et al reported the presence of perillyl alcohol triacontane cadeleric hydrocarbon and cadeleric tertiary alcohol. Depasquale and Silvestri reported that the main constituent of the oil other than chamazulene were exeyne bi cycle ethers herniarin farnesene and bisablol other compounds such as thujone and borneol were present in very low amounts. All these and other compounds were found in different amounts and rations in various parts of the inflorescence depending on the growth stage and on time of picking during the day. Jasicova and Felklova have presented a review of the content of total essential oils chamazulenes and bisabolol in Matricaria blossom from several Europeon regions Matricine chamazulene and guajazulene have different antiphlogistic activities and these substances can cont be replaced by each other arbitrarily in chamomile preparations . Gasic et al identified chemical types A C & D in Matricaria chamomilla samples from different regions of Yugoslavia. Two of the samples contained farnesene in approximately the same amount as (-) a bisabolol indicating the possibility of classifying these in separate chemical types. Kim et al revealed the presence of 31 volatile components in domestic M. chamomilla grown in Korea.

For manufacturing chamomile extracts of antiphlogistic effectiveness only such types of chamomile should be used which exhibit a high content of (-) a bisabolol and the synthetic recemic bisabolol (Jakovlev et al. Upto 50% of the oil of chamomile consists of (-) a bisabolol which is an unsaturated monocyclic sesquiterpene alcohol. Four bisabolol oxides were isolated from chamomile by Issac. Arak et al reported that the quantity of a bisabolol, bisabolol oxides A and B and bisabolol oxides A in the flowers reached a maximum at full bloom and then declined. Farnesene content of flower deciessed gradually with its growth and development. Accumulation of essential oils in flowers continued during drying. Harvestion at the early flowering phase and drying in shaded places is recommended. Franz in pot trials showed thta oil content was the lowest in decaying heads and highest in one week of flower initiation. Farnesene and bisabolol were highest in flower buds and lowest in decaying flowers. Chamazulene and bisabolol oxide content increased from buds to fully developed flower buds.

Some pharmaceutical concerns prefer chamomile flowers which on analysis give a minimum of 0.8% essential oil and contain 10% chamazulene 50% bisabolol 1 to 2% flavanoids mainly apigetrin and patulitrin. Schreiber et al. showed that apigenin did not actually occur in living chamomile flowers, it is the result of post harvest processes.

The quality of the dried flowers and blue oil from the crop raised on sub standard alkali soils at NBRI Lucknow analysed by Chandra et al gave the following results.

1.	Dry flowers	100 gm
	i. Bisabolol	7.4% by weight
	ii. Azulene	15.1% by weight
2.	Blue oil	100 gm
	i. Azulene	46.92 mg
	ii. Flavanoids	12.56 mg
	iii. Bisabolol	38.60 mg

3. According to I.P.C. specifications the drug (Flowers) should contain.

i. Stem	10%
ii. Other impurities	2%
iii. Total ash	10%
iv. Acid insol. ash	4%
v. Volatile oil content	Not less than 0.4% (B.P.C.)

CHAMOMILLA WASTE

Investigations of post distilled waste of Matricaria chamomilla L. grown in soil and in the ashes of a thermal power station showed that the waste contained an average quanitity of total proteins 20.1% sol proteins

18.7 mg/g fresh mass crude lipids 8.7% crude cellulose 24.8% and ashes 5.18%. Proteins of the post distilled waste contained all proteinous amino acids and were richer in lysine valine and methionine than alfalfa and clover. It cotained a singnificant amount of macro and microelements as well.

RAY AND DISC FLORETS

The main component of the essential oil from ray and disc florets is composed of (-) a bisabolol oxide A chamazulene cis en in dicycloether and (-) bisbolol oxide B. The receptacle contained cis en in dicycloether farnesene and spathulenol as mine component.

ROOTS OF MATRICARIA CHAMOMILLA

The essential oil from the roots contained sesquiterpenes chamomillol caryo phyllene caryophyllenepoxide and the polyenes chamomillaester I & II. The oil was accumulated in the schizogenous/oil passages and oil cells restricted to the roots.

ANALYTICAL METHODS

In recent years consierable advance has been made in the distillation of oil from flowers determination of the essential oil components of the inflorescence or its individual parts determination of the essential oil components of the inflorescence of its individual parts determination of structures of chemical constituents. Using modern methods of analysis DePasquale and Silvestri Padula et al. Schicher et al Verzar Petri et al Kunde and Issac Exner et al Hyvonex et al Kanamori et al Retamar et al have reported the presence of farnasene faresone patchoulene spiro ethers bisabolol bisabolol oxides I II & III chamazulenes flavones dicyclic ethers borneol thujone jaceidin chrysosplenol D eupatolitin and other unidentified compunds in the oil. These contribute to the oils fungicidal bactericidal antiallergic and separative properties. Chamazulenes pathoulene and bisabolol have structures amneable to conversion to azulenes.

With the use of the supercritical gases (CO^2 or N^2 O the active constituents e.g. bisabolol its oxides proazulenes coumarins and fragrant components are extracted unaccompanied by polysaccharides acids and flavonoids. Stahl et al. Lakszner et al showed that on the basis of O-FID (Oxygenate analyzer) chromatograms by measuring the relative peak areas of the characteristics compounds chamomilla oils can be classified and the oils unacceptable quality unambiguously distinguished.

Chapter-7

CULTIVATION OF DAVANA FOR ESSENTIAL OIL

INTRODUCTION

DAVANA (Artemisia pallens well.) belonging to family Asteraceae is an improtant annual aromatic herb, much prized in India for its delicate fruity fragrance. It is being commercially cultivated in Karnataka, Maharasthra, Kerala, Tamil Nadu and Andhra Pradesh. In these areas,davana springs are commonly used in garlands,bouquets and religious offering for most part of the year. The leaves and flowers contain oil valued for its exquisite and delicate aroma and is used in high grade perfumes and cosmetics.

The essential oil of davana which is a brown viscous liquid with rich fruity odour has acquired consierable reputation in the international trade particularly in USA and Japan where it is being used for flavouring cakes, pastries, tobacco and beverages.

BOTANY

Davana is an aromatic, erect about 60 cm tall herb with much divided leaves and small yellow flowers.The stem and leaves are covered with greyish white tomentum,leaves are alternate,petiolate and lobed. Inflorescence is capitulate which are peduncled to sessile,axillary or forming lax racemes,simple heterogamous having bisexual discflorets in the center and few pistillate ray flors on the periphery. Outer florets are glabrous except for a few cottony hairs, tubulur, generally 3-lobed.Stigma generally 2-loed. Inner florets are glabrous except for a few epipetalous filaments and dithecous et, syngenesious anthers, connective prolonged tapering, style bifid.

FLORAL BIOLOGY

The average length and diameter of fully opened flower head is 0.49 cm and 0.68 cm, respectively. Anthesis occurs between 7.30 a.m. and 12.30 p.m. with a peak at 10.30 a.m. Anthers dehice between 7.30 a.m. and 12.30 p.m. with the diameter under 40 magnification with 34.55 percent viability.Stigma is found to be receptive after anthesis and maximum receptivity is observed at 7.00 a.m.

The crop os highly influened by environmental factors with regard to the number of seeds per flower and percent seed setting. For obtaining the maximum seed set, the crop should be raised during November and December months, when low temperatures are prevailing. Under higher temperature, it is not only difficult to grow the crop but there is also very poor seed set.

Cytological studies have revealed that Artenisia pallens Wall. has a chromosome number of 2n =16.

CLIMATE

Season is an important aspect to be considered when davana is grown for extracting the essential oil. The oil content in plant was observed maximum when the crop was grown during winter season compared to other seasons. Thus when the crop was grown during for the production of oil, it should be planted during the first week of November. A few light showers with moderate winter conditions and no frost helps in allowing the plant to put on good growth. High temperature and heavy rains at the time of flowering have not only been found to affect the plant growth but also reduce the oil content and ultimately the oil yield.

SOIL

The crop is found growing on various types of soils from sndy loam to medium black. However, a sandy loam soil which is rich in organic matter and with a good drainags is ideal.

NURSERY RAISING

Davana is propagated by seeds. As the seeds lose the viability rapidly, seeds from the previous season crop only should be used for sowing . About 1.5 kg of seed is required to produce enough seedlings to transplant in an area of one hectare.

Usually nursery beds of 2 m long anbd 1 m wide are preferred. The surface of the beds should be clod free. It is then incorporated with the finely prepared farm yard manure at the rate of 10 kg per bed. Sowing of seeds at the rate of 1 gm per sq. m. is desirable. The seeds may be sown either dry or after wetting them with sand for about 48 hour. In the latter case, the seed is thoroughly mixed with sand at the rate of 4-5 times its volume. To this mixture, water is added so that the sand is sufficiently wet. It is then tied in a cloth bag and stored in a warm condition for 48 hours. This will hasten the sprouting of seeds and radicle will emerge at the end of 48 hours. The nursery bad is then flooded with water to provide a pool and the sprouting seed and send mixture is broadcast all over the bed, homogenously. The method helps in uniform distribution of seeds. When the seeds have settd down a thin layer of sand is spread over just to cover them. The seed will germinate in 2-3 days of sowing. Hand watering is done till the seedlings establish themselves (7 to 10 days) after which the beds are irrigated directly through the water channels.

Some farmers also sow the seeds directly. While sowing the dry seeds, they are mixed with sand in the ratio of 1:10 and broadcast homogenously all over the bed. A thin layer of sand is then spread uniformly to cover the seeds and the beds are hand watered twice a day. To prevent the ants from carrying away of seeds, application of 10 kg of 5% BHC per hectare into the soil about 10 days prior to sowing has been helpful. Using this method, the germination of seeds is observed in about 4-5 days.

In area where there are rains at the time of nursery raising seedlings may be raised in raised nursery beds which will also help in reducing the incidence of damping off disease.

As there is very slow growth of seedlings initially, foliar sprays of urea (0.1%) at weekly intervals from 3-weeks after sowing may be given to boost their growth.

TRANPLANTING

The seeding will be ready for transplanting in about 6-8 weeks from the date of sowing. At this stage they will be about 10 cm tall.

Before transplanting, the field is thoroughly prepared by bringing the land to a fine tilth with repeated ploughings. It is then laid out into the plots of convenient size by laying out buds and channels. The size of the plot depends on the conditions prevailing locally. However, generally a plot of 3-4m x 1.5-2.5m size is preferred as it helps in proper management of irrigation, weeding and other intercultural operations. After the preparation of plots, soil is incorporated with 6 tonnes of well decomposed farm yard manure or compost. The plots are irrigated a day prior to transplanting. The seedlings are then transplanted at a spacing of 15 cm between the row and 7.5 cm between plants. Trials have shown that transplanting davana at closer spacing results in higher oil yeild compared to wider spacing which although productes in larger plants but lower herbage and oil yield per unit area.

MANURES AND FERTILIZERS

Davana responds well to the application of manures and fertilizers. Well decomposed farm yard manure at the rate of 6 tonnes per hectare is incorporated into the oil at the time of land preparation. Subsequently , a fertilizer dose of 40 kg of phosphorus and 40 kg of potassium per herctare is given at the time of transplanting. Whereas,nitrogen is applied at a rate of 120 kg per hectare in there equal split doses. The first dose is given at 10 days after transplanting and the subsequent two doses at 15 days intervals, thereafter.

IRRIGATION

After transplanting, the plots are immediately provided with light irrigation. Later the irrigation is given daily till the seedlngs are well established (10-12 days) and subsequently once in 3-4 days depending on the weather condition.

INTERCULTURE

The field is kept weed free by regular weeding as and when required. In all about 2-3 hand weedings during early period of growth will help to keep the weeds down.

GROWTH REGULATOR APPLICATION

Growth regulators have been used to boost the growth and yield in many crops. In davana also, application of GA aat 200 ppm after five weeks of transplanting has been found to increase the herb and essential oil yield per unit area.

PLANT PROTECTION

Insect pests

No serious attack of insect pest has been reported in davana. However, some insect pests like leaf eating caterpillars, aphids and termites have been observed to affect the crop.

Application of 10% BHC or Aldrex to the plots will control the attack of termites. While spraying of any systemic insecticide like 0.05% of monocrotophos or 0.2% of dimethoate will control the incidence of aphids and spraying of contact insecticides like 0.2% Metacid will control leaf eating caterpillars.

DISEASES

Damping off : This disease is caused by a fungus belonging to Rhizoctonia sp. It is usually severe at nursery stage, particulary when there is high humidity and cloudy weather conditions, resulting in the heavy mortality of seedlings.

Controlling the irrigation will reduce the disease incidence. Treating the seeds with Emissan 0.2% or Ridonil MZ at 0.1% before sowing and then drenching the seed beds with the above chemicals, a week after germination gives good control of the disease.

HARVESTING

The crop starts flowering after 110-115 days of sowing which will be aroung 2nd or 3rd week of February. In order to obtain the maximum essenntial oil yeild, the plants should be harvested when about 50 percent of them have come to flowering. This stage will be reached by the end of

February or 1st week of March at 120-125 days after sowing. Harvesting is done by cutting the plants from the base. Although there are reports about the possibility of obtaining a ratoon crop in davana, no where it is being followed practically as the main crop is harvested only during the month of March and the ratoon starts sprouting by the end of March or beginning of April which due to the high temperatures prevailing during these periods results in poor growth of plant and mutilated flower beds which even fail to open. The crop thus obtained becomes uneconomical as flower heads are the major contributors of oil.

DISTILLATION

The harvested material before distillation, is dried under shade for 2 days. It is better to distill this immediately rather than store it. The dried material is steam distilled for obtaining the good quality oil. However, for estimation of essential oil under laboratory condition particularly of small samples, the shade dried material is hydro-distilled.

In case of hydro distillation, the material is taken in glass still and water is added to it so that around three fourth the material is immersed in water. The material is then heated. During boiling, water vapours along with vaporized oil moves into condenser, gets condensed and collects in graduated receiver. Based on the amount of oil collected, the oil content in the material can be determined.

However, for commercial purposes steam distillation should be used. The distillation equipment consists of (i) Boiler-which produces the steam; (ii) Distillation still-in which the material is filled and steam passed ; (iii) Condenser wherein the vaporized oil gets condensed into a liquid form and (iv) Receiver to collect the oil.

The boiler and the distillation still are made of steel. The boiler is connected to the distillation still by a steel pipe through which steam passes. A perforated grid (plate) is placed at the bottom of the still on which the plant material kept. The distillation still is connected to the condenser through a pipe. The condenser consists of many metallic pipes mounted inside a jaket. It is provided with an inlet and outlet. Water is passed through the gap between the pipes in order to cool the steam and essential oil vapours into liquid form, which then gets collected in the steel receiver. The oil being lighter than water and insoluble, floats on the water surface.

For distillation the air dried herbage is chopped into smaller pieces and then charged into the still. While filling, the material should be tightly packed inside the still, as otherwise steam, channels may be formed during distillation resulting in poor yields. About 5-6 hours are required to complete the charge.

After decantation of the top clear layer oil, the bottom layer which consists of small quantities of water and oil has to be clarified. To separate the oil, saaturated solution of sodium chlride is added to this mixture so that a separate layer of water and oil is formed. The lower water layer is drained off witt the help of separating funnel and the upper of oil is collected.

YIELD AND OIL CONTENT

The yield of fresh herbage including flower heads is around 12-13 tonnes per hectare. Though under laboratory conditions, the oil content in whole plant after drying it in shade for 2 days is 0.29 percent, an average recovery of around 0.2 percent under scale distillation yielding 12-13 kg of oil per hectare may be considered satisfactory.

When oil is extracted from the whole plant, flower heads contribute the major protion of the oil. The contribution of leaf and steam towards percentage oil content in a whole plant is very less. The percentage oil content in different plant parts worked out under laboratory conditions on v/w basis is as follow:

Plant part	Percentage oil content (2 days air dry basis)
Flower heads	0.53
Herbage (leaves+stem)	o.14
Whole plant	0.29

CHEMICAL CONSTITUENTS

Davana oil has a deep mellow, persistent rich fruity odour. Freshly ditilled oil has sharp herbal top note which disappears on keeping, leaving a mellow and pleasant note. The oil at room temperature on (about 23^0 C) is viscous and is slow to filter. The main component of the davana oil is Davanone which is a sesquiterpene ketone. Other components isolated in a fraction of davana oil are Linalool, Dehydro-L-linalool, Terpinene-4-ol, Nordavanone (C-terpenoid) and Davanafurans. These compounds are reported to contribute for the characteristic odour of davana oil.

PHYSICO-CHEMICAL CHARACTERISTICS OF DAVANA

1.	Colour and appearance	Oil obtained at CIMAP,Bangalore, Brown, viscous clear liquid,very aromatic some what balsamic and persistent odour
2.	Specific gravity	0.9587 at 28^0 C
3.	Optical rotation	$+41^0$ C
4.	Refractive index	1.4852 at 28^0 C
5.	Acid value	4.315
6.	Ester value	44.27
7.	Saponification	48.56
8.	Ester value after acetylation	117.58
9.	Solubility	Opalescent even upto 10 volume 80% ethyl alcohol

Chapter-8

CULTIVATION AND IMPROVEMENT OF SWEET MARJORAM

INTRODUCTION

MARJORAM (Majorana hortensis Moench.) is an aromartic perennial herhfaceous shrub belonging to the family Lamiaceae. The plant is native to Southern Europe, North Africa and Asia Minor. It is an important kitchen herb having a wide range of uses and it is cultivated throughout Europe, Mediterranean region as well as North and South America. France and Egypt are the major exporters of marjoram oil in the world. United States of America alone consumes about 300-400 tonnes of majoram oil per annum but France and Germany have large markets with over 600 tonnes requirements.

In India, this crop finds it cultivation only on small scale in several states. It is being grown in home gardens of Karnataka, Andhra Pradesh and Tamil Nadu as a flavouring and herb spice from time immemorial; fresh springs of this plant are also used to flavour garlands bouquets and other kind of wreathes for hair adornment. In the traditonally growing countries the leaves of the plant are used fresh or dried and highly esteemed as a condiment for seasoning food. Fresh leaves are employed as garnish and incorporated in salads and vinegar. Dried flowering tops are used for sachets and potpourri. The aromatic seeds are used in confectionery and french contitures.

Steam distillation of leaves and flower heads yields a volatile oil known in the trade as Oil of Sweet Marjoram. The oil is pale yellow to yellow green or colourless depending upen the material used for distillation.

The oil content in fresh leaves of marjoram ranges from 0.3 to 0.5 per cent. Although dried plant gives higher yield of essential oil upto 1 per cent it is better to distill fresh leaves and flowering heads than dried herhage as there is possibility of lower yeild of oil with flat note in case of dried leaves.

The oil is mainly employed in flavouring the food articles. It is very much in demend in food processing industries for flavouring the canned food. To a small extent it is also used in high grade flavour preparations leck this paragraphs for sprins bruises stiff and paralytic limbs and tooth ache and for hot fermentation in acute diarrhoea. Sweet marjoram is considered to be carminative expectorant and tonic leaves and seeds astringent. An infusion of the plant is used as stimulant sudorific emmenagogue and galactogogue it is reported to be useful in asthma hysteria and paralysis.

The essential oil obtained from the leaves of marjoram has got antimicrobial activity aginst Bacillus anthracis, Proteus vulgaris, Salmonella stanley, streptoicocus agalactiae, Staphylococcus guneus, Salmonella newport and Aspergillus fumigatus.

FLORISTICS AND CROP IMPROVEMENT

(I) FLORISTICS

There exists some confusion with regard to the so called marjoram oil and the botany of plants from which these oils are derived. The vernacu!alrterm marjoram comprises several sromatic plants belonging to different species. The best known is undoubtedly Origanum majorana which grows wild as a perennial herbaceous shrub. It is cultivated extensively as sweet marjoram Majorana horensis. It is also called as knotted majorana and is being cultivated in its native Mediterranean region since ancient times.

Sweet marjoram is a perennial plant which is often grown as an annual because it does not survive well in wet cold winters. It grows as an upright compact bush about 20 to 40 cm in height with a woody main stem and many softer branches. The leaves are round soft matt green and of a marvellous sweet smell. In the bud the flower heads (spicules) are the same grey green colour as the leaves and are like little ovel knobs. These expand slightly to show the frill of tiny white flowers only just protruding from their overlapping bracts.

There are other marjorams	—	some of them are:
Common marjoram	—	Origanum vulgare
Dittany of crete	—	Origanum dictamus or Amaracus distamus
Golden marjoram	—	Origanum aureum
Pot marjoram variegated	—	Origanum onites variegatum or Origanum Prismaticum
Winter marjoram	—	Origanum heracleoticum

Botanically the Origanums differ from other labiates in that flowers are collected in to condensed little cylindrical heads called spicule this formation can easily be seen in sweet marjoram. The species are them divided into three section according to its shape of the calyx which can be seen with a magnifying glass.

1. Section Origanum has a calyx with five even teeth Ex.O. vulgare and O. heracleoticum
2. Section Marjorana has one lipped deeply slit calyx Ex.O. majorana and O. onites.
3. Section Amaracus has a two lipped calyx. Ex. Dittany.

It is reported that the flavour and aroma vary enormously not only between the different species but also according to the type of soil in which they are grown, the amount of sunhine and water they receive. The name Origanum means, Joy of mountains, and they are indeed a joy to grow.

(II) STUDIES ON FLORAL BIOLOGY

FLOWERING ANTHESIS AND POLLEN STUDIES

Although the number of days taken for first flowering varies from 55 to 70 days after planting the cuttings the average time taken for first flowering is 61.7 days. Flowering in marjoram is observed almost throughout the year under Bangalore conditions. It normally starts two months after planting the cuttings and continues for one more month. However during the winter flowering is delayed by about 15 days thus extending the duration of the crop. On an average duration of flowering is observed to be 37.3 days.

The anthesis takes place from 8.00 a.m. to 3.00 p.m. and the peak period (38%) is between 12.00 noon and 1.00 p.m. The anther dehiscence takes place from 10 a.m. to 4 p.m. after the flowers are fully opened and maximum anther dehiscence (32%) is observed from 1 p.m. to 2 p.m. Stigmatic receptivity is found to be maximum (60%) on the day of anthesis. While it is reduced to 40 per cent receptivity one day after anthesis. The size of pollen grains of marjoram is found to be 43.749 p.m. in length and 27.707 h.m. in breadth. The pollen grains are white in colour when observed in light. They are oblong to oval in shape when dry and round in acetocarmine solution.

Flower: Bracleate sessile complete bisexual both calyx and corolla irregular zygomorphic and hypogynous. Bract porminent spatulate 4 mm dia hairy along the margin and on the abaxial surface. It encloses calyx.

Calyx: Five sepals united to farm a single spatulalte structure with wide and large (5 mm dia) bilobed anterior and narrow small posterior parts hairy along the margin and abaxial surface.

Corolla: Five petals gamopetalous bilobed with 3 petals (paseterior) and 2 petals (anterior): imbricate aestivation. Corolla tube 4 mm long and 5 mm dia. white in colour corolla tube is wider (2 mm) above and narrow (1 mm) below each limb measures 1.5 to 2.0 mm.

Androecium: Four epipetalous didynamous stamens the anterior shorter (3 mm) than the posterior (4 mm) ones. Staminode is absent. Anthers two celled dehiscing introrsely or by longitudinal slit hypogynous disc fleshy.

Gynoecium: Superior bicarpellary syncarpous ovary four partite by a secondary division with a single anatropus erect basal ovule attached to an axile placenta in each locule style gynobasic (5 mm long) simple with bifid stigma.

Fruit: Four one seeded nutlets included within the persistent calyx.

Seed: Seed oblong colour brown size 3 mm long and 1 mm wide testa thin endosperm scanty embryo with flat cotyledons parallel to the fruit axis and a short inferior radical.

(III) CROP IMPROVEMENT

EVALUATION OF GERMPLASM

In an evaluation trial five genotypes viz Bangalore Tirupattur Guntur Krishnagiri and Dharmapuri types were evaluated for 15 characters at Bangalore. The results indicate significant differences among the genotypes for fresh weight of the herb total weight per plant dry weight of the spikes oil content in spikes and oil content in whole plant. High PCV and GCV coupled with high heritability leading to high expected genetic advance is observed for fresh weight of herb per plant total fresh weight fresh weight per plant dry weight of spikes per plant oil content in spikes and oil yield per plant.

Plant height plant spread fresh weight of the herb dry weight of spikes and the total dry weight of whole plant are significantly and positively. correlated with total fresh weight while oil yield per plant correlated non significantly with all the characters studied.

Path analysis revealed that the direct effects of total dry weight of plant fresh weight of spikes plant height and fresh weight of herb are of high magnitude. In addition to this, these also served as main channels to direct the indirect effect of other characters towards fresh herb yeild per plant.

Ontogeny of oil bearing structure revealed that the oil gland originates from a protodermal cell which undergoes continuous divisions and finally it consists of 12-14 cells of which four small cells are located in the centre and 8 to 10 large cells are peripherally arranged.

CROP PRODUCTION AND MANAGEMENT

(A). SOIL AND CLIMATE

Marjoram prefers well drained and nutrient rich soil for its successful growth. Soils which have a tendency to form crusts will retard germination greatly and hence are not suitable for marjoram unlike most other herbs fron the same family. Marjorams have a strong flavour when grown in a rich soil. It is one of the few crops which can be grown even on saline or alkaline soil as well and can withstand high salt content in the soil. The plants resist drought but prolonged period of drought are harmful.

Marjoram is primarily a warm climate plant and as such rather sensitive to cold. Yet it is hardy enough to grow in colder regions provided the plants are well mulched with straws or leavles for protection against winter killing or still better grown as an annual crop and planted a new each season. It requires sunny position though mid day shade is preferred.

Planting time is one of the important factors in obtaining optimum yields from a unit area. Raising the crop in proper season is necssary as due to prevoailing optimum conditions the plants put on maximum growth and result in good yield. Under Bangalore conditions November planting is found to be superior to its counterparts for all the growth and yield attributes.

(B) PROPAGATION

(I) NURSERY RAISING

Marjoram can be propagated by seed. The seeds can be sown twice a year during June-July and September-October. They are sown in well prepared nursery beds in rows spaced at about 15 cm apart. About 50 g seeds give seedlings sufficient to plant one hectare area. As the seeds are tiny they are mixed with dry sand in the ratio of 1:10 and broadcasted in rows of nicely prepared nursery beds. A thin layer of sand is spread uniformly over the seeds to cover them. The seeds germinate after 8-10 days. Sprinkler irrigation and thorough after care of seedlings is taken after germination. The seedlings are ready for transplanting when they are about 2 months old.

As this method is rather cumbersome and the initial growth of seedlings is slow it is followed only where growing of crop through seeds is necessary.

(II) VEGETATIVE PROPAGATION

Sweet marjoram is commercially propagated through cuttings. The plants propagated through this method are not only true to type but also grow faster initially. Stem cuttings obtained from the second ratoon are the best for planting. Herbaceous cuttings of 15 cm length the cuttings. After planting they should be transferred to mist propagation chamber or in shade where they are watered twice a day. Cuttings take about one month to root. Ikndividual polythene bags of small size may also be used to raise the cuttings. In this method the roots do not get damaged during the transplanting and establishment of rooted cuttings in the main field is about 90- per cent.

Healthy seedlings or rooted cuttings with well developed root system only should be used for transplanting into the main field.

(C). STUDIES ON NUTRIENT AND SPACING

In an experiment under Bangalore conditions to determine the influence of nitrogen (80, 160, 240 and 320 kg/ha) and phosphorus (40, 80, 120 and 160 kg/ha) revealed that all the levels of nitrogen had significantly affected almost all the characters studied. While the application of phosphorus had no signigicant effect on any of the vegetative characters. Thus it is advisable to apply nitrogen at 240 kg/ha phosphorus at 40 kg/ha and potash at 80 kg/ha in three equal split doses in order to obtain maximum herbage and oil yield in marjoram.

In order to find out the effect of plant spacing and planting date on growth yield and oil content in marjoram the experiments were conducted at Bangalore. The results revealed the influence of the planting date on the growth of marjoram in all the three harvest except in case of days taken for flowering in the first harvest. July planting requires the maximum number of days of flower, while those planted during November needed the least number of days. The essential oil content and fresh herbage yield per hectare also are found significant. The plants grown during November recorded the maximum oil content and it was least in the October planting. November planting is found to be superior to its counterparts for all the growth and yield attributes.

Different spacings were also found to influence the growth and yield of marjoram significantly. The plants spaced at 30x30 cm recorded maximum oil content. While it was minimum in case of plants spaced at 15x7.5 cm although they recorded the maximum herbage and oil yield. This may be attributed to the reason that the closer spacing accommodates more number of plants per unit area which ultimately results in higher herbage and oil yield per hectare when compared to wider spacing having less number of plants per unit area.

(D). USE OF GROWTH REGULATORS

Studies conducted at Bangalore revealed that the application of GA3 at 200 ppm increased the fresh herb recovery recording the maximum oil yield (0.397% oil content and 55.54 kg/ha of oil yield). Although cycocel at 500 ppm and triacontanol at 6 ppm increased the fresh herb recovery and oil yield over control but were next to GA3.

(E). CROP ROTATION/SEQUENCING AND INTERCROPS

In many places sweet marjoram is essentially a short term winter crop. Of the several possibilities of crop rotation raising of coriander cumin methi is promising. These crops can be gorwn as a monsoon crop. After their harvest the land is rested for three months and then it can be planted with marjoram.

(F). IRRIGATION AND INTERCULTURE

After transplanting the crop is irrigated by a sprinkler for 5-6 days and then a light surface irrigation is given. Subsequently the crop may be irrigated once in 4-8 days depending upon the season and the soil type. The crop is weeded as and when required which is followed by hoeing to provide good aeration in the soil.

(G). INSECT PESTS AND DISEASES

Marjoram is comparatively a hardy crop and no serious pest and disease has been reported on the this crop in India. Among the insects it is found to be some times attacked by termites which may be controlled by the application of termex 20% E.C. With regard to the diseases some times leal frust disease is found to affect the plants particularly during the cloudy weather. It can be easily controlled by spraying 0.2 per cent Blitox at weekly intervals.

(H). HARVESTING PRODUCTION OF ESSENTIAL OIL AND YIELD

Under Bangalore conditions the crop behaves perennial. The first harvesting is done after 90 days of planting when the crop starts flowering. While harvesting about 10 cm of the shoot above the ground level is left for further growth. The subsequent harvests can be carried out after 45 days of the first harvest. On an average about 4-5 harvests are taken annualy. Also there are reports that the crop can be retained up to seven cuttings under good management. After every harvest the crop is applied with the top dressing of nitogenous fertilizers preferably urea. To obtain the oil of export quality the first harvest should be done only after 90 days of planting.

(I) CHEMISTRY OF OIL

The oil of marjoram is a colourlelss or pale yellow to yellow green liquid with a tenacious odour reminiscent of nutmeg and mint.

The essential oils obtained from the seven germplasm collections viz Bangalore Tirupattur Krishnagiri Dharmapuri Guntur Mysore and Milan (Italy revealed the presence of more than thirty compounds.

The composition of the oils of the Indian germplasm revealed that they resemble the oil of the germplasm from Milan (Italy) in varied proportions. However the oil of Italian germplasm contained the maximum amount of cis sabinenehydrate (32.75%) while that of Krishangiri (Tamil Nadu) germplasm had the least amount (16.43%) Terpenin 4-ol was highest in the oil Krishnagiri germplasm and lowest in Milan oil whereas alpha terpinene is not detected in the oil of Mysore germplasm.

By and large the composition of oils of the seven germplasm collections investigated were found similar to the composition of the marjoram oils from USA and Europe but differed from the marjoram oil from North India which are reported to contain high amounts of phenolic contituents like thymol eugenol and carvacrol that are not recorded in the oils of seven collections.

(II) INFLUENCE OF HARVESTING STAGE ON THE ODOUR VALUES OF ESSENTIAL OIL

The major components in marjoram oil are found to show the variability in their percentage with respect to the oil constituents at different harvesting stages. There was a definite trend observed in their production and retention.

Some of the components like alpha thujene, alpha terpinene gamma terpinene, terpinolene linalool and cis sabinenehydrate alpha terpineol transabinenehydrate and beta caryophyllene are present in higher quantities at 30 days which gradually decline with the age and are least at 90 days. Whereas the compounds like p cymene and terpene '4' ol on the contrary are least at the beginning (30 days) but increase gradually to reach to their maximum at the end (90days). Thus indicating the possibility of their exploitation depending upon the requirements of the aroma chemicals for the purpose. However in the early days because of lesser availability of biomass the recovery of the oil and ultimately of the compound per unit area will be poorer.

The oil obtained from the plants harvested at 90 days is found to be most nearer to the International quality needed for export. Thus unless one wants to obtain some specific compound in larger quantities for definite reasons the crop for general purposes should be harvested only after 90 days of its growth.

(III) PRODUCTION OF ESSENTIAL OIL

Fresh herbage of Marjoram is team distilled for obtaining the oil. The distillation equipment consits of a boiler, distillation still, condenser and receiver. Distillation still is made of steel. It has a perforated metal sheet at the bottom to supprot the herbage which is loaded into the still for distillation.

Loading and unloading can be mechanised with the help of an overhead chain pulley block. The lid of the sitll can be swung aside during loading and unloading. It is important that the herbage should be evenly packed inside the still, as otherwise steam channels may from during the distillation and result in poor oil yeild. The condenser which cools the hot vapour received from the still, consists of many tubes made of copper or stainless steel and mounted inside a jacket.

The condenser is provided with inlet and oulelt for the circulation of cooling water. The hot vapours are cooled in the condenser tubes and the condensate flows out into the receiver and only the water gets drained out. The oil can be drawn off separately at the end of distillation. The receiver is fabricated out of two compartments, so that any oil escaping from the first compartment can be retained in the adjoining compartment, although this rarely happens.

Distillation is carried out preferably at atmospheric pressure as this will prevent any sort of burnt odour in the oil. Usually about four to five hours are required for completing one distillation. The oil should be made free from sediment, suspended matter and moisture before storing. It is stored in aluminium containers. The containers should be filled to the brim to exclude all air in order to prevent deterioration during storage.

(IV) YIELD

On an average marjoram may yield about 16-18 tonnes of fresh herbage per hectare which in turn may yield about 35-40 kg marjoram oil by distillation. An oil recovery of 0.3 to 0.4 per cent on fresh weight basis may be considered satisfactory.

Chapter-9

EXTRACTION OF ESSENTIAL OIL

The sliced and dried rhizomes are steam distilled for 3-5 hours for obtaining the essential oil. Froathing is noticed during due to the presence of starch in the rhizome. Paincker et al. found that dried and powdered rhizomes gave 2.40-3.88 per cent volatile oil. The essential oil of rhizomes collected from Chowgule college campus was found to vary depending on the month of collection of plant materials. Maximim oil content of 3.98 percent was observed in October when the plants were in dormant stage while a minimum of 2.4 per cent was noticed in June when the plants were in vegetative stage.

PHYSICO-CHEMICAL PROPERTIES OF OIL

Nadkami reported that the tuberous rhizome of Kacholam contained an alkatoid, starch, gun, fatty matter with a fragrant liquid essential oil and a solid white crystalline substance and mineral matter. The rhizome possessed a camphoraceous odour with somewhat bitter aromatic taste resembling Hedychium spicatum.

The essential oil has the following physical properties.

Specific gravity at 3^{0C}	0.8792 to 0.8914
Specific optical rotation at 3^{0C}	-236 to -430
Refractive index at 3^{0C}	1.4173 to 1.4855
Acid number	0.5to 1.3
Saponification number	99.5to 109.0

Petroleum ether extract pf tubers yield 2.05 per cent of residual essential oil. The presence of cinnamic acid derivatives such as ethyl cinnamate and ethyl-p- methoxy cinnamate in K. galanga was reported by Bindin and Sumsudin. Four major classes of chemicals namely cinnamate esters,flavanoids, diterpenoids and cyclohexane oxide derivatives were reported in seven species of Kaempferia including K. galanga (Tuntiwachwuttikul). The composition of essential oil of rhizomes of K. galanga in Malaysia has been investigated by Wong et al. and they reported 54 components of which the major constituents were ethyl -trans-p-methoxy cinnamate (16.5%),pentadecane (9%), 1,8 cineole (5.7%), gamma carene (3.3%) and borneol (2.7%). Terpenoid constituents amounted to 16.4 percent. Hussain et al., reproted the presence of p-methoxy trans-cinnamic acid and cinnamic aldehyde in the oil.

UTILISATION

Kacholam rhizome is pungent, hot, sharp, bitter, aromatic and light. The rhizomes find an important place in indigenous medicine as stimulant, expectorant, diuretic and carminative. It promotes digestion and cures skin diseases, piles, phantom tumours, coughs, oedema, fever, epilepsy, spleenic disorders, wounds, asthma and diseases caused by the mobidity of vada and kapha. It removes bad odour of the mouth. It has also the power of destroying parasitic organisms such as worms. It is used as an ingredient for the treatment of skin disorders and rheumatism. The rhizomes are used for protecting clothes against insects and are eaten along with betel and arecanuts as a masticatory. The rhzomes are attached to necklaces for their perfume. Leaves are also used as a perfume in washing hairs. Powdered tubers mixed with hoeny is given for coughs and pectoral affections. Oil in which they are boiled is used to remove obstructions in the nasal organs.

Steam distillation of rhizome yield essential oil which is utilized in the manufacture of perfumes and curry flavouring. They are also employed in cosmetics, mouth washes, hair tonics and toiletries.

Chapter-10

ESSENTIAL OILS

The essential oil content at the final harvest (240th day) varied from 1.2% in Arippa to 2.5% in China. Even though the essential oil content was more during the initial stage of growth, per hectare yield was maximum at full maturity in all the cultivars except in Jamaica, cv 646 and Arippa . Among 25 ginger cultivars studied by Nybe, Sivaraman Nair and Mohanakumaran, cv. Karakkal contained highest essenial oil level in ginger generally varied from 1.5% to 2.5%. A wide range of 0.8-4.4% essenial oil is reported by Connell form the ginger grown Australia, India, Africa and Jamaica. Lewis et al. observed a variation of essential oil from 0.9 (Tura) to 2.1% (Maran) among 27 cultivators. (Natarajan et al. observed a minimum oil content (1.0%) in Nadia and maximum 2.7% in 'Mysore' among 26 cultivars analysed by them.

OLEORESIN

The oleoresin percentage was generally maximum in immature crop (i.e., 150th day) in all the cultivars except in Maran and CV 646 and thereafther the tendency was to decrease steadily with maturity. This is in conformity with earlier reports; Jayachandran et al.,; Maurya et al.,. The calculated yeild of oleoresin per hactare (Table 3) is maximum in all the cutivars at 240th day in spite of the decreasing percentage of oleoresin. This is understandable since the fresh as well as dry weight of rhizome increase rapidly after 15th day. In view of this though the percentage of oleoresin is maximum during the initial period of growth, it is advisable to harvest the crop at full maturity to obtain maximum yield of oleoresin/ha. Among different cultivars, the maximum oleoresin per hectare at 240th day was in cultivar Nadia (336.68 kg) followed by Ernad Chernad (312.82kg) and Maran (272.14kg). Generally the oleores in content varied from 4 to 6% significant variation in oleoresin in 25 ginger cutivars, maximum (10.5%) being in Rio de Janeiro followed by Maran (10.0%) Sreekumar et al. observed a wide variation in oleoresin content in 30 ginger cultivars and the range of variation was observed to be 3.0% (Poona) to 10.8% (Rio de Janeiro). According to Mathai oleoresin decreased with maturity which is broadly in conformity with the present day.

GINGEROL IN GINGER OLEORESIN

The pungent principal in ginger is gingered and the estimation of gingerol presented in Table 1 shows that it varies from 9.10% in Venegara Selection to 28.05% in Jugijan in different cultivars at varying maturity. Natarajan and Lewis reported 18 to 20% gingerol in oleoresin though they did not mention the cultivar. There seems to be a concentration of gingerol in oleoresin about a month before the rhizome reaches full maturity (between 180 and 210 days) in majority of the cultivars except in, No.464 Ernad Chernad, 'Sleeva local' in which the gingerol content was maximum at full maturity.

Starch, the dominant constituent and an index to maturity increased in all the cultivars with maturity. The maximum starch content in full maturity varied from 40.34% (in Arippa) to 49.72% (in Karakkal). Jayachandran et al. (1980) Maurya et al., also reported an increase in starch content with increasing maturity in cultivar Rio de Janeiro. Natarajan et al. observed maximum starch content of 59% in Naidia and a minimum of 40.4% in cv. Assam.

PROTEIN

Protein content reaches the maximum at 180th day in almost all the cultivars except in Jugijan , Ernad Chernad and 'Sleeva Local' and thereafter decreasing rapidly. Jogi et al. also reported a similar trend in protein content in different maturation periods in14 cultivars of ginger. According to them, the protein content at full maturity varied from 4.21% in Wynad Local to 9.29% in Rio de Janeiro. However, a Natarajan et al. reported a higher protein which varied from 10.3% (in Assam) to 15.0% (in Manjeri) among 26 cultivars analyzed.

CRUDE FIBRE

Crude fibre content also increased with increasing maturity. This is in conformity with the findings of Jogi et al. Janachandran et al. and Maurya et al. However Mathai obsered a decreasing value in crude fibre content during maturity in seven ginger cultivars studied by him. Sreekumar et al. reported a minimum crude fibre content 3.5 in Tura and maximum of 6.0% in Jorhat. Muralidharan reported a lower fibre content of 4.23% in Himachal Pradesh and maximum of 8.44%in 'Thodupuzha'. The present investigation indicated that minimum crude fibre content was in Jamaica (4.85%) and maximum (6.90%) in Sleeva Local.

Commercial exploitation of ginger should be limited to ginger oleoresin and essential oils alone and not for all the components as described above it is not economical to upscale the process meant for them. Hence the process description is limited to the these by products.

COMMERCIAL EXTRACTION OF GINGER OLEORESIN

A concentrated from of ginger which contains not only its aromatic and odorous constituents but also the non volatile pungent principles, is the oleoresin of ginger often called commercially as gingerin. In preference to natural spice, usage of oleoresin is gaining ground due to its high flavour intensity low microbial contamination and economy in use. Adamsan elaborated the problem relating to the production of ginger oleoresin with appropriate solvent or solvent combinations. A need for the specific solvent and extracts only aroma and pungent constituents prohibiting the admixing of non flavour constituents like organic acids sugars soluble oligosachharides and colouring include selection of raw materials combination of the spice, choice of solvent and extracting conditions solvent recovery and residual solvent in the oleoresin besides the overall quality are the factors that determine the efficiency of the process. Earlier reports on the oleoresin extraction give only brief summary and not the technical details of the process. A combrehensive account of continuous extraction give only brief summary and not the technical details of the process. A comprehensive account of continuous extraction process amenable to automation and control and quality of the oleoresin thus obtained are presented in this part.

PROCESS DESCRIPTION FOR OLEORESINS

Dried ginger samples used in this study were procured from the wholesale market of Calicut. They were powdered using a pestle and mortar and sieved through 20 mm mesh. Oleoresin was extracted by conuter current sequential soxlet and cold solvent percolation methods,.

Counter current extraction - A step-wise working pattern of counter current extraction is persented in Fig 2. Three glass colummss 45x4 cm were taken and filled with the solvent (125 ml). After 6 hours contact soluble from column I is taken to column II and from II to column III thereby solvent from step I comes in contact with spice of the successive step. Sequential extraction Sequential extraction adopted in this study as follows. There 45x4 cm columns are filled with 220 g spice and 75 ml of the solvent. After 6 hours spice solvent contact the elute from A is transferred to column B, from B+ to C and from C to A. This is repeated after 6 hours without either changing the solvent or spice. After operating this for 4 cycles the eluates are pooled up, solvent stripped under vacuum and thick viscous oleoresin in separeted.

Solvent extraction - In a solvent extractor 30 g of the spice powder is loaded with a cotton plug on the capillary of the extractor and extracted with 100 ml of the solvent for 3 hours at 90 C. Spice solvent in this process is ensured for 10 cycles then extract is removed, stripped of the solvent under vacuum an a thick mass is separated.

Cold solvent percolation method - 10 g of the spice powder is loaded in a glass column 45x1.5 cm and 125 ml of the solvent is percolated after overnight contact. The percolate is stripped of the solvent and viscous mass is separated for further analysis.

Gingerol and essential oil content are estimated as per the ISI and AOAC methods respectively. Hydro-distilled oil is evaluated for the aroma quality by gas chromatography as per the mothod of Narayanan and Mathew.

OLEORESIN QUALITY

The input of spice, solvent, the ratio of solvent to spice, oleoresin yield, gingerol and essential oil contents under counter current, sequential soxlet and cold solvent percolation methods are presented in Table 5. The spice holding capacity in the counter current extraction is maximum 2.5,5 and 15 times more as compared to sequential, soxlet and lab methods respectively. Spice solvent utilization in counter current extraction is minimum and maximum in lab method. Even though extractive yield maximum by soxlet method but it is comparable to lab and counter current methods. Similar trend is observed in case of essential oil contents. A heat treatment beyond 100 C is not desirable and is likely to remove some of the volatile constituents and soxlet extraction employing high temperature evidently reduce the volatile oil. A sliht increase in the oleoresin content may be due to influx of resinous matter. Gingerol content do not appreciably change due to various extraction methods. In the process desigining an ideal situation would be to reach the

Table 5 - Spice solvent input and utilization, extraction yield, gingerol and essential oil contents of ginger oleoresin under counter-current, sequential, soxlet and cold solvent percolation.

Method of extraction	Imput spice g	Solvent ml	Solvent spice utilization ratio	Percent extraction yield	Percent gingerol	Percent essential oil
Counter current	150	375	2.50	6.04	28.0	28.0
Sequential	60	225	3.75	5.71	26.0	25.0
Soxlet	30	100	3.33	6.84	27.6	25.0
Cold solvent percolation	10	125	12.50	6.31	27.0	32.0

laboratory mehtod of extraction in terms of efficiency which is noticed in case of counter current extraction

Yield of oleoresin, gingerol and essential oil contents obtained by different solvent combinations is presented in Table 6. Alcohol extracts more oleoresin and essential oil content in the latter is also more as compared to other solvents. Gingerol content remained more or less the same.

FLAVOUR QUALITY OF GINGER OLEORESIN

Gas chromatographic profile of the essential oils obtained by the hydro-distillation of the oleoresin are presented in Fig.2 and the data presented in Table 7. Flavour of the oleoresin depends on the individual composition of the oil constituents. Pinenes, which impart turpentine odour,

is the highest in acetone; alcohol extractive

Table 6 — Yield of oleoresin, % gingerol and essential oil contents with different solvent

Solvent	Extractive yield	Gingerol	Essential oil
Acetone	5.8	24.5	26.0
Aceton alcohol (50v/v)	5.4	26.0	28.0
Alcohol	6.3	27.0	32.0

Table 7— Gas chromatographic evaluation of essential obtained from ginger oleoresin with different solvent combinations

Constituent	% of the total constituents present in oil obtained from the oleoresin with			
	Oil direct distillation	Acetone	Acetone alcohol	Alcohol
a-Pinene	0.40	0.48	0.54	0.26
Binene	0.05	0.23	0.33	0.20
Camphene	0.17	0.32	1.16	0.79
Propionaldehyde	0.16	1.75	0.68	0.54
Cineole	2.35	0.69	2.99	1.26
Linalool	0.37	0.55	0.88	3.26
Zingiberene	4.69	12.86	20.04	17.13
ar-curumene	46.15	51.70	55.16	46.24
Sesquiphellandrene	37.87	24.20	12.28	23.57
Unidentified	6.04	6.89	4.63	5.84

are comparable to original oil. Camphene and propionaldehyde are high in all the extractive than the original oil suggesting that these constituents accumulate more in the extractive oil than in direct distillation. In acetone:alcohol extract more cineole content is observed. Cineole imparts camphory note to the oil or oleoresin. Interestingly, original oil also contains high cineole; whereas in alcohol extractive it is low. Linacol which is generally present in high concentration in fresh ginger is more in alcohol extractive. Even though above constituents account for 6 per cent of the total composition, these minute quantities may be sufficient to alter the sensory

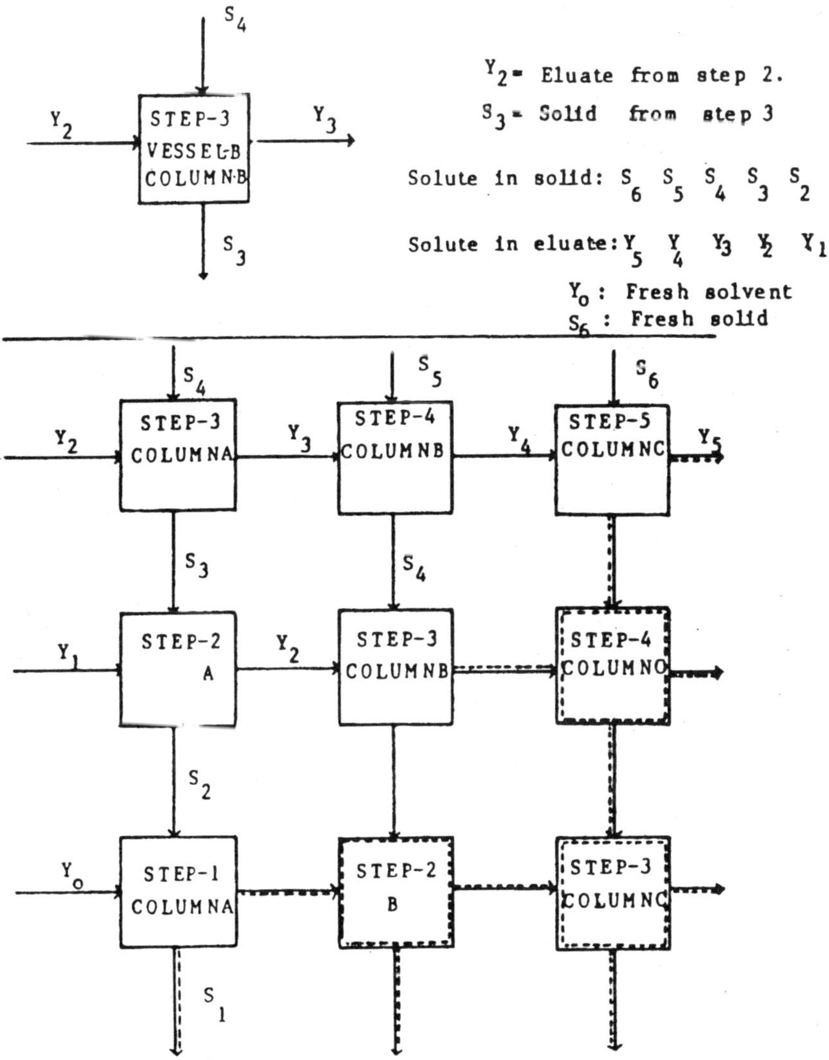

Fig. 2 - Schematic representation of counter current extraction of ginger oleoresin adopted in this study

profile of the ginger oleoresin. Zingiberene, B-sesquiphellandrene and Ar-curcumene are the most important compounds of the ginger oil. The algebraic sum of the zingiberene and sesquiphellandrene of alcohol extractive essential oil are more and comparable to original oil. Ar-curcumene is secondary product of essential oil and obtained on the conversion of sesquiphellandrene and zingiberene. This conversion appears to be more in acetone : alcohol extractive. The ratio of B-sesquiphelldrene adn zingiberene/curcumene which is indractive of the age of oleoresin is in the order of 0.88 adn 0.92 in case of essential oils of alcohol extractive and original oils respectively and are comparable.

To conclude the counter current extraction procedure described in this study is suitable for industrial upscaling as solvent : spice utilization is optimum with oleoresin yields comparable to that of the alcohol derived oleoresin is superior to all other solvent combinations.

ESSENTIAL OILS OF GINGER

Ginger oil obtainable by hydro or steam distillation of coarsely ground ginger rhizome is valued for flavour and perfumery. The yield of the oil in some of the important cultivars of flavour and perfumery. The yeild of the oil an some of the important cultivars of Indian ginger so far reported vary from 1.4% to 2.6% on dry weight basis (1,2). Reports on the detailed gas chromatograpgic analysis of the essential oils in the popular ginger cultivars are scanty.

PROFILE OF FLAVOUR IN GINGER CULTIVARS

Mature rhizomes of nine popular ginger cultivars; Wynad Local and Ernal Chernad from Kerala, Karakkal from Pondicherry, Maran from Assam, Narasapattam from Andhra Pradesh, No.646 from Himachal Pradesh (all from India) and Rio de Janeiro (ex- Brazil), Jamaica (ex-Jamaica) were washed with water to make them free of sand and soil particles. The rhizomes were dried in a cross flow draft air oven with temperature of 55 20 C and they were coarsely grounds to pass 20 mesh. Essential oils were obtained by hydro-distillation using a clevenger trap [4], oleoresin was extracted by cold acetone percolation mehtod [2], gingerol was determined according to the method of ISI [5].

Hydro-distilled oil was evaluated by gas chromatography using a flame ionization detector in Hewlett Packard 5730 A and gas chromatograph

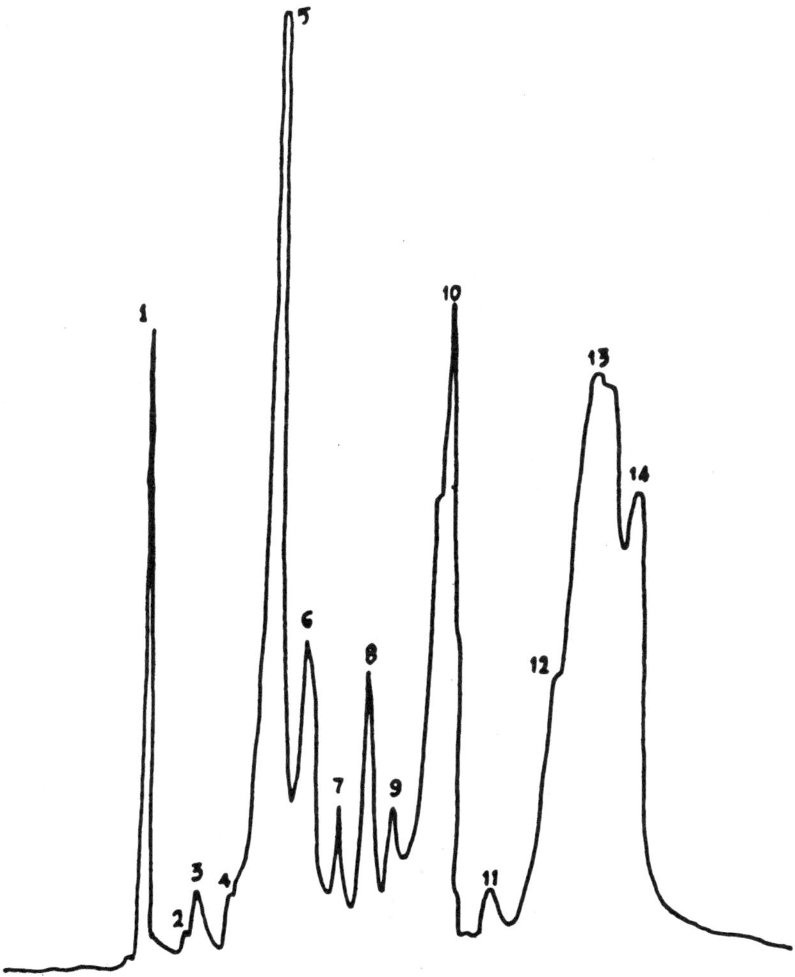

Fig. 3 - Gas chromatogram of essential oils from ginger oleoresin peak description - 1. a-pinine, 2. pinine, 3. camphene, 4. propionaldehyde, 5. cineole, 6. p-cymene, 7. linalool (peaks : 8, 9, 10, 11 are unidentifled), 12. zingiberene, 13. ar-curcumene, 14. B-sesquiphellandrene

interfaced with Anika 3200 series strip chart recorder. The operating conditions for gas chromatography were as follows: Detector temperature at 25^0 C, Injection port at 20^0 C and oven isothermal operated at 14^0 C (all the temperature were exclusive of ambient). The carrier gas nitrogen passed at 40 ml/min. Hydrogen and air flow was regulated at 20 ml/min and 20 ml/min and 220 ml/min respectively for detectable ionization. The range of FID was maintained at 1 to 100 at attenuation 2.1.8 matter 10% carbowax (100/120 mesh) on a support of chromosorb AWS60-80 mesh filled in stainless steel column (1/8 dia). Chart speed was maintained at 5 cm/min for the first 1.8 min and subsequently reduced to 1 cm/min for 14 min. The order of emergence of peaks were identifed as per the report [6] who have used similar test condition of gas chromatography with authentic standard for peak identification. a pipene (0.28 min) b pinene (0.30 min), camphene (0.44 min), propionaldehyde (0.48 min) cineol (0.64 min), P-cymene (0.8 min), linalol (0.94 min) 1-nonanol (1.10 min),zingiberene (2.06 min) ar-curcumene (3.06 min) and sesquiphellandrene (4.56 min), nerolidol (12.06 min) and zerumbone (13.56 min) could be identified. Peaks at retention times 1.26, 1.70, 5.86, 7.36, 8.55 and 10.36 minutes could not be identified. Peak areas were calculated by triangulation, areas added and respective components were expressed as per cent of total volatile oil.

A typical gas chromatogram of freshly extracted ginger essential oil is presented in Figure 4 and data in table 9. For ease of constituents are divided into four parts (1) pinene contents (ii) cineole (iii) zingiberene, B-sesquiphellandrene

Table 8 — Name of the cultivar, place of origin, per cent essential oil yield, oleoresin and gingerol in ginger.

Sl. No.	Name of the cultivar	Place of origin	Essential oil yield	Oleoresin	Gingerol
1.	Wyna- d local	Kerala	2.2	5.30	17.70
2.	Narasapattam	Andhra Pradesh	2.0	6.50	18.91
3.	Maran	Assam	2.0	6.05	19.25
4.	Nadia	Assam	2.0	6.05	20.09
5.	Karakkal	Pondicherry	2.0	7.75	20.85
6.	No.646	Himachal Pradesh	1.5	8.59	21.32
7.	Ernad Chernad	Kerala	2.0	8.10	24.66
8.	Rio-de-Janerio	Brazil	2.0	7.00	24.81
9.	Jamaica	Jamaica	2.0	5.37	26.67

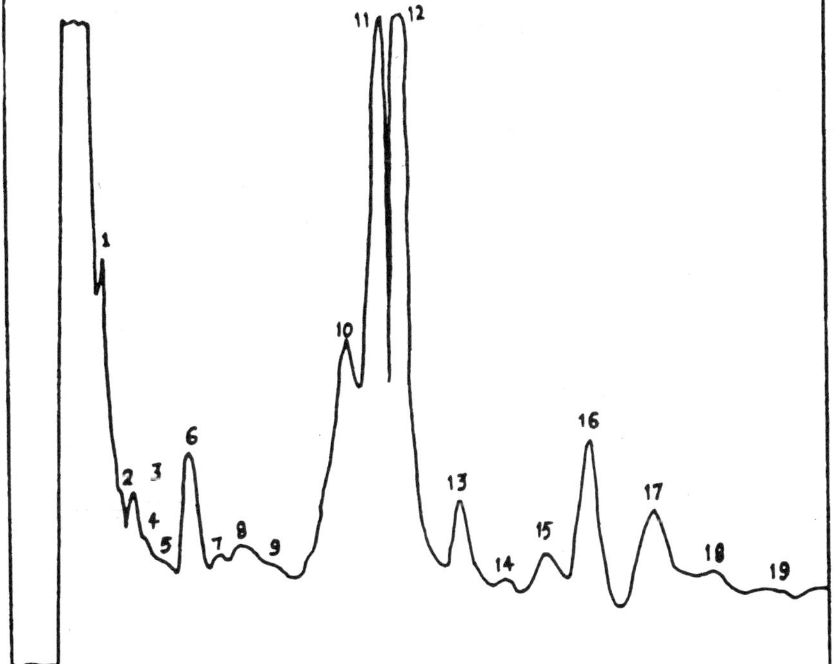

Fig.4. Gas chromatogram of essential oil of ginger (**Zingiber Officinale** Roscoe).

Compounds: Identified: (1)α-Pinene, (2) β-pinene, (3) Camphene (4) Propionaldehyde, (5) Cineole, (6) p-cymene, (7) Linalol, (8) 1-Noanol, (11) Zingiberene, (12) ar-curcumne, (13) Sesquiphe-llanderene, (18) Nerolidol, (19) Zerombone, Peak Nos. 9, 10, 14, 15, 16 and 17 are unidentified.

Table 9 - Essential composition in nine cultivars of ginger
(Expressed as per cent total essential oil)

Peak Compound	Hyand Local	Narasa Pattan	Maran	Nadia	No.646	Karakkai	Ernad Chernad	Rio-de-Janeiro	Jamaica
1. pinene	1.7	1.72	2.14	2.20	3.99	4.22	4.47	2.72	2.35
2. pinene	1.19	0.63	1.10	2.29	0.12	1.07	1.14	0.07	1.31
3. Camphene	1.40	1.46	2.95	2.83	2.15	1.28	2.22	1.47	1.41
4. Propinaldehyde	1.19	2.21	1.25	1.98	2.59	3.11	0.95	4.40	0.11
5. Cineole	8.53	0.49	1.97	13.29	0.07	1.55	1.61	5.13	0.97
6. p-cynene	2.88	0.16	3.45	5.24	7.77	1.07	7.70	6.88	10.80
7. Linalool	5.46	3.13	2.60	4.11	4.36	1.05	3.29	3.11	4.77
8. 1-Nonanol	5.85	5.64	2.95	5.14	6.35	2.38	7.85	2.09	2.81
9. Unidentifed	2.12	4.54	1.77	2.66	0.49	2.18	3.80	9.56	2.76
10. Unidentified	1.53	5.83	4.29	1.87	1.81	4.08	5.37	12.70	5.47
11. Zingiberene	27.56	20.23	43.69	30.50	35.61	50.89	11.34	21.77	27.69
12. ar-curumene	0.11	32.93	3.91	4.85	2.51	3.89	8.39	0.26	10.94
13.sesquiphellandrene	2.72	7.13	1.65	3.51	5.57	5.05	6.66	2.79	2.22
14. Unidentified	9.18	6.11	2.64	3.37	4.72	10.38	9.99	6.87	2.22
15. Unidentified	6.39	1.72	9.23	1.99	4.72	1.09	3.28	13.60	3.49
16. Unidentified	2.88	4.61	6.60	1.75	2.03	1.35	2.05	t	5.86
17. Unidentified-6	3.38	1.96	3.25	6.79	2.62	1.86	4.12	t	4.45
18. Neroliodol	4.67	t	3.38	6.89	7.30	1.52	8.94	t	6.80
19. Zerumbone	9.84	t	4.06	4.57	7.41	1.90	7.99	8.81	3.42

and ar-curcumene and (iv) nerolidol. Pinenes which generally impart turpentine odour were higher in cvs. Karakkal and Erand Chernal (4.22 and 4.77% respectively). The lower the contents better may be the quality of oil. Cineole content was high in cv. Nadia (13.29%) followed by cv. Wynad Local (8.55%). Bineole in the volatile oil impart camphory note to ginger oil. Zingiberene,sesquiphellandrene and ar-curcumene are the most important compounds of ginger essential oils and ar-curcumene is considered as a secondary product obtained by long storge [7]. sesquiphellandrene and zingiberene are the main components of freshly prepared oil and are converted to ar-curcumene varied from 0.11%(Wynad Local) to 23.93 (Naraspattam). The ratio of sesquiphellandrene + zingiberene to ar-curcumene which is indicative of the age fo the oil [9], varied from 2.73 (Jamaica) to 273.27 (Wynad Local). Nerolidol is reported to impart woody or soapy role by some workers [9] where as some other [11] relate it with sweet pleasent and balsamic notes. Zerumbone a constituent of wild ginger [2] was high in cv. Wynad Local followed by Rio de Janeiro. Zerumbone, a.

Sensory quality is not related to the increase ro decrease of one or more compounds [4]. Pinenes contributing to turpentine odour is more in cv. Ernad Cherand. Cineole contributing to turpentine odour is more in cv. Ernad Chernad. Cineole imparting camphory note is high in cv. Nadia. Zingiberene + sesquiphellandrene, imparting camphory note is high in cv. Karakkal ar-curcumene which is a product of a storage is high in cv. Narasapattam. Nerolidol is high in cv. Ernad Chernad. Zerumbone is high cv. Narasapattam. Narolidol is high in cv. Ernad Chernad Zerumbone is high cv. Along with major aroma bearing compounds imparting flavour to ginger essential oil the role of an identified peak is still to be elucidated. Until the contribution of the individual compounds alone and in combination with the other counter parts is established, it is difficult to characterize the aromatic profiles of ginger oil.

Turmeric and ginger are two aromatic plants which are valued for their by products more than the dried spice. An appropriate cultivar and method are two important criteria which promising entrepreneurs should select in order to develop spice based industry. By products of turmeric and ginger lead better economic returns to the entrepreneur if he / she is quality conscious and attempt to monitor the quality continuously. Caution should be exercised in selecting the food grade solvent and then also keep the solvent residues at their minimum levels so that the finished by product reach the prescribed national and international standards.

Chapter-11

ESSENTIAL CHEMICAL CONSTITUENTS PROFILE IN TREE SPICES

NUTMEG, Clove and Cinnmon are the major tree spices and are sources of essential oils among tree spice. The plant parts, nut and the mace (the seed and aril) of nutmeg, flower buds of cloves and leaf and bark of cinnamon are main sources of essential oils from where the oils can be extracted on the industrial scale. Well researched information on these tree spices and the profile of chemical quality is scanty.

NUTMEG (MYRISTICA FRAGRANS L.)

Nutmeg, Myristica fragrans L. is indigenous to eastern islands of the Mouluccas in Indonesia. The tree produces two separate spices nutmeg (the dry shelled seeds) and mace (the dry arillus). The nutmeg and 15 tonnes of total area under this crop in India is estimated to be 250 ha producing 180 tonnes of mace The major nutmeg tracts in India are Kerala and Tamil Nadu. Even though nutmeg oil and oleoresin are widely used in perfumery and confectionery, reports on the aroma quality are scanty.

Nutmeg Myristica fragrans L is a source of two spices viz. nut and the mace. Analytical characteristic of mace fat and is lipid composition studies confirm its suitability for perfumery. Even though nut is reported to contain 28.35% of solvent /fat, reports about its analytical characteristics and lipophilic profile are scanty.

At the National Research Center for Spices Calicut many studies on the profile of chemical constituents for elaborating the sex expression lipophilic profile of solvent extractable fat and chemical quality investigations in Germplasm etc. were conducted.

STEROID DEGRADATION COMPOUND ASSOCIATED WITH SEX EXPRESSION IN NUTMEG FRAGRANS)

Characterization of sex in nutmeg Myristica fragrans L. has been investigated without much success so far. Currently sex determination is possible only after flowering commences which is five to six years after transplantation. Identification of sex in nutmeg was attempted by morphological chemical and physiological methods. Quite interesting studies were made in this spice at the NRCS and the researchers conclusively proved the association of a steroid degradation compound.

(A) EXTRACTION AND ESTIMATION

Leaf samples from 32 males and female lines of eight year old nutmeg plants were collected and the enzymes were inactivated. Dried leaf samples were finely powdered and 5 g of the samples were extracted with chloroform for 24 hrs at ambient temperature. The extracts were centrifuged at 19,980 g for 5 min. Clear supernatant fraction was flash evaporated to near dryness adn redissolved in 2 ml of chloroform.

The leaf extract was chromatographed on thin layer plates coated with silica gel G (0.25 mm) and activated at 60^0 C (1 hr) using benzene and ethyl acetate (4:3 v/v)Two chrumogenic splphuric acid and 5 % alcoholic phosphomolybdic acid were tried respectively for consistency in identifying steroids and their degradation products. The plates were heated at 110^0 C for 2 min. B-sitosterad and stigmasterol were co-chromatographed and treated as above.

(B) IR AND MS OF EXTRACTED STEROIDS

Spectra om Perkin Elmer 3400 IR spectrophotometer (form 4000 to 600xcm) and in Hewlett Packard mass spectrometer operating at 70 ev and an ion source temperature of 170^0 C were recorded every 6 sec and processed by VG Digispec display data system which produced standard bar graphs for direct comparison.

The chloroform extracts were spotted on TLC plates-a typical chromatogram in chloroform is presented in figure 1. Under the conditions of TLC development stigmasterol and sitosterol have similar Rf values (0.8).

Sitosterol undergoes degradative changes on storage. These degradative changes resulted in a compound having Rf values 0.5. Chloroform extracts of the male line also exhibit a similar patton. Oogoniol, a sterol having a similar structure as sitosterol undergoes degradative change the resultant compound is reported by Popplestone and Unrau as precursor of steroid hormone.The structural details of sitosterol and probable cleavege sister aour indicated is figure 2. Even though sitosterol in if cited as an example of Barbier Wieland degradative change this compound can result from similar steroids like cholesterol, campesterol etc. Such type of degradation is found in the male lines of nutmeg. By changing the solvent proportions attempts were made to differentiate the sito and stigma sterols. When the Zones corresponding to stigma and sito sterols were re chromatographed after a preliminary clean up Rf values remain as in the pure compound. This indicates that degradation is partial and complete degradation does not occur. Phadnis and Choudhary reported difference in chlorophyll pigments, P, N and K contents as well as in the carbohydrates between the male and female lines but could not arrive at a tangible conclusion with any degree of certainty.

IR Spectra of purified fraction of plant origin (a) and sitosterol (b) at Rf 0.5 are presented in figure 3. A peak at 1680 cm and 1750 cm represent C=O and CH^3 CO groupings respectively. The fingerprint region of spectra indicates the long chain hydrocarbon. Super imposition of (a) over (b) indicates the similaruity in the nature of the compound.

Pure compounds obtained after TLC clean up are subjected to Mass Spectroscopy (MS) and scanned through 40 to 600 a.m.u.at a fixed voltage. The MS of the purified fraction of plant origin (a) and sitosterol (b) are presented in figure 4. Hundred per cent abundance of a compound having a molecular weight of 150 units is found in both the above fractions. A tentative indentification of the compound is made as 1-dimethyl 2-ethyl butyl methyl ketone on the basis of IR,MS and know reactions of sitosterol and its analogues.

Under ambient conditions of oxidation sitosterol and its analogues undergo degradative change resulting in steroid hormone and ketone (as qouted by Finar.

In nutmeg plants, the consistent association of the degrdation of steroids in the male and the absence of such degradation in the female

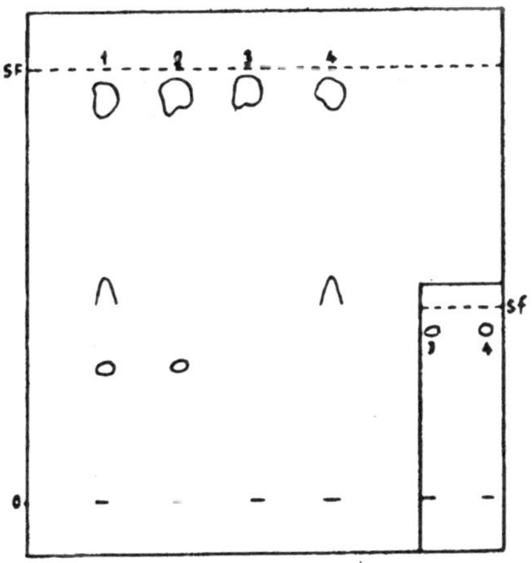

Fig-1

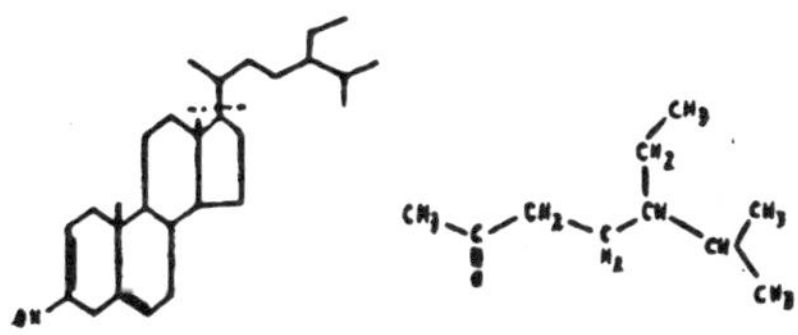

Fig-2

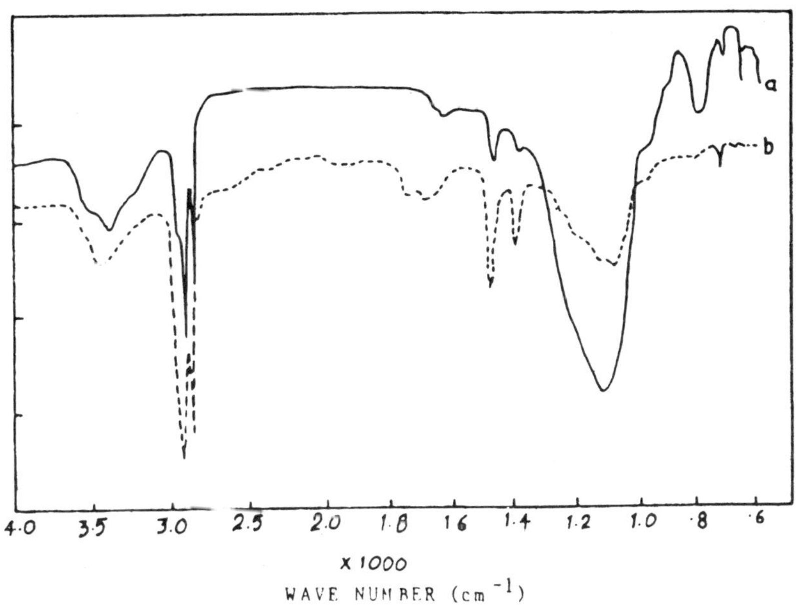

Fig. 3 - IR spectra of the degradation products of (opuriffied chloroform extracts) (a) male line of nutmeg and (b) B-sitosterol

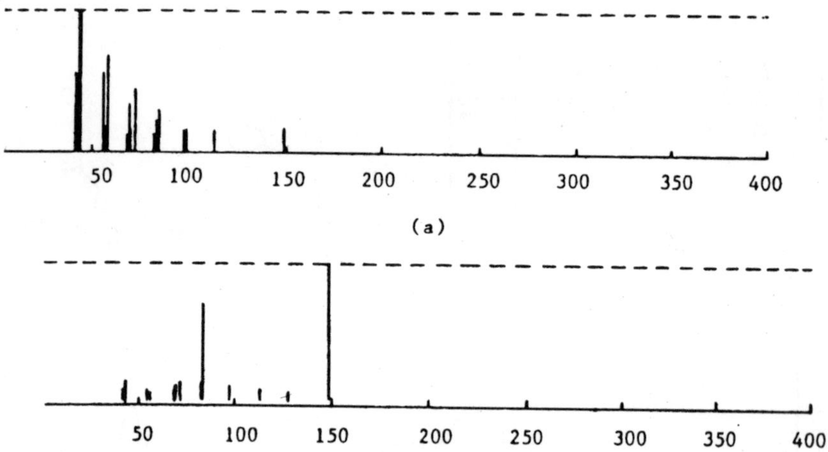

Fig. 4 - Mass spectra of degradation products (purified chlorofem extractive) of (a) male line of nutmeg and (b) B-sitosterol

seems to be indicating a role for steroids in the determiation of sex in this plant species. The author in a pilot study noted similar difference in one year old nutmeg seedling also. Out of 20 seedlings so evaluated steroid degradation was noted in eight seedlings only. It may be possible that the process of degradation of steroids sets in during the early devolpment stages itself and this may be influening the differentiation of sex in nutmeg. Efforts are now under way to screen the seedlings based on the above difference in order to correlate the data with adult plant sex later when the plants come to bearing.

SOLVENT EXTRACTABLE FAT

Nutmeg nuts were obtained from market accessions (from CPCRI Research Center Kannara) and dried ground fine to pass 40 mesh and fat extracted as per the flow sheet (Fig. 5). For obtaining the total fats hexane extract was dissolved and quantified by gravimetry. It is necessary to use wide open column in place of ordinary glass columns since the hexand extra during the elution bloks the column by the formation of semi solid fat. However, by using a wide open column such a difficulty could be overcome the extraction of 200 g nut flour yield about 60g of nutmeg fat. Analysis for the residual solvents in the extractable fat indicate the presence of spice fat only. A wide variation in the total extractable tatwas observed in different accession. in per cent nut weights. extractable fat and lipid profile in selected accessions are presented in Table 1. It is generally observed that the fat content depends on the percent nut weight and varied from 24-30 % .

LIPID SEPARATION

The chloroform solubles were resolved by step wise elution into neutral glyco and phospholipds as per the method of Prakashchandra and Chandrasekharappa and respective fractions were quantified by gravimetry.

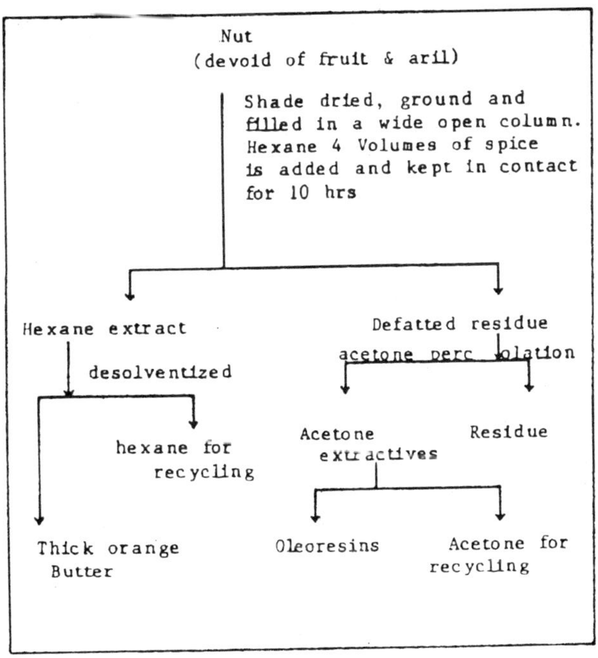

Fig. 5 - Flowsheet for the extraction of nutmeg butter and oleoresins

TLC OF LIPIDS

Known quantity of nutmeg fat from each accession was dissolved in chloroform along with lipid standards containing mono, di and tripalmitins (Sigma chemicals) in equi-proportions on a preactivated silica gel G (0.25 mm thickness) plate and developed in a solvent system containing petroleum ether (60-80^0 C) diethyl ether

Table 1 - Variation in nut weight total extractable fat and lipid profile in the selected Nutmeg accessions of CPCRI research center Kannara

Accession No.	Nut Weight	%** Fat	Lipid porfile*		
			Mono	di palmitins	tri
20	17	26.04	0.6	1.9	97.4
57	27	30.50	6.8	6.8	86.2
66	15	24.00	4.7	5.0	89.3
79	13	25.78	0.8	5.4	93.8

* Average of two determinations
** Hexane extraction

and acetic acid (90.10 v/v) and exposed to iodine vapours for visualisation. Another plate was developed and sprayed with o.5% Bromothymol blue in aqueous ethanol and exposed to ammonia vapour to confirm the above results.

TLC OF FATTY ACIDS

Fatty acids in nutmeg fat were separated by TLC with a linoleic acid as a marker standard as per the method of Morrison et al.

GAS LIQUID CHROMATORGRAPHY OF FATTY ACIDS

GLC of representative sample of the (methylead) fat was accomplished by using Hewlett Packard 56730 A GC interfaced with Varian Techtron recorder as per the method of Marta I. Aveldans and Lioyd Horrecks. Individual fatty acids were quantified and presented as the b% total of the acids.

A preliminary TLC after dissolving nutmeg fat in chloroform and visualized by iodine vapour exposure has revealed besides fatty acids, some saturated and unsaturated lipids. Hence a selective TLC was conducted for lipids and fatty acids. TLC profile for saturated lipids is presented in Figure 6. It is observed that along with the saturated lipids the unsaturated counterparts are totally absent which indicates that rancidity of this fat is negligible. As linear relationship is observed between concentration and the area the unknown lipids could be extrapolated. Mono di and triglyceride content in different accessions indicate the triglycerides vary from 86.2 to 97.4% whereas mono and diglycerides vary from 0.6 to 6.8 and 1.9 to 6.8% respectively. Out of three triacyl glycerols only tri-Myristicin was present in nutmeg while triolein and tripalmitin were absent.

fractionation of nutmeg fat into neutral, glyco and phospholipid resulted in 33% glycolipids followed by neutral lipids (28%) and phospholipids (10%). The unaccounted lipid fraction may be a lipoprotein. As neutral lipid portion is considerably high a detailed estimation

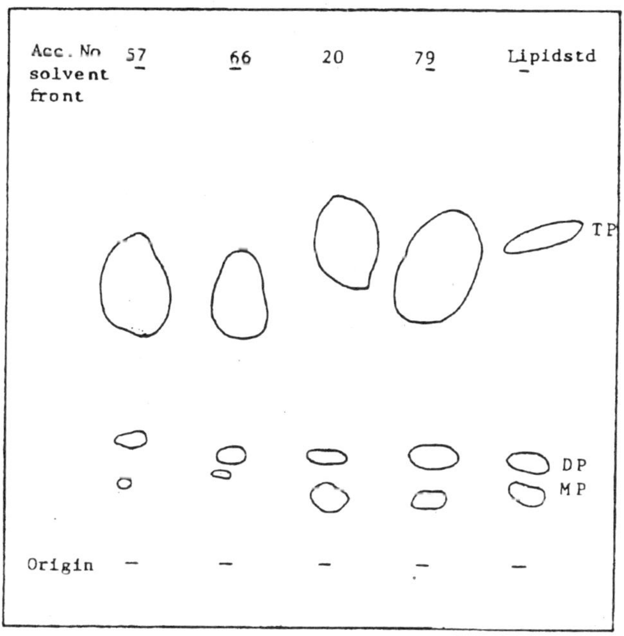

Fig. 6 - TIC trace diagram of saturated lipids in Fat extracted from nutmeg solvent system : Pet:ether Diethly : Acetic acid 90:19:1 (v/v) TP: Tripalmitin
DP: Dipalmitin
MP: Monopalmitin

on the fatty acid composition was taken upto understand the lipophilic profile of this fat.

TLC porfile of fatty acids is presented in Figure 7. Due to the paucity of fatty acid standards linoleic acid standard alone was co-chromatographed and the unknowns were identified on the basis of Rf values of Morrison et al. And presented in Table 2. Gas liquid chromatography of the fatty acids trimethylsilyl derivatives confirm the results of TLC. The acid value and the saponification value of the hexane extractable fat was found to be 8.98 and 196 respectively.

High saponification vlaue and low acid value indicate its suitability in perfumery. In spite of its easy extractability and desriable physical and

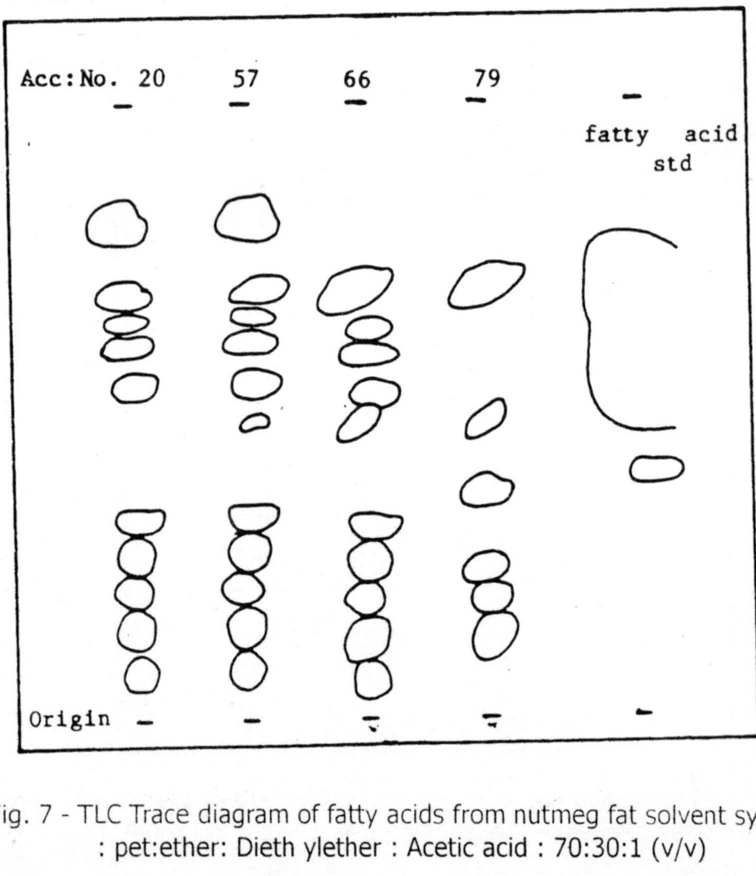

Fig. 7 - TLC Trace diagram of fatty acids from nutmeg fat solvent system : pet:ether: Dieth ylether : Acetic acid : 70:30:1 (v/v)

chemical characteristics, reports on the use of this fat either in perfumery or in confectionery are scanty. High glycolipid content (Finlay Macrutchie makes the fat desirable for confectionery and low lipolysis of triglycerides (Ahuja et al.) confirm the suitability of this fat for bread making.

AROMA QUALITY OF NUTMG OIL AND SOLVENT EXTRACTABLE FAT

Aroma quality of nut and aril of nutmeg accessions maintained at Central Plantation Crops Research Institute, Research Central located at Kannare, Trichur district is studied. Extractable fat, oleoresin and essential oil of nut and oleoresin and essential oil of aril are the main constituents analysed for evaluating these accessions. Acc. Nos.66 and 78 are superior as far as aroma quality is concerned. The quality components are projected to give per plant yields. Acc. No. 66 is found to yield 1.60 kg of extractable fat, 1.15 kg of oleoresin and 133.8 ml of essential oil. Aril

Table 2 - TLC profile of fatty acids in different accessions.

Fatty acids	% of total fatty acids
Caproic	1.8-3.6
Caprylic	4.2-5.2
Capric	3.6-4.1
Lauric	3.6
Myristic	5.2
Palmitic	2.6-3.6
Stearic	4.1
Oletic	0.2-2.4
Linoleic	4.3-6.7
Linolenic	0.9

of Acc.No 66 is found to yield 0.28 kg of oleoresin and 36.9 ml of essential oil (Data not presented). The aroma quality of aril which embraces the nut is importent to assess the overall performance of an accession. It may be a desirable to utilise this accession for further propagation.

OIL OF NUTMEG & OIL MACE

The extraction of volatile oil from nutmeg and mace is done by steam di stillation. The yield of oil varies according to the geographical distribution.

Wormy nutmeg in commercial distillation give much better yield of essential oil then sound nutmeg. Sound nutmeg as a matter and physicochemical properties the volatile oils of nutmeg and mace are so similar that trade rarely distinguishes them. Since mace is costlier than the nut, the essential oil is producted from nut and not from the mace.

Prior to distillation, nutmeg are powdered and the fixed oil is removed by hot pressing. This process is not economical as the fixed oil tends to lower the yields of essential oil. The physico chemical properties of the oil are presented in Table 3.Pinene and camphene account for 80% of the total oil whereas linalool 'borneol' 'terpineol' account for about 6% only. An aldehyde with citral odour is reported in traces by Power and Sahay. Myristcin and elemene the known hallucinogenic principles in nutmeg are 4% and 8% respectively.

CLOVE (EUGENIA CARYOPHYLLATA.L)

The yield and the physico, chemical properties of clove oil depend upon the distribution quality of cloves and their condition prior to distillation and the type of distillation employed viz, water and distillation, water and steam distillation or direct steam distillation.

Table 3 - Physico Chemical properties of the volatile oil of nut and mace of nutmeg and the chemical composition

	Nut	Mace
Specific gravity at 15	0.865 to 0.925	0.923 to 0.947
Optical rotation	+8 too +30	+2 to +11
Refractive index at 20^0C	1.479 to 1.488	1.486 to 1.494
Acid number	Upto 3.0	2.0 to 3.9
Ester number	2 to 9	1.2 to 7.3
Chemical composition	pinene, camphene, pinene, Dipentene, P-cymene, Linalool, terpineol, Broneol, terpinene 4-ol-,Geramiol, Safrole, Myristicin, Eugenol, Formic acid, Acetic acid, Butyric acid, Caprylic acid, A mono carboxylic acid: $C^{12}H^{17}O$, COOH, Myristic acid	

If whole cloves are employed, the forces of hydro diffusion play a vital role and the first fraction of oil contains high eugenol levels. Water distillation gives colve oil with 81% eugenol, suitable for perfumery whereas dry distillation yield strog oil contains even 95% eugenol. The yields of oil from clove buds, clove stems and leaves are 17%, 6% and 3% respectively The physico-chemical properties and chemical composition of oil from clove bud, stem and leaves are presented in Tabel 4. Besides the compounds listed, some steroid glucosides and phenolics are also reported to be present in clove oil.

Volatile oil obtained at lower maturity stage of clove is found to have more eugenol acetate and less eugenol. In fully mature clove, 4 months after the onset of flowering the eugenol acetate buds has mellow odour Organised research studies are yet to be conducted for elaborating the chamical quality of this spice.

CINNAMON

(CINNAMOMUM VERUM)

Cinnamon (Cinnamomum, verum Bercht & Presl.) is an important tree spice. Cinnamomum verum is the true cinnamon of commerce. The genus Cinnamomum belongs to the family Lauraceae, which has some 32 genera and 2000-2500 species. The dried bark (quill) of the tree is the cinnamon of commerce. Leaf and bark oil

Table 4 - The Physico chemical properties and chemical composition of clove buds stem and leaf oil.

	Volatile oil Buds	Clove stem Oil	Clove leaf Oil
Yield of oil	17.46%	1.050	1.054
Specific gravity	1.051	-0^0 36	-1 20
Optical rotation	-0^0 32	1.5352	1.5379
Refractive index	1.5318	1.5352	1.5379
Total phenol	91%	91%	88.5%
Solubility	1 vol.of 70% alcohol	1 vol.of 70% alcohol	1 vol of 70% alcohol
	Eugenol	Eugenol	Same as stem oil
	Eugenyl acetate	Eugenyl acetate;	
	Carophyllene	B-caryophyllene	
	Caryophyllene		
	Oxide	furfural	

Methyl salcylate	Mythl alcohol
Mehtyl n heptyl ketone	Methyl amyl
	Napthalene
Valeraladehyde	
Methyl n amyl carbinol	
Furfuryl alcohol	
n- mehtyl furfural	
Methyl heptyl carbinol	
Methyl furfuryl alcohol	
Dimehtyl furfural	
Vanillin	

are also extracted for commercial use. India imports cinamon bark for domestic consumption and as such there is ample scope for genetic improvement for higher yields. Cinnamon is propagated through seeds and the spceies is reported to be cross pollinated. No systematic evaluation of variability in cinnamon germplasm has been done. Ponnuswami et al. reported good variability for five growth characters in a six year old seedling population of cinnamon. Krishnamoorthy, Gopalam and Abraham also observed significant variability for bark oil content in cinnamon germplasm maintained by the National Research Centre for Spices, Calicut.

ANTHOCYANIN PIGMENTS OF YOUNG FLUSHES OF CINNAMON

A cinnamon tree in full flushing is a sight to behold owing to the beautiful coppery red to purple colour of the juvenile leaves. Interestingly many of the wild cinnamons such as C. malabatrum the most common species of Cinnamomum distributed in the peninsular India produce only coloured juvenile while in C. verum alone the juvenile leaves are coloured either green or purple. A correlation between the flush colour and essential oil content has been reported by Krishnamurthy et al. (in press), thereby making the character an important on that can be used in selection programmes.

Cinnamon produces juvenile leaves (flushes) during monsoon season (June-July) and again in December-January prior to flowering. The Juvenile leaves are either green or purple covering the entire emerging leaves and purple colour is restricted to a part of the leaf. A study was undertaken to characterise the pigments that contribute to the purple or flowers, fruits and young leaves are imparted mianly by anthocyanins. The biological role of these anthocyanin pigments is not very much understood though in flowers they are associated with pollination by insects.

Young leaves from C. verum were immediately excised into methanol hydrochloric acid (1 % v/v) as per the method of Markham. Thin layer chromatography of crude mehtanolic extracts of cinnamon was carried over on cellulose (0.5 mm thickness) Sigmacel Sigma Chemical Co, USA) with solvent system comprising of n butanol acetic acid and water (6:1:2 upper layer). Preparative TLC was carried out on cellulose (2 mm thickness) and subjected to visible and UV spectroscopy from 750-360 mm respectively. Sugar mouety was characterized after acid hydrolysis by TLC and co chromatography with known standards and standard mixture (Markham) using the solvent system n butanol; benzene: pyridine: water (5:1:3:3). Visualization was accomplished by the metheod of Touhstone and Dobbins.

Developed chromatogram when exposed to long wave uv gave a fluorescent pink spot at rf 0.4, which changed to blue under ammonia +uv thereby indicating its anthocyanin nature. Co-chromatography with cyanin extracted from red rose (Hiroake et al,) cinfirmed the presence of cyanidin class of antocyanins. Visible and ultra violet scan of the purified fraction gave a sharp absorption maximum at 523 mm in visible region which indicates the presence of cyanidin glycoside.

Analysis of the sugar moiety revealed glucose xylose and galactose indicating the occurence three cyanidin glycosides. Uv scanning spectra coupled with regenerated sugars by TLC indicate that the anthocyanin glycoside present in the cinnamon flushes are cyanidin glycoside cyanidin xyanidin xyloside and cyanidin galactoside. The leaves of the cut cinnamon stalks are removed prior to the preparation of the quiils. Before distillation the leaves are dried in shade. Approximately 100 gm of leaf is loaded into the extractor and distillation is continued for 7 to 24 hours depending upon the region and quantity of leaves charged. A change of 4 kg normally yields 37 to 50 ml of leaf oil. Approximately 30 to 35 lbs of leaf oil are obtained from one acre of cinnamon plantation. Florentine flasks separate the light oil from heavy oil. The distillation water is collected and used again to avoid any loss of oil. The method of distillation condition of the chips their age presence or absence of outer bark are of importance not only to the yield of oil but also to the quality. Usually Ceylon cinnamon bark contains 55% cinnamaldehyde and 18% eugenol.

QUALITY PARAMETERS OF CINNAMON (CINNAMOMUM VERUM) IN RELATION TO FLUSH COLOUR

Colour variations of young flushes from pure green to pure purple were observed in different plants with varying degress of purple pigmentation present in the intermediate categories. Earlier workers aimed their study on the distribution of volatile constituents in cinnamon obtained from different geographical regions. However they did not elaborate further to the wide range of variability in the morphological and quality attributes in this heterogeneous species. Attempts were made in this direction to correlate the flush colour to the quality parameters of cinnamon viz, bark oil bark oleoresin and leaf oil.

A sample of 239 cinnamon accessions planted at National Research Center for Spices were used for the study. Detailed study of colour patterns of young flushes was carried out and based on the dominance of one or the another colour these accesions were classified into four major classes viz, pure purple, purple dominated with green colour green dominated with purple colour and pure green. Quality parameters like the percentage to bark oil, bark oleoresin and leaf oil were estimated and these were correlated with colour to study whether or not there is any correlation between these characters. Distribution of the plants according to the four classifications is presented in Table 5.

It is observed that the number of plants falling into the first three categories comes of 44.4% and those in the fourth category 55.6% which shows that the ratio of purple and purple pigmented one to green was nearly 1:1 Hence' for statistical comparison purpose the first three groups were pooled and 'test' was carried out to see whether the flush colour has any indication on the quality parameters. The results are presented in Table 6.

Table 5 -- Distribution of cinnamon accessions of National Rescarch Centre for Spices according to colour categories

Category	No. of plants
I Purple	22(9.2)
II Purple dominated with green	53(22.2)
III Green dominted with purple	31(13.0)
IV Green	133(55.6)

Figures in parenthesis are percenteges.
Total accessions planted are 239.

Table 6 -- Mean values of thc quality parameters for the Two broad colour classifications

Quality parameters	Colour Groups to value			
	Purple		Green	
Bark Oil (%)	1.84	1.43	3.58	**
Bark Oleoresin (%)	8.41	7.90	0.97	NS
Leaf Oil (%)	1.68	1.73	1.72	NS

Table 7 -- Mean range and coefficient of variation for nine characters in cinnamon

Character	Mean	Range	CV(%)
Leaf length (cm)	13.08	8.75 - 20.69	17.83
Leaf breadth (cm)	5.06	3.31 - 8.30	18.74
Leaf size index	0.67	0.29 - 1.71	35.13
Fresh weight of bark (g)	207.41	30.00 - 840.00	67.19
Recovery of bark (%)	32.08	10.70 - 80.00	34.00
Bark oleoresin (%)	8.48	1.32 - 20.02	57.08
Bark Oil (%)	1.81	0.51 - 3.85	36.28
Leaf Oil (%)	1.97	0.72 - 4.80	48.46
Dry weight of bark (%)	64.70	8.00 - 305.00	74.73

Number of accessions :71

Table 8 — Inter-character association in cinnamon

Character	Leaf length	Leaf breadth	Leaf size index	Fresh weight of bark	Recovery of bark	Bark oleoresin	Bark oil	Leaf oil	Dry weight of bark
Leaf length	1.00	0.70**	0.91**	0.067	0.071	-0.00	0.069	– 0.034	0.062
Leaf breadth		1.00	0.90	0.18	0.063	– 0.106	– 0.048	– 0.006	0.21
Leaf size Index			1.00	0.13	0.029	-0.053	0.020	-0.021	0.13
Fresh Weight of bark				1.00	-0.069	-0.006	-0.165	0.19	0.94**
Recovery of bark					1.00	-0.13	-0.015	0.17	0.21
Bark oleoresin						1.00	0.17	-0.16	-0.046
Bark Oil							1.00	-0.37	-0.20
Leaf Oil								1.00	0.29**
Dry weight of bark									1.00

**Significant at 1% level

Table 9 -- Physico chemical properties chemical composition of Ceylon cinnamon leaf and bark oil.

	LEAF	BARK
Specific gravity	1.037	1.023 to 1.040
Optical rotation	-1^{0}96 to - 0^{0}40	Slightly laevorotary
Refractive index	1.5288	1.581to 1.591
Aldehyde content	4%	65 to 76 %
Eugenol content	77.3 to 90.5 %	4 to 10 %
Solubility	1.5 volumes of 70% alcohol	2 to 3 volunes of 70%
		Methyl an amyl Ketone
	Dipentene	Furfural
	Phellandrene	Phellandrene
	Pinene	p-cymene
	Benzaldehyde	Benzaldehyde
	Linalool	Nonyl aldehyde
	Geraniol	Hydro cinnamic
	Borneol	aldehyde
	Terpineol	Cinnam aldehyde
	Safrole	Cinnamic aldehyde
	Caryophyllene	Linalool
	Eugenol	Linalyl iso-butyrate
	Cinnamaldehyde	Eugenol
	Benzyl benzoate	Caryophyllene
	Cinnamanol	
	Foliol	
	Combanol	

The results show that there is a highly significant difference between the two groups with reference to bark oil content. Plants with purple coloured leaf flushes recorded about 29 % more bark oil.

Chapter-12

MEDICINAL USES OF INDIGENOUS AROMATIC PLANTS

INTODUCTION

THE IDENTIFICATION of plants useful to man from natural stands commenced in pre historic times. Experiments and trials were the two main ways through which man has learnt the various uses of plants : Only a few of the useful plants have so far been domesticated while a majority of them are still used from the wild. The wealth indigenous flora of a country is therefore one of the vital resources having significant bearing on health economy and environment (Bhattarai). Although considerable ethnobotanical studies have been carried out in the country identical studies on essential oil bearing plants are scant. The present communication is an attempt to scientifically update indentification investigation and documentation of their traditional therapeutic uses in Nepal.

THE STUDY

Nepal extends along the great Himalayan range south eastward from 80^0, 15^1 E to 88^0, 10^1 E longitudes, a distance of some 800 km has an area of 147, 181 sq. km where the altitude ranges from 60m to 8848m above the sea level. Being a mountainous country, it provides a great variety of habitats which is vidly reflected in the richness of its flora estimated to comprise about 7000 speices of higher plants. Species diversity in Nepal can be well illustrated from the fact that over 1000 species of Himalayan plants have been originally discovered and described from the Nepalese flora among which 252 species are endemic to the country

Stearn has identified Nepal as the meeting place of the eastern and western flar The country occupies the central part of the Himalaya and is a transition zone between the flora of west Himalaya containing many west Himalayan elements and the east Himalaya. with many Sino Japanese elements. It also has plants representative of Tibet in its many northern frontiers' especially in the trans Himalayan regions. Numerous plants representative of the Indo-Gangetic plants are also found in its tropical regions.

The types of vegetation in the country are governed chiefly by the altitudes and the corresponding climatic factors with tropical' sub tropical' temperate' subalpine and alpine zones. Each zone has the representative domonants types and other secondary forms. The type of vegetation' however' tends to overlap the adjoining zones at places in relation to local climatic factors and aspects. Like the rich flora ranging from the tropical to the alpine zones' Nepals geographical isolation and climatological diversities provide a home and protection to a large number of ethnic groups. People living in villages and remote areas constitute more than three quarters of the 19 million people of Nepal. The country appears to be a cross road between the Aryan Influences of the southern Indian flatlands and the Tibetan the southern side' the Indo Aryan cultural elements have usally been stronger than the influences from the north. At the same time' it is not very surprising to note that the rural Napalese people have developed and preserved an old and strong tradition in the use of plants and plant products for their varied basic requirements. Hence' there appears immense opportunities for ethnobotanical studies in the country.

METHODS OF STUDY

Different parts of the country were surveyed repeatedly between 1984 and 1993, in different seasons and along different transects. Oral interviews were conducted with the cooperation of the village or tribal chiefs, staff of the local Forest Offices and the country school teachers because the majority of the population are illiterate and are afraid to deal with the outsiders. Informants included the native traditional herbal faith healers 'priests,' monks as well as the ordinary villagers belonging to different ethnic and linguistic groups who had knowledge of the traditional uses of plants. Information on medicinal use was documented in considerable detail. Each information was considered authentic after confirmation by 3 or more sources from distant localities. The quantity of herbs and preparations were' however not measured but estimated carefully at the site. Plant specimens were collected by the investigator with the help of informants later indentified and deposited in the National Herbarium (Kath) 'Kathmandu' Nepal.

FOLK MEDICINAL USES

In the following enumeration plants are arranged alphabetically followed by the family and English (E), Hindi (H), Sanskrit (S), and Nepali (N) names, where available. One collection nember of each species is given which is followed by the folk medicinal uses. The traditional uses of the plants considered are as reported by the informants, irrespective of any published source.

Abies spectabilis (D.Don) Mirb. ("Pinaceae"), East Himalayan silver fir (E), Talispatra (H), Talispatram (S), Gobre salla (N) (86/291).

About 10g of the fresh leaf tops are boiled in 400ml of water, until boiled down to half this amount. The resultant decoction with a little sugar or salt is administered orally warm twice a day for 3-5 days to treat cough especially the whoooing cough.

The leaves with those of Pinus wallichiana A.B. Jaks and Tymus linearis Benth. ex Benth 5g of each are boiled in 300ml of water with common salt and drunk twice a day for 2-3 days warm to relieve bronchitis and whooping cough.

Acorus calamus L (Araceae). Sweet flag (E), Ssfed bach Ghora bach (H) Bhadra (S) Bojho (N) (87/81).

As paste of the rootstock is considered antiseptic to wounds both in men and animals.

Two grams of the rootstock are boiled in 300ml of water with sugar or molasses and drunk warm 'regularly' before bed time as a curative measure for throat infection. A piece of the rootstock may also be chewed regularly for the indentical curative action.

A warm decoction of the rootstock is used regularly to wash the mouth to treat gingivitis pyorrhoeo and scurvy .

Two to three grams of the powdered rootstock is ingested with warm water for 3 or more days, before going ro bed, for its alleged anthelmintic action.

About 2g of the rootstock are chewed slowly twice to thrice in a day to loosen the phlegm to facilitate expectoration.

A decoctain is prepared from 1 g of the rootstock with 5g of the crushed leaves of neem tree (Azadirachta indica A Juss) with salt drunk twice a day in the morning and before bed time, for 2-4 days, warm to cure sore throat acting as an expectorant .

Infantile diarrhoea is treated by prescribing the patient goats milk boiled with 0.5g of the dried rootstock thrice a day 2 days or longer.

About 50g of the rootstock is pounded with 50g of salt and diluted in 1 litre of water. It is orally prescribed to the cattle having dyspepsia. In case of goats sheep and pigs the dose is nearly halved. The course is tewice a day until cured.

The crushed rootstock is made into a paste with mustard oil then warmed and applied on the anus 'regularly' to treat piles.

Ageratum conyzoides L. (Asteraceae). Goat weed Appa grass (E) Gandhe jhar (N).(88/477).

The leaf juies is applied to cuts and wounds for its alleged antihemorragic and antiseptic properties.

Two to three drops of the leaf juice are used as a nasal dose 2-3 times a day for 2-3 days to treat catarrh. It is said to increase the expulsion of phlegm. Based upon the severity of the ailment the juice may be prescribed for 5 or more days. It is also said to relieve sinusitis.

The dried leaves are powdered and inhaled as sniff 4-6 times a day for 3 or more days to treat catarrh.

Allium hysistum Stearn (Alliaceae). Jimbu (N) (93/198). About 300 ml of a decoction is prepared from 0.5g of the dried leaves of jimbu and 3g of the fresh leaves of holy basil (Ocimum sanctum L.) with common salt and drunk twice a day for 3-4 days warm to treat catarrh as well as the accompanying mild fever.

About 200 ml of a decoction is prepared from the leaves of Allium hypsistum Stear stem bark of Indian cassia lignea (Cinnamomum tamala Nees et Blume Lauraceae; Tejpat (H) Tamalapatra (S) Tejpat (N) (90/1243) and common salt about I g of each and the rhizomes of turmeric (Cinnamomum domestica Val). and ginger (Zingi ber officinale Rose) and fruits of Nepal pepper (Zanthoxylum armatum DC.) about 2g of each. The reultant decoctain is drunk warm inhaling the vapour through mouth and nostrils as well. It is administered before bed time for 3 or more days to cure catarrh and cough to control excessive flow of mucous through the nostrils and to loosen the sputum to facilitate expectoration.

Allium stracheyi Baker (Alliacrae). Jimbu sag (N) (87/112).

The leaves are cooked like vegetables and eaten regularly to relieve constipation and throat infection. Dried and preserved leaves may also be used.

Allium wallichii Kunth. (Alliaceae). Ban lasun (N) (93/140).

A decoction of the leaves is claimed to possess carminative property. Used as a vegetable it is considered beneficial for the mild laxation.

Artemisia vulgaris L (Asteraceae) Indian wormwood Fleabane (E) Nagdona (H) Nagadamani (S) Titepati (N) (90/418).

Ten to twenty grams of the fresh root is boiled in about 500 ml of water until this quantity is reduced to about 200ml. The warm decoction is drunk inhaling the vapour as well to reduce fever. The course is given thrice a day for 2-3 days. Two to three powdered fruits of black pepper (Piper nigrum L.) may also be added during boiling. It is also claimed to possess antiashmatic property.

The fresh leaf juice is applied to bleeding wounds and cuts as a haemostat and antiseptic in both man and cattle. The leaf juice may also be mixed with equal quantity of ginger juice (Zingiber officinale Rose) for the indentical action.

A thick layer of the leaves is spread on a heated flat stone and the patient suffering from diarrhoea or bloody dysentery is subjected to sit down on it with the naked hip for 2-3 minutes 2-3 times a day for 2-5 days for the cure.

About 50ml of the leaf juice is given with curd to the children twice to thrice in a day as an anthelmintic drug more particularly to rid ringworms.

Children are given 5-10 drope of the leaf juice mixed with equal amount of that of spearmint (Mentha spicata L) diluted in water twice a day for 1-2 days as an anthelmintic.

Five to eight millilitres of the leaf juice is diluted in about 200ml of water with I g of asafetida (Ferula assaefotida L) and warmed. This preparation is injected into the bowel through the rectum as an enema as a vermifuge. This treatment is said to be more effective in case of children.

Infantile cough and colds are treated by smearing the crushed leaves on the throat and at the same time 2-3 drops of the leaf juice are given with milk for 3-4 times each with an interval of 3-4 hours.

The fresh leaf top is smelled regularly as a protective measure against epidemics. It is considered to be more effective with infants and children. The common epidemics included cholera chicken pox measles and typhoid.

Azadlrachta Indlca A. Juss (Mellaceae) Neem tree Margosa tree (E) Neem (H) Nimbe (S) Neem (N) (88/541).

The leaf decoction is used to wash cuts and wounds as an antiseptic both in men and animals.

A decoction prepared from 2-4g of the crushed leaves and 2 teaspoonsful of butter is taken warm once a day for 6 months or longer to treat leprosy.

A decoction prepared from 5kg of the bruised leaves or seeds is used to wash the vagina regularly to relieve leukorrhoea.

A leaf paste is smeared on the affected parts reglularly to relieve skin infections like eczema ringworm and scabies.

Ten to fifteen crushed fruits are eaten with curd and molasses twice a day for 3 weeks or longer to treat bleeding piles.

To treat boil or carbuncle 2-3 teaspoonsful of the leaf juice are eaten with honey or molasses 2-3 times a day for 3-5 days and at the same time a leaf paste is applied on the boil or carbuncle leaving the top area clean. It is and to accelerate the maturation of the boil or carbuncle shrink and expel pus with the curative result.

Five to seven grams of the fresh leaves are boiled in 400ml of water then the resultant decoction i sieved and drunk warm 2-3 times in a day each with an interval of 4-6 hours to cure intermittent fever.

Two teaspoonsful of the leaf juice are mixed with an equal amount of honey and taken twice a day for 2-3 days as a vermifuge.

Five to eight grams of the leaves are boiled in I litre of water until reduced to about 200ml. The warm decoction is drunk with honey or molasses to arrest diarrhoea and dysentery. The usual course is thrice a day for 3 or more days.

The endosperm is mixed with equal amount of that Persian lilac (Meliaazedarach L. Meliaceae: Bakainu (N) 86/97) and crushed into paste. About 5g of this paste is eaten in the morning before breakfast for 3-5 days as an anthelmintic. Alternatively the oil extracted from the endosperm of neem tree is mixed with equal amount of that of Persian lilac. Half a teaspoonful of this preparation is orally prescribed in the morning for 3-5 days for its alleged anthelmintic property.

The fresh leaves and common salt 50g each are made into a paste and diluted in water. It is orally prescribed twice a day 2-4 days to the mature cattle as an anthelmintic.

About 30g of the leaves are made into a paste with equal amount of common salt and turmeric powder (Curcuma domestica Val). This preparation is orally given to the cattle once in every morning for 3-5 days to cure constipation and indigestion.

About 100g of the fresh leaves are crushed and boiled in 2 litres of water until this quantity is reduced to about I litre. The warm decoction is sieved and used to wash the ear of the cattle regularly to cure otorrhoea. The decoction is also used to wash and massage the throat to relieve swellings. Generally one dose per day for 3-6 days is recommended.

Betula utils D Don (Betulaceae). Himalayan silver birch (E) Bhujpattra (H) Bhojapatra (S) Bhojpatra (N) (84/44).

About 10g of the leaves are boiled in 400 ml of water then the cooled decoction is taken 2-3 times daily for 5-7 days as a diuretic. It is also recommended to relieve dysuria. The decoction when taken warm 2-3 times a day for 2-4 days is claimed to have antipyretic property.

Boenninghansenia albifora (Hook) Meisn. (Rutaceac). Pissumar buti (H) Damplate (N).

The bruised leaves are sniffed continuously to cure headache. It is also said to cure migreine.

Carum carvi L.(Apiaceae).Caraway (E) Shia jira (H) Sushavi (S) Jangali jira (N) (90/938).

The fruits are used as a spice or condiment to give flavour and relish to vegetables and pickles. Used as a spice it is considered to be carminative and also effective to overcome anorexia.

Cedrus deodara (Roxb) Loud (Pinaceae). Deodar Himalayan cedar (E) Devadar (H) Devadaru (S) Davadar (N) (85/237).

The essential oil extracted from the leaves is massaged on the relish to vegetables especially to meat. Used as a spice it is considered beneficial against dyspepsia and anorexia.

Cyperus rotundus L (Cyperaceae) Nut grass (E) Motha Nagar mohta (H) Naagarmusla (S) Mothe Siru (N) (87/237).

A decoction prepared from 10g of the crushed tubercles in 100ml of water with a little salt is given twice a day for 2-5 days to treat bronchitis. Its prolonged use is also said to relieve bronchial asthma.

The rhizome is made into a paste and 10-20g of the crushed tubercles in 100ml of water with a little salt is given twice a day day for 2-5 days to treat bronchitis. Its dose is usually halved.

The rhizome is mixed with an equal amount of the root of sabai grass (Eulaliopsis binata (Ritz) C. E. Hubbard; Poaceae; Babiyo (N) (84/542) and crused to extract juice. Two to three teaspoonsful of this juice are taken 3-4 times once in 3-4 hours as an anthelmintic drug.

Five to ten grams of the rhizome are eaten in the morning for a week or longer as an appetizer.

About 5g of the tubercles are crushed boiled in about 300ml of water obtained from rice wash (Chaulani) and the decoction is given with 2 teaspoonsful of honey thrice a day for 3 or more days to relieve diarrhoea.

Didymocarpus villosus D. Don (Gesneriaceae). Kumkum dhup (N) (86/168.).

The dried plant is burnt in the patients room as as incense to purify air and to repel evil spirits that are supposed to cause the disease. It is believed to accelerate the recovery of the patient together with increase in the efficacy of other drugs used.

Eupatorium odoratum L. (Asteraceae). Banmara (N) (87/141).

Leaf juice is said to have antihemorrhoid and antiseptic properties and is frequently applied to cuts and bleeding wounds.

Leaf paste is used to massage on the sprained part, regularly to relieve pain and swelling .

Gaultheria fragrantissima Well (Ericaceae). "Fragrant", wintergreen Indian wintergreen (E) "Dhasingare" Patpate (N), (88/255).

About 3 teaspoonsful of the young leaf paste are orally administered to relieve cough and colds. The usual course is 2-3 times a day for 3 days or longer.

The consumption of 3-4 teaspoonsful of the juice expelled from the stem bark is taken with cows milk to induce menopause. This treatment is prescribed twice a day for 2 weeks, beginning from the 4th day of menstruation, and is said to suppress the menstrual cycle for about a year.

Gnaphalium affine D. Don (Asteraceae). "Cotton weed", Cats foot ,

Jersey cudweed "(E)", Boke phul (N) (85/863).

The leaves and flowers are made into a paste and applied over cuts to stop bleeding and to promote healing.

Heracleum nepalense D. Don (Apiaceae). "Chhatare" (N). (90/1234).

Two to three grams of the fresh fruits are made into a paste and eaten with warm saline water once a day for 4 or more days as a carminative. It is also said to possess antipyretic properties.

The pounded fruits are applied on open wounds as a disinfectant both in men and animals .

Houttuynia cordata Thunb. (Saururaceae). "Gane" (N), (90/441).The aerial paste are cooked like vegetables and eaten regularly to treat various types of abdominal pains.

The leaf juice is largely used to alleviate dysentery. About 3 teaspoonsful of the juice are taken with sugar or molasses 2-3 times a day for 2-5 days.

The tender leaves and roots are cooked like vegetables and eaten "feed" regularly to cure diarrhoea.

Jasminum humile L (Oleaceae). Yellow jasmine Italian jasmine Nepal jasmine (E) Peeli chameli, Pilajui, Malto (H), Suvarnajuthica , Hemapushpike (S), Masino jai, Jangali jai (N), (90/796).

About 10 fresh leaves are chewed and ingested thrice a day for 2-3 days to treat throat infection. It is also said to promote expectation.

Leucas cephalotes Spreng. (Lamiaceae). Dhurpi sag, Deldona, Goma, Motapati (H), Dronapushpi (S), Takure jhar, Guma , Dronapushpi (N), (86/365).

Six to ten flower heads are boiled in about 600 ml of water for 1-2 minutes and sieved. The warm decoction is drunk to cure jaundice. The course is thrice a day in the first week twice a day in the second week and once a day in the next two weeks. In the course of this treatment fatty foods are to be avoided completely.

A decoction is prepared by boiling 10-15 flower heads in 400 ml of water and drunk warm as an antipyretic drug. The course is twice a day for 2-3 days or longer.

It is also drunk to treat various types of gastric pains food poisoning and to accelerate the healing of wounds.

About 5g of the crushed flower heads are mixted with equal amount of the leaves of holy basil (Ocimum sanctum L. Lamiaceae: "Tulashi" (N) 84/536) and boiled in a litre of water with continuous stirring until the liquid boils down to about 100ml. Two teaspoonsful of this decoction are orally prescribed twice a day for 3-4 days for its alleged antipyretic action.

A decoction prepared from 10kg of the crushed flower heads in 300-400 ml of water with salt is drunk twice a day for 4-5 days as an anthelmintic drug. It is also said to relieve dyspepsia and act as an appetizer.

Ligularia fischeri (Ledeb) Turcz (Asteraceae). "Nangreu" (N), (90/1018).

Root paste is used to massage the sprained parts regularly for the relief.

Mentha longifolia (L). Nath (Lamiaceae). Horsemint (E), "Podina" Jongli Pudina (H) Babari , Pudina.

The leaves are considered an effective coolant as well as an appetizer. It is mostly consumed in the form of fresh pickle.

Three to four grams of the leaves are boiled in 300ml of water with some common salt and the decoction is drunk warm twice a day for 3-5 days to cure throat infection.

About 10 fresh leaves are chewed one by one regularly to cure boils on tongue. It is also said to relieve sore throat.

Micromeria biflora (Buch Ham ex D.Don) Benth, (Lamiaceae) Indian wild thyme (E) Pinase jhar Pinase ghans (N) (85/310) .

Two to four drops of the plant juice are inhaled through each nostril 2-3 times a day for a week or longer to treat sinusitis.

Nardostachus grandiflora DC.(Valerianaceae). Spikenard, Indian nard, (Y), "Jatamansi,Bal chir, Balchhar, "Chhad" (H), "Jatamansi" (S), "Jatamansi", "Bhulte" (N),(93/88).

About 3g of the root paste is eaten in the morning , regularly, as a bitter tonic, It is also to be effective against dysentery.

Nyctanthes arbor tristis L. (oleaceae). Nibht jasmine , Coral jasmine Tree of sorrow (E), Harsinghar. Seoli (H) parijata, Sephalika, Parijataka (S) Parijat , Rudilo (N) (90/332).

About 5g of the bruised leaves are boiled in 500ml of water, and sieved. This decoction is drunk 3 times a day for 3 or more days. Warm to relieve cough and colds acting as an expectorant. It is also considered an antipyretic.

Two to three mature seeds are chewed and swallowed 5-8 times each with an interval of 2 hours to cure boils in the throat.
Osyris wightiana Well. ex Wight (Santalaceae). Nundhiki (N) (86 / 264).

Two kilograms of the leaves are crushed and boiled in 10 litres of water with constant stirring. When the amount is reduced to about 5 litres it is sieved and the filtrate is evaporated again until a sticky mass called nundhiki ko khoto is obtained. It is cooled and preserved. The drug "nundhiki ko khoto" is mixed with double the amount of cows butter or mustard oil and the ointment is used to massage on the sprained parts twice a day for 2-3 days for relief. Usually this treatment is also accompanied by the consumption of a teaspoonful of the drug with honey or milk to accelerate the relief.

About 2g of the durg is eaten with honey or milk thrice a day for 4 or more days to treat profuse diarrhoea and chronic dysentery more particularly the bloody dysentery.

The drug "nundhiki ko khoto" is made into a paste with mustard oil and a thick plaster is applied over bone fractures. The plaster is usually, wrapped with a cloth or "Nepali paper" (made from the stem bark od Daphne bholua Buch Ham. ex D. Don; thymelaeaceae; "Kagatpate" (N), 86/182) and the injured part is kept immobile with the help of bamboo splints. This treatment is followed by the consumption of 2-3 g of the drug with milk or honey thrice a day for 3 weeks after which the plaster is removed with the help of warm water. A root paste may also be used identically for the treatment of bone fractures and plastered or massaged to relieve pain and swelling due to sprains.

A warm decoction prepared from 20g of the crushed stem bark in 500 ml of water is orally prescribed twice to thrice each with an interval of 6-8 hours to relieve post natal abdominal pains. It is also considered to be galactagogue carminative and tonic.

The leaves are fermented in an earthen vessel for a week then "dried" in the sun and preserved. It is used as a substitute for tea leaves. When taken as a tea regularly it is believed to act as a blood purifier and a vital tonic.

Equal amounts of the leaves with that of "baklopate" (Hoya arnottiana Wight; Asclepiadaceae; 88/364) and the stem bark of guava (Psidium guajava L.) are made into a paste then plasted over fractured or dislocated bones and maintained for about a month for the curative effect. The patient is not permitted to do heavy works affecting the injured part for months. Pinus roxburghil Sarg. (Pinaceae) Chir pine, Himalayan long leaved pine (E), "Chir", Chir, "Sarala", Salla (H), "Sarala" (S), "Rani salla", Sallo (N) (85/571). About 2g of the resin with an equal amount of common salt is boiled in 250-300 ml of water and drunk warm before bed time for 2-4 days to relieve cough.

The roasted seeds are eaten by the post partum mothers to promote lactation.

Pinus wallichiana A.B. Jacks (Pinaceae). "Blue pine" (E) "Kali" (H), "Lek sallo" (N), (85/673).

The resin is used as a plaster for bone fractures. It is warpped with Nepali paper, (made from the bark of Daphne bholua Buch Ham ex D. Don). The injured part is kept intact with the help of bamboo splints. After 3 week or more the plaster is removed with the help of warm water.

The resin is mixed with an equal amount of butter then warmed to make a paste. The ointment is applied to the affected parts before bed time regularly to soften scar tissue.

Pleurospermun dentatum (DC.) Benth.(Apiaceae). Gandainu (N) (93/

142).

About 2g of the root is east together with additives like sugar, molasses or honey twice a day for 3 or more days to relieve various types of abdominal disorders including colic and constipation. It may also be administered in the from of a decoction.

Rosa serices Lindl. (Rosaceae). Jangali gulal, Sano ben gulaf (N), (90/802).

A decoction of the petals is used regularly to wash the eyes to treat opthalmia. Skimmia anquitelia N.P.Taylor & Airy shaw (Rutaceae) Chumlani Narapati (N) (90/911).

The fresh or dried leaves and flowers are burnt in the diseased house as an incense to purify air and to ward off evil spirits in the belief that it accelerates the recovery of the patient.

Syzygium cumini (L) Skeels (Myrtaceae). "Jave plum", Black Plum, Jambolan, "Jaman" (E), "Jaman", "Jambu", "Jambeva" (H), "Jambu" (S), Jamun (N), (87/113).

Ten to twenty five milliliters of the syrup of ripe friuts are given according to the age of the patient 4-6 times a day for 3-6 days to treat chronic diarrhoea and dysentery.

About 40ml of the juice from the crushed stem bark is mixed with double the amount of curd and consumed to cure profuse diarrhoea. A single dose is considered enough for the relief but usually a second one after 2-3 hours is given. The dose it lowered proportionately according to the age of the patient and patients below the age of 3 years are not given this medicament. This treatment is also prescribed to the livestock having diarrhoea or dysentery. The course "however" is thrice a day for as many as days necessary.

The stem barks of Java plum (Syzygium cumini L. Skeets). guava (Psidium guajava L.) and variegated "bauhinia" (Bauhinia variegata L. Caesalpinaceae; "Kachnar" (H) "Kanchanara", "Kovidara" (S), "Koiralo", Chaite phul (N), 86/1260) are mixed in juice are given orally 4-5 times, each with an interval of 3-4 hours, to equal proportions, then crushed and the juice extracted, two tea spoon of the control profuse diarrhoea and dysentery.

Thymus linearis Benth. ex Benth. (Lamiaceae). "Wild thyme" (E), "Bana jwain" (H) "Ghora marcha" (N) 84/23.).

A decoction of 3-5g of the aerial parts is taken warm twice a day for 3-4 days to cure cough and cold. It is also reputed to relieve various types of gastric complaints.

The aerial part is used to treat animals more particularly to treat horses. It is usually given with salt and other additives as an appetizer and carminative and also to overcome debility.

Valeriana hardwickii Wall (Valerianaceae). "Tagger" "Shumeo" (H), "Sugandhawal" Nakali Sugandhawal (N) (85/551).

A root decoction is used to wash wounds regularly as it is said to have antiseptic porperty.

A paste of the leaves or of the root is applied on the boils as an alleged cure.

Valeriana jatamansi Jones "Valerianaceae". "Indian Valerian" (E), "Mushkbala" (H) Sugandhawal "Samayo" (N), (86/180).

The rihzome juice is applied on the forehead to relieve severe headache. It is also used as a nasal drop to overcome nose bleed.

The rhizome is crushed and mixed with water which is used to wash the child having weeping sickness. After the bath some pieces of the dried rhizome are placed on fire and the resulting fume is inhaled by the patient.

Vitex negundo L. (Verbenaceae). "Chinese chaste tree" (E), "Sambhalu", Shivari , "Nisinda" (H), "Nirgundi" (S), "Simali" (N), (88/330).

The leaves are wrapped in thin cloth and plastered with an earthen paste then boiled in water for a minute. The leaves are then made into a paste and plastered on the swollen parts of the body, especially those of the joints and testicles for the comfort and accelerated recovery.

The tender leaves are cooded like vegetable and 30-40g of it is eaten twice a day for 4 or more days as an antipyretic drug.

Two to three teaspoonsful of the leaf juice are diluted in water and given orally 2-3 times each with an interval of 6-8 hours to relieve various types of abdominal pains.

Zanthoxylum armatum DC. (Rutaceae). Wingleaf prickly ash , Nepal pepper (E). "Tejphal", Darmar (H), "Tumburu", "Gandhalu" (S), "Timur", Timmur (N),(88/410).

About 250ml of a decoction prepared from 2g of the fruits with a little salt is drunk warm before bed time to treat various types of abdominal complaints including flatulence and constipation. This treatment when continued for 3 or more days is said to act as an anthelmintic.

About 1g of the fruits are boiled in 300ml of water with salt until reduced to half this amount. The resultant decoction is used warm to wash the mouth before bed time "regularly" to relieve toothache and pyorrhoea.

DISCUSSION

In Nepal like in most other developing countries home herbal remedies have been emploued and appreciated by the masses for centuries. due to its long period of existence folk medicine has in fact become an intergral part of the culture of the people. This type of medicine is fairly well accepted, easily available bearing a minimum cost and therefore expected to remain in use for a long time to come . The present communication has brought to light the traditionally verified curative properties of 41 indigenous species of essential oil bearing plants of Nepal along with considerble details on ues. These remedies are used by the majority of the rural populace, regularly to treat most to the frequently occuring ailments . Among isolated people these remedies appeared to be much alive and functioning being often the only available medicaments.

Floristic elements in Nepal are to some extent, the same as those in India where there is a rich ethnobotanical literature. Consequently many of the species considered in the present documentation are treated in the ethnobotanical literature but the majority of use regarding the ailments treated and the manner of use are partially or wholly different in the majority of the cases. Usually very interature but the majority of uses regarding the ailments treated and the manner of use are partially or wholly different in the majority of the cases. Usually, very incomplete and confusing information regarding the usage has been provided in most folk medicinal studies, leaving readers to the wild guess. It is urgent "therefore" to pay due attention on how the plant or plant product is utilized its dosage form and the route of administration. At the same time, like in most developing countries tribal cultures are fading fast in Nepal due to urabanization, industrialization and acculturation, with consequent loss of knowledge and tradition. The environment where people learnt and experienced useful lores is shrinking on account of deforestation and other forms of destruction of habitat. It is "therefore" important that the ageold folklore about plant resources be explored and properly documented for future uses before it is lost.

Ethnobotany is becoming pertinent to economic botany because it has much to do with the fulfilment of the basic human needs and the conservation of biological diversity. Although ethnobotanical study involves plant uses in general medicinal use is an important factor. Ethnobotanical studies can also be utilized to understand the social cultural and economic factors influencing ideas and activities prevalent among the people of the region. Such studies may help to provide the basic requirments to the greater part of the rural population in an effective way provided that such studies are conducted hand-in-hand with other related disciplines.

WHO has estimated that 80% of the world's population rely chiefly on traditional medicine and Nepal is no exception. Today in many countries modern medicines has displaced plants with many synthetic products but almost 30% pharmaceutical preparations are still obtained directly or indirectly from plants (Marino bettolo). According to Farnsworth out of 1.532 billion prescriptions dispensed in USA in 41.2% contained one or more constituents from natural products and according to Sticher 50% of the prescriptions in Europe contained natural products or their constituents. There is thus resurgence of natural products.

Apart from traditional medicinal uses the majority of the lay poputation use wild plants in a variety of ways that are also inevitable for their livelihood the additional uses being for food fodder fibre fuel, and a variety of domestic articles. They are also used for dye, tannin, gum, resin, agricultural and hunting tools, weapons and for witchcraft and magic. Some species are also used in worship and other mythology. Considering the medical practices, the folk herbal medicine is still the method of therapy of choice in the country. At the same time, it has been realized that many of todays tools used for the cure of diseases are blunt, brutal, combersome and costly. We have made significant progress in health services by introducing expensive modern drugs and technology, no doubt. It is not a matter of complacence although it is not wise to understate the future significance of these advances. In the present state of rapidly expanding population the rural challenges are enormous. The paramount question, of course, is how the concerned authorities are going to fece these challenges. A comparatively tolerble solution would be to bring health services and facilities to the rural people by helping to apply what are available in their environment and what is known to them, but otherwise for the rural scenario to get better with more equality and evenly shared health services the struggle ahead is likely to be long and difficult one.

Chapter-13

ESSENTIAL OIL BEARING PLANTS STATUS

THE EIGHT hill districts viz, Uttarkashi, Tehri, Pauri, Dehradun, Chamoli, Pithoragarh, Almora and Nainital of U.P. are administratively known as Uttarakhand. Uttarakhand can be divided into three main climatic zones: (i) The Alpine Zone, (ii) The Temperate Zone, and (iii) The Sub tropical or Sub temperate Valleys. The Terai Bhabar region of Uttar Pradesh, which is also a part of Uttarakhand (Now utlarakhand has become anindividual state) has not been included under this study.

(I) THE ALPINE-ZONE:

It consisite of two subzones: (a) the dry alpine found in the interior Himalayan ranges nearing Tibet borfer ar an altitude about 2750 to 4000 m. With low precipitation and xerophytic conditions. It gets snow fall from November to May and the inhabitants migarate to lower hills during this period. The inhabitants of this region are mostly Bhotias of Niti, Mana, Malari, Bruphu, Railkot, Kuti, etc. (b) the wet alpine zone that exists from an altitude 2500 to 4000m. This is further divided into two parts: the Alpine forest between 2500 to 3500, and above 3500m. the alpine meadows. The rainfell in this region is high and therefore it bears a lush vegetation. e.g. Tungnath, Madhyayamheshwar, Gangotri, Vedini fall in this region.

(II) THE TEMPERATE ZONE:

It exists in the outer ranges of Himalayes commencing from 1000 to 2700 m. With moderate rainfall to high rainfall. The towns like Uttarkashi, Pauri, Tehri, Nainital, Almora, Pithoragarh, etc. fall in this zone.

(III) THE SUB- TROPICAL OR SUB-TEMPERATE VALLEYS:

This zone mainly exists in the valleys of the temperate zone. The valleys are warmer and rainfall is moderate and mostly rice is cultivated in these valleys though the snow falls in this region but never stays. The places of this region are Karnprayag, Rudraprayag, Bageshwar, Garur, etc. Uttarakhand having such varied climatic zones, is rich in vegetation and so about 100 assorted herbal plants are collected from these zones. These herbal plants are either used by the local people as incense, condiments, medicine or for some other purposes or traded for economic gains. The herbs which are taeded from Uttarakhand are used variously in different industries such as indigenous pharmacies for manufacturing ayurvedic and unani medicines indigenous veterinary pharmacies for manfacturing medicines for domestic animals; homeopathic and modern medicines indigenous perfumeries for manufacturing attar incense havan samigri, tobacco curing, etc. and in modern perfumeries and cosmetic industries for extraction of essential oils used in preparation of scents, soap, talcum powders, etc. in flavour industries. The harbel plants therefore, are the resource commodity; a single herb used in various industries.

The aromatic herbs of Uttarakhand yield essential oils can be divided into the following categories for present discussion:

1. The Utilization of Wild Growing Aromatic Herbs

The herbs are used variously as follows:

(a) The herbs exclusively used by the local people as incence, condiments, etc. and not traded out of Uttarakhand. These herbs need investigation, exploration and evaluation to be used outside Uttarakhand as incense, condiment, essential oil be utilized in perfumeries cosmetics flavour etc.

(b) The herbs which are locally used as well as collected for trade purpose and sent to plains in good qualities for economic gains.

(c)The aromatic herbs not used locally but collected and traded for economic gains.

(d) The herbs which are well known in national and international markets but never been investigated evaluated and exploited.

2. The Utilization of Locally Cultivated Aromatic Herbs.

The aromatic herbs already cultivated or introduced in this region need further investigation, evaluation and exploration of market and finally extention of cultivation if found successful.

3. The introduction of new aromatic herbs and essential oil bearing horticultural crops (mostly citrus fruits) in suitable localities and their market exploration.

At suitable climatic locations there are possibilities for introduction of aromatic crops like lavender, clarysage, rose, rosemary, sage, etc, and citrus fruits, which apart from their main use as edible may also be utilised for processing of cordials, squash, marmalade, etc, and side by side be used for exrpression of oil as a by product.

4. The establishment of extraction units for essential oils oleoresin from wild growing lichens and cultivated ginger crops.

1 (a). Seriphidium brevifolium (Wall.) Y. Ling et Y.R.Ling (Artemisia brevifolia Wall ex DC. A.maritima HK.f.non L.) Asteraceae Sufed purcha (LN).

Plant perennial 0.5-1.5 m. high, gregariously growing in dry alpine zone from 2700-3500m.

Locally the Bhotias collect the immature infloresence and leaves and use it as incense by simply placing the dried material on burning charcoal in an earthen or tin bowl.

The analysis of essential oil, (Shah & Thakur) from immature inflorescence and leaves yielded 0.3-0.4% of oil and the main constituents identified are: a thujone (77%), B-thujone (4.4%), 1-8 cineole (3.3%) and the nature infloresence and leaves yielded 0.4 to 0.5% of essential oil and the major constituents are, a-yhujone (60.2%), thujone (4.4%), 1-8 cineole (1.5%). The authors further believe the reason for preferring the use of immature inflorescence and leaves could be the high percentage of thujone and 1-8 cineole (1.5%). The authors further believe the reason for preferring the use of immature inflorescence and leaves could be the high percentage of thujone and 1-8 cineole. Thujone is a mild intoxicant if inhaled and it is postulated by the authors that the psychoactive property of this incense is beneficial to the Bhoties who use it as incense to forget the fret and worries due to severe cold conditions and other hardships of the region.

There are every possibilities to explore the dry inflorescence and leaves as incense material for agarbattis and the use of essential oil distilled in situ for its use in incense, perfumery, cosmetic and other industustries. The material is in abundance and easily collected without any threat to environment.

Artamisia gmelini Web. ex Stechm. (A. sacrorum Ledeb) Asteraceae.

Kala purcha, Gangatulsi (LN); Russian wormwood (CND)

Herb is 0.5-0.9 m high found in dry alpine region from 2300-3000 m. Locally the herb is used as incense and due to its fragrant nature offered to deities.

The author collected the sample material from Niti valley and the essential oil was subjected for analusis.

The yield of essential oil was 0.3 to 0.5% and the major constituents limonene (45.6%), borneol (11.1%), farmesol (9.2%), thujyl alcohol (9.0%), geranyl acetate (6.9%), pinene (6.5%), nerol (3.6%), thujone (2.8%), thujyl acetate (0.9%, cineole
(0.2%);

The material may further be investigated and evaluated like Serphidium brevifolium.

Allium consanquineum Kunth (A. stracheyi Baker) Liliaceae
Jambu, Faran (LN); Himalayan seasoning Allium (CN)

Scapigerous herb with 30cm long narrowed leaves occuring in wild state in the dry alpine zone above 3500m.

Locally the dry leaves and inflorescence used as conditment for seasoning curries dal and other cooked dishes. The people of Mana and Niti,etc. cultivate the herb for their own use and for trade purpose. The herb is often found on sale in all the important towns of Uttrarkhand. Allium wallichii Kunth is also used for seasoning purpose.

No report on chemical analysis of the material is available. This commodity needs further evaluation and research as a flavouring agent and efforts should be made to prepare its oleoresin and evaluate it. The flavour of the herb is very appetising.

Pleurospermum brunonis (DC) C.B.Clarke. Apiaceae

LASER OR TAKKER (LN)

Stemless hairy herb with long tapering roots and found over 4000ml in the wet alpine zone. Its occurrens has become rare due to merciless collection by the local people.

Locally it is considered as a prized incense which is offered to deities. No chemical work on its essential oil or the herb is available. The aroma of the herb is very sweet and pleasant and the herb needs protection from the local people.

Rhododendron hypenanthum Balf.f. (R. anthopogon D.Don). Ericaceae Paul, Kalu-kutti, Poh, Bhallu-sallu, Kodya (LN); Sufer Rhododendron (CN). Evergreen aromatic herb, 40-60cm high occurs gregarious in patches in wet alpine zone at 3000-4000 m beyond tree line and before the alpine meadows.

Locally the decoction of the herb is used for treating asthma and leaves used as incense material. The plant burns even when green therefore much collected by the local people as fuel (Shah & Jain). Leaves are used as one of the ingredients of a non alcoholic beverage known as bhtiya chaya (bhotia tea), specially prepared in a wooden apparatus for mixing known as bubong. Leaves are crushed and applied on forehead in headache.

No chamical analysis of the herb or oil is available from Uttaranchal. The commodity needs further investigation and evaluation for its possibilities to be used as incense or the use of essential oil in perfumery, cosmetics and flavour industries.

Artemisia indica Wall (A. vulgaris auct non Linn.). Asteraceae
Kunjapati, pati (LN)

A fairly tall shrub about 1.0 to 2.5m high with gregarious growth distributed throughout the temperate region from 1000-3000m.

Locally, the plant is not used for any purpose except as an offering to deities possibly due to its strong aroma. If a single twig is kept in a room after some time the whole room is scented with its pleasing aroma.

Uniyal, Singh, Shah and Naqvi obtained essential oil from its aerial part 0.2% and the major chemical constituents are camphor (9.7%), 1-8 cineole (6.5%), B eudesmol (7.98%), borneol (5.29%), artemisia alcohol (3.4%), camphene (2.59%), cymene (1.6%), terpene 4-ol (1.2%), pinene (1.2%) gujuneme (1.92%).

The material is abundantly avilable and the oil distilled in situ could be used in soaps and other cosmetics but further evaluation is required before taking any step.

I (b). Juniperus communis L. var. saxitilis Pallas (Pinacear)

Bhitaru, parpanja, pama (LN); Juniper (CN)

The shrub is 1.5m high and commonly found in the dry alpine zone from 2700-3200 m.

Locally the leaves are used as incense.

Juniper berry oil is extracted from the fruits and in Juniper plant equally serve the purpose of Juniper berry oil which is presently imported and the present market rate of the oil is Rs. 1653/- per kg. The material needs further investigation and evaluation and exploring possibilities for its use in havan samigri and evaluation of oil.

Angelica glauca Edgew. (Apiaceae)

Chora, gandrayan, chipi (LN); Himalayan Angelica (CN)

A herb 1-2m high and found in wet alpine zone mostly near ponds and rivulets above 3000m.

Locally used as prized condiment for seasoning purpose also used as medicine in digestive disorders.

In Himachal Pardesh, the Himachal Angelica has been exploited by few perfumers as a good substitute of European Angelica oil, which is used as toner in masculine note which gives a musky odour and has good demand in the market. In Uttaranchal, the local people have mercilessly depleted the herb. The Bhotias and other people sell the roots @ of Rs. 6/- per tola (10gm) for local use as conditment and for seasoning purpose and for medicine in digestive disorders. It is suggested that the exploitation of Himalayan Angelica from Uttarakhand be planned and efforts should be made for it systematic cultivation at suitable localities.

The international market rate of European Angelica oil is Rs. 12,600 per kg.

Jurinea dolomiae Boiss (J. macrocephala (DC) Benth) Asteraceae Dhup guggul (LN)

A stemless perennial herb found growing in the meadows of wet alpine zone form 3000-4000.

Locally the root and rhizome of the herb are used as incense and also traded occasionally.

From Himachal Pradesh the herb is collected in huge quantities and mostly used in havan samgri.

The rhizome and roots on extraction with organic solvents yield a sticky material, chemically a hydrocarbon caoutchouc. The higher the content of caoutchouic material, superior is believed to be the quality of the herb.

In Uttaranchal the collection of the herb is to be conducted in a planned manner otherwise the herb may deplete.

Skimmia anguetillia Tailor & Airy Shaw (S. laureola Wall) Rutaceae

Nair, nairpati, kasturpatta (LN) Himalayan Skimmia (CN). A shrub 0.5-1.0m high found in shady localities in the temperate region or below alpine region from 2000-2500m.

Locally the leaves are used as incense.

About two decades ago the Regional Research Laboratory, Jammu had found out the market potential of the oil of Skimmia to be used in perfumaery as it contains two importants perfumery linalool and linyl acetate.

Sharma et al. (1966) found the yeild of oil from the leaves 0.5 to 0.8% and chemical constituents, Esters of linyl acetate (71.5%); linalool (17.5%); phellandrene (12.7%) and 8 other minor constituents.

About ten years ago few entreprising entrepreneurs of Uttarkashi installed a distillation unit extraction of oil and the herb was collected from nearby forest but after some time the forest authorities imposed ban on collection of the herb with the argument that the leaves of skimmia are the main food of muskdeer. Mr. Green, scientist working at Department of Biology University of, Cambridge U. K. made detailed study about food for the muskdeer and found out that Skimmia is not a staple food of muskdeer and mostly it feeds on Rhododendron species (Shah). Skimmia oil is used in high grade perfumeries and it has good demeand in the perfumery industries. The plant can be propagated by stem cutting and the U.P.Forest Authorities should allow the collection of Skimmia in a planned way.

Valeriana jatamansi Jones (V.wallichii DC) Valerianaceae Sumeo, sumea (LN); tagar, sugandhbale (TN); Indian Valerian (CN).

A perennial herb 15-65 cm high found throughout the temperate region from 1800-2500 m in shady and moist localities mostly in oak and rhododendron forests.

Locally the whole vegetative herb used as incense and mature herb, rhizame, in collected for trade purpose.

The rhizome of Indian valerian are in good demand as these are used in various industries. It is used us indigenous pharmaceutical industries for manufacturing number of proprietary medicines of Ayurveda, Unani, Sidha and Tibetan system of medicins; in the perfumery industries in the process of curing; and recently it had found its use in the modern medicine as a number of epoxy iridoid esters collectively known as valepotrates discovered in 1966 used to improve coordination' diminishes restlessness anciety and aggressiveness in young students and increases the power of concentration.

The herb needs immediate production in nature as it has been collected in huge quantities from the wild and it needs systematic cultivation at suitable locations.

Selinum condolleii DC. Apiaceae

Moor bhudkeshi (LN); Nard selinum (CN); Nakli jatanmasi (TN)

A perennial herb 25-50cm high found in temperate forest at 1800-2100m.

Locally the rhizomes are used in magicoreligious ceremonies mostly to drive away the evil spirits. The rhizomes look like jatamansi. The rhizome of S. vaginatum (Edgew) C.B. Clarke are also used as bhutkeshi.

I (c). Cedrus deodara (Roxb,) Loud. Pinaceae

Deodar, diyar (LN); Cedrus (CN)

A high tree found above 2000 m in the temperate zone.

Earlier when the trees were cut freely and the saw dust was available and which after distillation yielded cedarwood oil and the saw dust was also used as an ingredtent in "haven samigri". But now there is a complete ban in cutting of trees in the hills and therefore the saw dust is not available from the saw hills. But there is a good demand of the cedrus oil in the perfumery industries etc. Aggrwal et al. had found out the root of old cut tree stumps can yield in optimum condition more economically as high as 8-12% of essential oil in comarison to 2. 6-4.5% usually obtained from the saw dust and chips.

Uttarakhand can also be a good source of the old dead tree stumps available commonly in the cedrus forests. The forest department of U.P. should allow the young entrepreneurs to dig out the old stumps of dead trees and side be side replace the pit with new seedlings of cedrusy plants which would grow into a tree in due course of time.

Cinnamomum tamala Nees & Ebern. Lauraceae

A medium size tree found in between 2000-2500 m in shady forest in the temperate zone.

The leaves and bark of the trees are under the trade name "taj" and tejpat respectively and marketed to the plains where these are used in various industries like indigenous pharmacies condiment manufacturers and dealers. The essential oil from the leaves of C. tamala have been analysed by Gulati with following main constituents the yield of oil is 0.23-0.36% cinnamaldehyde (41-55%) linalool (15-15.67%), eugenol + cinnamic acetate (4.23-13.3%) caryophylline (4-7.26%) eugenyl acetate (2.06-12.45%) benzaldehyde (2.0-4.11%) camphor (0.9-3.19%) phellandrene (0.10-3.95%). It is interesting to more that the essential oil obtained from the leaves of C.tamala of Assam does not contain eugenol.

In recent years the plants of C. tamala from Uttaranchal have been mercilessly lopped and debarked' due to which a number of trees have died. It is needed that necessary steps may soon be taken for their systematic and scientific collection so that the tree is not harmed and destroyed and efforts should be made for its systematic cultivation and regeneration in the forest.

Presently only leaf and bark are marketed but no efforts have been made to distil cinnamomum oil for commercial purpose from the leaves in Uttaranchal .

During 1987-88 cinnmon leaf oil worth 4.6 Lakh rupees was imported from Sri Lanka and Indonesia. Cinnamon oil has good market within the country. In the recent year the leaves under the name Tejpat worth Rs.6.43 Lakhs were imported from Nepal.

Zanthoxylum armatum DC (Z alatum Roxb) Rutaceae

Timur timru (LN); tejbal (TN); Wartara (CN)

A spiny "shrub" 1-2 m found in the temperate region from 1300-2500m.

Occasionally the aerial shoots are used as tooth brush like neem. The fruits are collected for trade purpose as these are used in indigenous pharmacies and indigenous perfumery industries.

Sharma et al. and Adhikari et al. have reported the oil yield from the fruit 0.4-0.5%. The author collected fruits from Uttarachal and the pericarp of the furit was removed and subjected for distillation and the yield of oil was found 10-12% and on analysis the following main constituents were indentified; linalool (72%) 'methyl cinnamate (12.20%)' limonene (6.2%) phellendrene (5.3%) and 25 other minor constituents.

Tejbal could be a good source of linalool which has good demand in the perfumery and cosmetic industies. recently about 20 tonnes and 70 tonnes of linalool were exported and 30 to 70 tonnes were produced in the country (possibly from Bursera delpechiana cultivated in S. India) Varshney. The oil needs further research and investigation and evolution as in USA the oil of allied species of Zanthoxylum are used in insecticidal sprays.

Hedychium spicatum Smith Zingiberaceae

Vanhaldi siaru (LN); kapurkachri (TN)

A herb 0.5-1.5m high and found mostly in shady and moist forests in the temperate zone.

The rhizomes of the plants are collected by the local people for trade purpose. The rhizomes are mostly used in indigenous perfumery industries for prepatation of attar and in indigenous phamacies. Recently few oil distillers have brought its oil in the market from Himachal Pradesh.

The herb now needs planned collection from the wild and systematic cultivation at suitable locaeities as the rhizome in the market is sold Rs. 25-30 per kg and the oil yield is 0.4%.

Acorus calsmus L.Araceae

Bach, boja (LN); Ghurbach (TN); Sweet flag (CN)

A herb 0.3 to 1.0m high and usually found in marshy and damp localities in the temperate region near lakes' ponds and rivulets. Occasionally the rhizomes are used to cure cough' cold and asthma but mostly traded for economic gains. The rhizomes are used in the indigenous pharmacies and perfumeries and in veterinary medicine mostly in preparation of flea powder, etc.

The essential oil contains asarona 80-84% and which has been reported to be cancerous therefore not used for flavouring purpose in India. The North American A. calamus' a chemical strain does not contain asarone therefore much used for flavouring food and liquors. Research is needed either to make the oil free from asarone or to develop a strain free from asarone. Essential oil of A. calamus is being produced from Himachal Pardesh and being marketed.

In recent years the rhizomes of A. calamus have been mercilessly collected from the hills of Uttaranchal and now it needs cultivation and suitable places would be the temperate valleys near rice fields on the river banks.

Didymocarpus aromatica Wall. and D. pedicillara R.Br.Gesneriaceae

Patharachatta patharphori (LN); Patharlaung Kumkum (TN)

A stemless herb found clinging to rocks found in shady and moist localities in the temperate zone from 1000-1500m.

Earlier the curl young leaves were collected from this region and traded to be used indigenous perfumery in preparation of high grade attar. Now it is seldom collected because it was mercilessly cellected by the local people. It is recommended that a complete ban on its collection may by imposed by the government.

1. (d) *Hyssopus officinalis* L. Labiateae

Zufa, zufeyabis (TN); Hyssop (CN)
Herb is about 1.0m high and found in gregarious patches in dry alpine region at an altitude of 2300-2500m.

Local use is none but in Unani system of medicine the herb is referred as "Zufa" or "zufa yabis", nut presently in India under this name some other herb is available.

It is reported that earlier the herb was cultivated in Germany France USSR and USA as potherb; Guenther Bianchini and Lawrence. The present position of the herb cultivation in these countires is not available.

The author collected the herb from Malari (Chamoli) which yielded 0.4 to 0.5% of oil characterised by 47 chemical constituents. The, 1-8 cineole (12.2%), B-pinene major components are isophenocamphone (38.1%) pinocarvone (20.3%) 'pinene (10.2%) and pinocamphone (0.61%) Shah.

On comparison with the oil cultivated in North America and with Hyssop growing wild in Himachal Pradesh it was found that the essential oil from Uttarakhand region is characterised by lesser quantity of pinocamphone, i.e, 0.61% while the cultivated one from North America and the wild from Himachal Pradesh is characterised by 42.66% and 38.4% respectively.

The lower quantity of pinocamphone may be useful so that the oil could be used for flavouring purpose as it is reported that higher quantity of pinocamphone in the oil causes cancer therefore the use of oil for flavouring purpose is banned in USA.

The essential oil of hussop and the hyssop herb from Uttarakhand needs proper evaluation and its market exploration.

Origanum vulgare L. Labiateae

Vantulsi (LN); Wild marjoram or Oregano or Pizza (CN and TN)

An annual herb 30-60 cm with orange flower found in moist and shady localities from 2000-3000 m in the temperate and alpine zones.

Locally' at Badrinath the herb is used as an offering at Badrinath temple and sometime the decoction is taken in cough and cold. There are two main types of Organo the carvacrol type and thymol type. The carvacrol type is considered as good Oregano which contains about 70% of Phenyl carvacrol.

The herb was collected by the author from Joshimath region and on analysis yielded essential oil 0.6% charcterised with the following main constituents; thymol (71.3%), terpinene (12.7%) = pinenene (10.10%) camphor (3.2%) pcymene (0.5%) carvacrol (0.7%) (CIMAP Annual Report.

Origanum is well known culinary herb in tabe as its dried herb tincture and essential oil are used in flavour industry and certain liquor formulations etc. The U.S.A. Italy France and Germany are some of the countries which consume oregano in huge quantities. The main suppliers are Maxico and some of the European countries like Greese "Turkey" "Spain" Egypt etc.

Though the origanum of Uttarakhand is the thymol type and it may have its use in flavour and other industries 'however' the0 oreganum of uttarakhand needs further investigation evaluation and exploration of market. Presenlty' the Spainsh oregaum oil is sold @ Rs 1026/- per kg.

Thymus linearis Benth (T. serphyllum L.ssp. quinquestatus (Celak) Kitamura. Labiateae

Banajawain (LN); Himalayan Thyme (CN)

A common prostrate herb is found in temperate and wet alpine zone from 1500-4000 m.

Locally the herb is used in cough and cold. Chemical analysis of Himalayan thyme from Kashmir 'Himachal Pradesh' and Uttar Pradesh hills (Uttarakhand is tabulated here under):

	Yield of essen. oil (%)	Thymol	P-cymene	Borneol	Broneol acetate	Linalool
Kulu (HP)	0.5%	64.6%	9.1%	5.6%	5.4%	3.1%
Manasbal (JK)	0.5%	59.3%	13.4%	7.9%	1.3%	7.4%
Chakrata (UP)	0.45	19.1%	46.9%	3.9%	1.9%	5.7%

	Carvacrol	=terpenene	Nerilodol
Kulu (HP)	5.0%	3.6%	2.6%
Manasbel	1.9%	4.7%	1.8%
Chakrata	2.5%	5.0%	5.6%

Himalayan thyme has great resemblance with Thymus vulgaris the true thyme which is an important culinary herb much used in meat and other dishes with good market in European countries and the thymol content varies form 20 to 60% and true thumc oil is sold @ Rs. 1080 per kg.

Himalayan thyme of Uttarakhand requires detail investigation of the herb and its essential oil from different altitudunal regions and evaluation of the herb and oil in the trade market. Owing to the increasing availability of synthetic thymol the demand of thyme oil has considerably decreased but still there is perference to natural oil than the synthetic thymol. It is further to note that most of the botanical and chemical investigastion undertaken on this plant have referred the plant under Thymus vulgaris while T. vulgaris is not found in India and whatever work is reported it is on

T. linearis and its subspecies.

Tagetes minuta (T. galandulifera) Compositae (Asteraceae)

Vanhazari (LN); Wild marigold (CN)

An annual herb 1-1.5 m high found in the temperate region of Uttarakhand. The plant is nativ to Mexico and probably introduced about a century ago in the country.

Locally, the juice of the flowers is dropped in aching ear.

The herb of Uttarakhand yielded 2% of oil but no chemical analysis is available from Uttarakhand. However the oil from African with marigold has been characterised with the following main constituents; ZB ocimene (41%) dehydrotagetone (13.5%) 'Z&E ocimenone (26.5%)' (De Villers et al. Lawrence et al. reported 104 chemical compounds 'the major' ones are cistbocimene (40.42%), Dihdrotagetone (17.64%) 'cis tagetone & germacrene D (13.50)' and cis-tagetone (9.96). One of the perfumer from Himachal Pradesh in Kulu has distilled the oil from the wild growing marigold and produced essential oil for market sale.

The essential oil of tagetes needs futher exploration of market for its ready sale. It is required that the essential oil samples may be brought to the notices of leading perfumers of the country for evaluation purpose. There will be no diffculty in the availability of the material from Uttarakhand as it is found growing in waste lands abundantly and in situ distillation of oil would be profitable.

Carum carvi L. Umbelliferae (Apiaceae)

Thoya kala jiri tibbati zeera (LN); Himalayan caraway (CN)

A perennial herb 20-60 cm high found above 3500 m in the dry alpine zone. The people of Niti Mana and Milam collect it from the wild and cultivate it in their kitchen garden or waste fields for their own use. Locally the fruit is used as main condiment and for seasoning purpose. The seeds collected by the author from Niti valley yielded essential oil 4.1% and the main constituents characterised are; carvone (64.05) limonene (30.04%) dehydro carvone 91.35%) and euggenol methyl ether(0.47%) (CIMAP Annual Report.

In caraway fruits the quantity of carvone plays an important part more the carvone content is the quality. The caraway oil contains 53..50% of carvone. Lawrence made a detailed analysis of caraway oil and found that main constituents are; carvone (47%) and limonene (49.8%) with other minor constituents. Therefore, the fruits of caraway of Uttarakhand has wider prospects for application in flavouring beverages. Only thing required is the exploration of the market for ready supply and when market is assured then encourage the local people of border region to cultivate it in big way. recently caraway worth Rs. 42.67 lakhs and caraway oil worth Rs. 4.13 lakhe was imported in to India.

Saussurea costus (Falc.)Lipsch (S. lappa)

(Decne) Sch. Bip.) Compositae (Asteraceae)

Kuth (LN); Costus (CL and TN)

Plant is 1.5 m high with big triangular leaves. The plant is reported to be cultivated occasionally in Milam, Mana, Laspa, Railkot, Burphu, etc. for the roots which are locally used for curing asthma, gastric, disorders,etc.

Kutu plant originally belongs to Kashmir and it was the Kashmir state monopoly in kutu trade. From Kashmir it was hrought to Himachal Pradesh by the missionary people who cultivated the plant for economic gains as there was a great market of kuth in China. In 1929, Kuth was introduced in Bhuna nursery (Chamoli) and cultivated in commercial scale by the Forest Department to be exported to China. Kuth was exported to China under the name Puchuk and used as incense in monastries. But after the IInd World War the trade was abandoned and the Bhuna nursery was converted into an experimental medicinal plants nursery by the forest department.

It is well established from the eariler experiments that the plant can be easily cultivated in cool and humid localities above 2500 m in the wet alpine zone where monsoon rains are not much. The essential oil of kuth has good demand in high class perfumery mostly in France. If there is a large scale demand of the kuth then the cultivation of the plant can easily be taken up in Uttarakhand and distillation of oil and olresin extraction units can easily be established in situ.

Perilla frutescens (L) Britt (P,ocimoides L.) Labiateae

Bhangira, Bhangjira (LN); Selum (Nepal & Sikkim) (Common perilla CN)

Plants is 0.5-1.2 m high and mostly cultivated in the temperate region from 1500 to 2000 m for the seeds, which was are locally used as condiment for flavouring purpose.

Common perilla is among the oldest food and condiment crop cultivated throughout the east Asian countries' and mostly in Japan.

The aerial parts of the plant after seeds harvest were collected by the author from Uttarakhand and subjected for analysis. The oil by hydrodistillation of the aerial part is 0.6% and the main constituents reported are carvone (57.08%) in carvyl acetate (32.72) methyle chavicol (2.8%) and linalool (1.5%). This was preliminary analsis.

Mishra & Husai experiment raised the crop at cimap Lucknow from the seeds collected from Bangladesh and hydrodistilled the inflorescence that yielded 0.15% of essential oil with main constituents as rosefuran (58%) B-caryophylline constituents of rose oil the authors propose the use of the common perilla oil for blending of the oil for rose odour.

In Japan the perillartine a monoteroene extracted from the essent ial oil (not mentioned either from the plant inflorescence or the seeds) is used to sweeten and flavouring tobacoos.

INTRODUCTION OF ESSENTIAL OIL BEARING CROPS

There are possibilities for introduction of essential oil bearing crop like lavender, clarysage, rose, etc and the horticultural citrus fruits in Uttaranchal.

AROMATIC HERBS

The inner valleys of dry alpine zone like Niti has been identified climatrically suitable for cultivation of crops like lavender and rose.

Lavendula angustifolia P. Miller subsp angustifolia Labiateae

Lavander (CN & TN)

The aerial part on hydrodistillation yields oil of lavender and this crop was introduced for commercial cultivation by CIMAP though it was long been introduced in the country for experimental purpose by RRL Jammu in Kashmir.

The oil is used in high grade perfumery colognes lotions etc. The present production of the oil in the world is about 1000 tonnes per annum and the main producers are Bulagaria USSR and Tasmania. India imports oil of lavender worth 52.3 lakh of rupees and the present Indian market rates are Rs. 600/- per kg. In the year 1992-93 lavender oil worth Rs. 79.57 lakhs was imported into India.

Salvia sclarea L. Labiateae

Clarysage Sage oil (CN & TN)

The inflorescence part of the plant on hydrodistillation yields clarysage oil which is mostly used in perfumery as well as in flavour industries for flavouring liquors and confectionarls etc. The aroma of the oil blends easily with other oils aroma. The present production of the oil in the world is more than 100 tons per annum and the main countries to produce the oil was USSR and Bulgaria and the present international market rate for the oil is Rs. 3000/- per kg.

Rosa damascena Mill Rosaceae

Desigulab Bulgarian rose (CN)

The petals on hydrodistillation yield rose oil. The rose oil has good demand in the perfumery and flavouring industries including the pharmaceutical. Present porduction of rose oil in the world is 15-20 tons per annum and the main producer is Bulgaria and the international market rate is Rs. 1.34 lakhs per kg. and in Indian market the rate is Rs. 1.0 lakh per kg.

Rosemarinus officinalis L. Labiateae

Rosemary (CN)

Rosemary is mostly used as herb in cooked dishes because of its antioxidant properties and also used in the manufacture of meat based products. The essential oil from the leaves is an important ingredient in cosmeties perfumes and insect repellent. The world production is about 970-1020 tons per annum and the main producer is mediterranean basin Mafeti. Though the crop has been experimentally grown in Kashmir but large scale cultivation has not been tried.

Salvia officinalis L. Labiateae

Sage. Sage oil (CN)

The dried herb as well as essential oil are used in home cooking commercial meat processing etc. It is used in herbal teas in Europe. Its essential oil is used to flavour liquor bitters condiments and cured meats and as an ingredient in perfumery formulations.

Oleoresin of sage is also prepared which is used as flavouring agent in industrial meat processing. Annual production of sage oil is 1750 tons per annum and international market rate of the oil is Rs.800/- per kg. The main producing countries are Albania Greece and Turkey. What is needed is to cultivate the above stated crops experimentally at suitable localities extract their essential oils and get it evaluated by the foreign buyers before large scale cultivation is undertaken.

Expressed Essential Oils

The hills of Uttarakhand are found very suitable for cultivation of citrus and orange fruits and already a number of species are being cultivated which are mostly sold as fruits and not processed for squash cordial marmalade etc. If suitable varieties and species introduced in the hills mostly for processing purpose then as a byporduct cold expressed essential oil may be obtained .

Citrus sinensis Citraceae

Orange sweet oil

The peels of Citrus sinensis on cold expression yield the orange sweet oil which is mostly used as flavouring soft drinks baked goods and confectionaries and in soaps and other cleansing products and aerosols. It is also a source of 'd' limonene an important flavouring compound which has good demand in the market. The total world production of orange sweet oil is about 15000 tons per annum but demand is estimated to be 2000-2500 tons per annum. India imports orange sweet oil worth Rs. 54.16 lakhs. The other byproduct obtained from it could be pectin and animal feeds etc.

Citrus limon (Linn.) Burm. f. Citraceae

Pahari nimbu (CN)

Cold expressed lemon peels yield lemon oil which has also good demand within the country as it is used in soft drinks confectionary and pharmaceutical porducts. The world production is about 2000-2500 tons per annum.

To establish these two above stated industries in the Uttarakhand hills it is required that a horticultural survey for the citrus and orange growing regions should be made where these are being cultivated in considerable quantities and the regions where citrus crops can do well. The Horticultural Department of Uttarakhand is the most appropriate agency which could supply this information as the department has already established the canning and processing fruit industries in some of the localities for processing squash cordial etc. A leading fruit processing company is already collecting lemons oranges malta etc. from Mandal (Chamoli) and transporting these to plains for processing squash marmalade etc Information is not available whether this company is using the fruit peels for expression of oil or not.

Present market rate of lime oil is about Rs. 400/- per kg and India imports lemon oil and other citrus fruit oils worth of about Rs. 70 lakhs per annum.

Establishment of Grading and Processing Units

Lichens (Parmelia spp; Usnea ssp; ramalina ssp.)

Jhoola, charila, (LN); Stone flower, Oakmoss (CN & TN)

Different species of lichens are mostly found in oak rhododenron and pine forests in Uttarakhand. These lichene are commercially traded in huge quantities from this region which are used in indigenous perfumery (attar industry) modern perfumery (oleoresin used in cologne soaps and fragrances) incense industry (havan samigri) in flavour industries (in sambhar and garam masala and in tobacco curing) and in indigenous systems of medicine in Ayurveda under the name shailya and unani under the name ushna.

In the year 1983-84 about 7500 quintals of lichen was traded from Uttarakand. Mostly to Kanpur, Luckhnow and Nagpur. It is estimated that about 100 m tons of lichen of high grade is exported from India to produce concrete, absolute and resinoids. The main regions from where lichens are collected are Assam, Nepal, Uttarakhand and Himachal, Prdesh.

Presently lichens which are collected from Uttarakhand are transported to plains at railheads like Kotdwar, Ramnagar, Kathgodam and Tanakpur where these are graded to cater the needs of above stated industries.

Mostly these are graded into four grades which are detailed below.

Grade 'First'— It consicte of Parmelia niegherrensis exclusively.

Grade Second— It connnsists of P. nilgherrensis P. nepalensis Taylor and P. cirrhata Fr. about 90-95% mixed with Usnea susordida Triton Ramalina inflata (JD. Hook & Tayeolr) JD. Hook & taylor and R. subcomplanata about 5-10%. This grade is used mostly in indigenous perfumery.

Grade 'Third'— It consist of Parmelia spp. of grade IInd about 60-75% mixed with Usnea and Ramalina spp. about 20-25%. This grade is mostly used in flavour industry as an ingredient of garam masala and in havan samigri.

Presently all grades of lichens are collected from Uttarakhand but not graded in situ. It is required that the grading should be done in situ and possibilities for establihing extraction units for oleoresin may be explored.

Zingiber officinale Rosis. Zingiberaceae

Adrak (CN & TN); Ginger (CN)

It is a well known agricultural crop and is cultivated near Chakrata (Dehra Dun) in a big way. There are possibilities to establish ginger oil and ginger oleoresin extra ction units nearby Chakrata hills.

Ginger oil is largely used as flavouring material in alcoholic and non alcohlic beverages. The oleoresin is used in confectionary and perfumes.

Present market rate of the oil is about Rs. 900/- per kg.

During 1992-93 ginger worth Rs. 286.433 lakhs was imported from Nepal.

CONCLUSION

It is concluded that the aromatic herbs of Uttarakhand need the following action for establishing the essential oil industry and for their conservation and preservtion.

The locally growing species like the Himalayan angelica, Skimmia, Indian valerian, hedychium, cinnamomum, etc which have been much exploited in recent years need systematic and planned collection and regeneration in the forest or in the farmers fiedls.

The locally growing herbs like sweet flag. caraway costus which have good market demand should be encouraged for cultivation in farmers fields at suitable localities after working out their economics of cultivation.

Proper markets may be explored for the essential oil cosmetics modern perfumeries etc. which could be easily obtained from zanthoxylum hyssopus juniper and wild marigold. Side by side the forest authorities may by approached to allow the collection of stumps of cut deodar trees and the skimmia leaves.

There is need for establishment of field units at suitable localities for the extraction of cold expressed essential oils from lemons and orange peels as a byproduct and oleoresin from lichens and essential oil and oleoresin from ginger.

It is suggested that in Uttarakhand some leading perfumers should come forward and act as entrepreneur and install hydrodistillation units for essential oils and extraction units for oleoresin in situ and encourage the cultivation of the aromatic crops.

The aromatic species which are commonly available like Serephidium brevifolium Artemisia gmelinii Rhododendron anthopogon Origanum vulgure Thymus linearis Perilla frutescens either need detailed analysis of essential oils or evalutaion in the international or Indian markets or chemical analysis and evaluation both.

Chapter-14

PROMISING AROMATIC PLANTS OF INDUSTRIAL VALUE

INSPITE of the spectacular advances and high use levels of synthetic chemicals matural products still occupy a formidable position in industry. Infact there has been an increasing demand for aromatic raw material for industrial formulations. It is because the natural products obtained as plant isolate may be useful directly or may serve as starting material for the synthesis of active agent. In addition these porducts are suitable as lead compounds for subsequent design of structurally related molecules that are more active or less toxic. Most importantly, the natural products are still indispensable for producing homogeneity and rounding off effect and tempering harshness of the synthetics in a perfume composition. Thus a revival of interest has been paid worldwide on the natural products. This growing interest in plant originated substances over the last few decades has brought essential oils to the forefront of the international trade. Moreover an increasing number of plant based medicines and cosmetics are on the market and intensive trade between the nations has enhenced the availability of new products in the Western world. In India alone about 20 percent of 4000 tonnes of chemicals estimated to be used annually in perfumes and flavours are obtained from the essential oil representing an important class of indigenously produced starting material for perfumes and flavour industry. Some of them are used in pharmaceuticals and other industries as well.

North Eastern region of India basically a tribal and aboriginal inhabited area harbours a rich flora on account of its varied topography climate and altitudes. There are about 8000 flowering plant species bolonging to this region representing 50 percent of the flora of the country. This region also endows with a vast resources of medicinal and aromatic plants, many of which have been in use over the millennia among the local people in the promotion of health and as drugs and fragrance materials. These factors coupled with the socio economic condition of the people provide a good deal of scope for developing agrobased industry in the region based on the local resources of medicinal and aromatic plants. However adequate attention has not so far been paid on these resources of North east India either in research or developmental activities. Furthermore this region of Iadia is at present becoming a highly vulnerble geographical area so far as the man made activities continuing in its various places are concerned. Meanwhile many plants of this region are becoming endangered and some of which are already on the verge of extinction. Considering the importance of the above facts Regional Research Laboratory Jorhat has taken up a programme of R&D work on North East Indian plants. The results achieved so far on certain plant species are highlighted in this communication.

CINNAMOMUM SPECIES

The genus Cinnamomum (Family Lauraceae) comprsing about 270 species of tropics and sub tropics represents a group of industrially important economic plants due to many of its species having perfumery, flavour, cosmetic and pharmaceutical values. There are about 20 species occur in India; most of them are found in its north east part some of which are grown by the local people for their domestis consumption and even for trade. Two new essential oil sources of industrial potential discovered from the region are presented here.

1. *Cinnamomum impressinervium* - A small evergreen tree found in North Cacher Hills of N E India at an elevation between 800m, 1050m the leaves possess an odour similar to Cinnamomum tamala eugenol type (Tezpat of commerce). The leaves of this Cinnamomum species are also known locally as "Tezpat" and used as spice. Apart from being found sporadically in wild stands, it is also seen under cultivation in the homestead gardens of many tribal people in the region. The local people consider the cultivated form as the "quality" clone of the species and its leves are even sold in the market under the name 'best quality Tejpat' Fresh leaves of the plant on hydrodistillation give 1.8% and 2% of a yellow and yellow brown essential oil from wild and cultiveted sources respectively. Physicochemical constants of the oils are as follows: Wild sources nD=1.5236 d=1.03320 and d=+15; cultivated source nD=1.5320 d=1.0350 and d=+16.

Eugenol was the main component of the oils, the concentration of which was however higher in cultivated sources (88.3%) than in the wild ones (83.2%). Other components indentified in the oils were pinene (0.5-1.2%), B pinene (0.1-0.2%), 8-3 carene (1.6-7.2%), limonene (2.3-4.1%) B cymene (0.6-0.7%) guaicecol (0.1-0.4) terpineol (0.3-0.4%), B caryophyllene (0.1-0.2%) B and eugenol acetate (1.0-1.1%).

The eugenol occuring as a main component in the oil of C. impressinervium leaf was a first ever record (Nath and Baruah, 1994) in contrast to cinnamic aldehyde as main component in the oil of same plant native to Burma. Thus the eugenol type C. impressinervium is a new source providing a good deal of scope for commercial use.

In India C. impressinervium is also growing in Sikkim Himalaya at an altitude 1200-1800m. In traditional sustem of medicine its leaves are used as hypoglycaemic stimulant carminative antirheumeticy antidiarrhoeal, antidote for scorpion sting in colic and bark as antigonorrhoeal.

2. *Cinnamomum sulphuratum Nees-* A new addition to the flora of North east India recorded from the Mahur area (600-800m) of N.C. Hills, Assam was earlier reported from Southern India.

It occurs as a small evergreen tree known locally as "Jungli Dalchini" and "Chasing Jola" among the people of N.C.Hills. Leaves are aromatic and used by the tribal people for preparation of an infusion said to be useful in fever dyspepsia and cholera besides being useful as flavouring agent in their local dishes. On hydro distillation, the fresh leaves yield a colourless sweet smelling oil (0.6%) with the following physico chemical properties: d=0.8510 nD C =1.4622 and (a^) $D^{28}/D5^{0}$=-19.5. Eight components (98.01%) were indentified (Nath et al . 1994) of which l-linalool alone accounted for 92.66% of the oil. Other components were (a^)pinene (0.50%) camphene (0.08%) pinene (0.28%) limonene (0.73%) citronellol (1.47%) nerol (0.09%) and geraniol (2.20%).

There was no record of chemical investigation so far on the essential oil of this plant. Moreover linalool from natural source is a high valued aroma chemical (Present New York market price Rs. 3900/kg) extensively used for flavour application. The present production of this chemical in India is insufficient even for internal consumption and as a result, the country imports on an average 55 tonnes of the product every year. Commercial cultivation of additional or alternative source of linalool in India is 25 therefore desirable to meet the industry's demand. Thus C. sulphuratum containing 92.66 percent linalool in its leaf oil seems to be a promising source for commercial use.

A FEW OTHER WOODY PLANTS

Woody plants on account of their significant role to ecology and economy have, in the recent years received increasinq popularity as raw materials of agrobased industry. Meanwhile, this group of plants has occupied an important positioin essential oil industry too. About 65 percent of the present world production of essential oil (45000 tonnes) is now obtained from this group of plants (tree and bushes) alone. However as compared to some other essential oil producted in India, little attention has been paid on this group of plants either in research or developmental activities. Few plant species of this category other than the Cinnamomum spp. brought to light by RRL Jorhat are highlighted here.

Betula alnoides Buch-Ham: A large tree (Betulaceae) with aromatic bark. In North east India it is found sporadically in the subtropical forests at an elevation between 800-1400m. It is locally called "Khiringjau" Kadinglen "Sour" and "Bhujapatra" and its barks are used by the aboriginal people for the treatments of jaundice rhieumatic pains, sprains and for severs bleeding of women after child birth.

An essential oil characteristic of wintergreen aroma obtained from the fresh stem-bark, on hydro-distillqation, is 0.18 percent. Methyl salicylate was identified as the main component (98.2%) in the oil.

B. alnoides wood is also a good quality timber being utilized from the fresh stem bark on hydro distillation is 0.18 percent. Methyl salicylate was identified as the main component (98.2%) in the oil (Nath 1991).

Clausena heptaphylla W&A: A bushy undershrub (Rutaceae) sporadically found in the everqreen forests of North east India upto an altitude 1400m. In the region it is locally known as "Netang tabu" "Arhuksi" and "Panmachala" where the leaves are used by the people for flavouring food stuff tobacco (Kanjilal et al) and also for the treatment of ailments like malaria and fever.

Both the leaves and fruits of C. heptaphylla possess a swet aromatic odour and on hydro distillation, their fresh materials give a pale yellow essential oil in 0.82% and 2.22% respectively with the following physico chemical properties nD=1.5291 and 1.5270 D==+0.1228 and +0.68 and d= 1.2215 and 1.1765. Methyl chavicol was identified as main component (57%-75%) followed by (E) anethole (12.7% -40.3%) in both the oils. (Nath and Bordoloi 1991 ;1992). The fruit oil contained higher amount of methyl chavicol (86.2%) than that of the leaf oil (57% - 75%). In contrast (E) anethole was higher in the leaf oil (40.3%) than in the fruit oil (12.7%)

C. heptaphylla containing anethole as a main component in its leaf oil has also been reported elsecwhere. C. heptaphylla is also a medicinal plant. From its roots two pyranocoumarins viz causenin and clauseniden were isolated.

Litsea cubebea Pers: A small deciduous tree (Lauraceae) found in the Eastern Himalayan region upto an altitude of 2700 m. Its fruits are edible carminative and used as preservative for fish in Indonesia and for headache, dizziness, hysteria paralysis and loss of memory in Indochina (Chopra et al). Almost all parts of the plant are aromatic and yield volatile oil. The fruit oil has gained importance in China as a source of citral.

In North least India particularly in Assam it is known as, Mejankari and was once extensively used as host plant for rearing Muga sikworm for production of 'Mejankari' silk. The tribal people of North east Hills, on the other hand, use the fruit as condiment and also for the treatments of ailments like colic, heart diseases, eczema and scabies.

On investigation of stem bark and fruits of L. cubeba growing wild in North "east Indian" Hills a pale yellow essential oil is obtained. Yield of oils their physico chemical properties and the constituents identified in the oils are presented in the Table.1.

The fruit essential oil reported previously for the L. cubeba growing elsewhere (Naves and Grampoloff,) other than North east India contains citral 80% only. Hence the fruit oil of the same plant native to India seemed to be significantly superior. Average yield of fresh fruit as studied in the field for a plant of average growth (6m height) yielding average total biomass (aerial) of 195 kg was 6 kg. Likewise, 8 kg of bark on an average could be easily obtained in a single harvest. Based on this observation and also on oil yield data, per hectare annually the production (single harvest) of fresh biomass (bark and fruit) and oil were estimated. This showed that 947.64 kg of total oil could be obtained annually on cultivation of this crop at a spacing of 2.m from plant and row to row, out of which 825 kg of the oil would be from the fruit alone. Like wise at the spacing of 2.5 and 3.0 m, oil yield would be 604.8 and 419.95 kg respectively.

It is seen that per hectare annual yield of essential oil so far obtained from cultivation of Lemongrass is around 380 kg. Thus Litsea cubeba could be contemplated as better source for citral to be commercially exploited. Meanwhile 'a' L cubeba oil has occupied a position in international market and consequently production of lemongrass oil has declined considerably. The present production of this oil is essential at only 300 tonnes against 2000 tonnes.

CYMBOPOGON SPECIES

Cymbopogon species are well known for their use in essential oil industry. C. winterianus, C. flexuosus and C. citratus are the major crops cultivated in North eastern India for commercial purposes. A programme of selecting better yielding strains of these species was undertaken by RRL Jorhat over the last couple of years. Two strains screened out so far are presented here.

Cymbopogon citratus (DC) Stapf RRL- J-1180 : A delayed flowering strain of the species with superior yield attributing characters. The strain gives more tillers (116.20/plant) higher herbage (0.990 kg/plant) oil (0.7%) and citral content (84.65%). Likewise on large scale cultivation it porduces herb and oil yield of 53.77 tonnes and 376.36 kg respectively per hectare per annum and hence appeared to be a supeior strain as compared to existing ones for commercial cultivation.

Table 1 - Essential oil and its constituents of Litsea cubeba native to North east India

Oil yield phusico-chemical constants and constituents	Value of the physico chemical constants percentages of oil yield and constituents		
	Stem bark oil	Green fruit oil	Ripe fruit oil
Oil yield	0.60	5.40	5.60
d^{26}	0.8023	0.8693	0.8562
nD^{26}	1.2345	1.4802	1.4802
(a^) D^{26}	$+6.85^0$	$+5.81^0$	$+5.79^0$
mehtyl heptenon	4.80	1.31	1.46
liomonene	4.30	0.33	0.17
linalool	4.40	3.30	2.84

Citral -A	43.50	50.31	51.90
Citral -B	33.80	40.57	40.68

Table 2— Chemical composition of the oil of Cymbopogon flexuosus growing in North east India

Components*	Peak area percentage	Component	Peak area percentage
Tricyclene	0.2	neral	10.3
pinene	0.2	citronellol	24.1
camphore	1.3	geraniol	30.5
6- methyl-5-heptane-2one	0.4	geranial	13.6
Myrcene	0.5	bornyl acetate	0.3
B phellandrene	0.2	eugenol	0.2
limonone	1.9	citronellyl acetate	2.2
4-nonanone	0.3	geranyl acetate	2.1
linalool	1.0	B caryophyllene	0.4
B armevl	0.4	V-Candinene	1.0
citronellal	4.0	cubebene	0.5
terpineol	I.3	cadinene	1.0
decanal	0.2		0.3
		Total	96.4

* Listed in order of elution from an OV-1 column.

Cymbopogon flexuosus (Steud) Wats - RRL-J-1280: In the courses of resource surveys in Arunachal Pradesh of North east India the authors have come across some population of the crop distinct from the existing strains of the same crop on account of their higger leaf size and bushy habits. The strain has been raised and multiplied in experimental farm and evaluated for essential oil characters (Nath *et al)* On hydro-distillation, a pale yellow essential oi is obtained from the grass with the following physico chemical properties: Specific gravity (27^0 C) 0.262, optical relation (27^0C)+3.12^0 and refractive index (29^0C) 1.4662.

Twentyfive components of the oil as identified are presented in Table2. Instead of citral, geraniol was the main component (30.5%) in the oil. It is followed by citronellol (24.1%), citral (23.9 (%), citronellal (4.0%) etc. Further developmental work of this crop is under progress.

Chapter-15

ESSENTIAL OIL INDUSTRY WASTE UTILIZATION

SUBSTANTIAL quantities of ligno cellulosic residues are available after the distillation of essential oil, which are not being put to any use rather pose disposal problems. Utilisation of these residues will not only fill up or narrow down the gap of present shortages of cellulosic raw materials needed for paper and board industry, but will also form a potential source of its development. These ligno cellulosic residues can be economically utilized for the manufacture of straw boards, fibre boards and paper pulp.

Some of the basic requirements of cellulosic raw material needed in the production of paper pulp and board are:

(i) The cellulose content that is available in the form of a fibre;

(ii) The ease with which it can be isolated in the form of a pulp;

(iii) Economic recoveries of the pulp;

(iv) Quality, shape and size of the fibres;

(v) Availability in bulk quantities at an economic price.

CYMBOPOGON MARC

The potentialities of ligno cellulosic waste available from the essential oil distillation units should not be underestimated. Different varieties of Cymbopogongrass (also called lemon grass) are being distilled in large quantities in Assam, Kerala and other places. The residues are available for a period of 8-9 months, only three months being the learn season. It is also reported that on an averaga about 12-15 tonnes per ha (bone dry basis) is available per annum. With the new trends of setting up mini paper mills these materials will go a long way in meeting the raw material demands of such small units. Moreover, the pulping os such materials is easier than those of wood, requiring less drastic pulping condition. No chemical recovery units may be needed. The final product resembles with agricultural residues and short fibre hard woods which have recently made inroads into the paper pulp and board industry. The black liquor formed during cooking of the rew material contains dissolved organic matter thus causes disposal and pollution problem. Therefore it will need additional affluent treatment unit the same way as is required for straw based paper and pulp mills.

Studies carried out in this laboratory revealed that these left over lignocellulosic marcs respond well to pulping by chemical and semi chemical methods and pulp recoveries are as good as any other pulpable raw material.

Our experiments also indicate that Cymbopogon marc can be converted into straw board and fibre board. Fibre board is a kind of board generally made in thickness more than 2.5 mm in varying density range. It is made from the isolated lignocellulose fibres which are converted into a wet sheet from water suspension on a screen and dried under compression to a haid rigid board. The board is much stronger than straw board or the ordinary card board/paper board.Table 1— Composition and fibre dimensions of different materials

	Cymbopogon marc	Mentha marc	Rice straw	Eucalyptus citriodora
Extractives				
a. Ether(%)	2.00	2.00	-	0.45
b. Alconol benzene (%) (1:2 by vol.)	3.23	2.65	4.60	1.1
c. Hot water (%)	8.75	22.7	13.3	4.20
II. Pentosan (%)	20.1	12.3	24.5	21.8
III. Holo cellulose (%)	67.8	78.0	-	77.8
IV. Alpha cellulose*(%)	43.8	-	36.2	41.2
V.Lignin*	22.2	25.0	11.9	22.8
VI. Average fibre(U)	1.112	-	1.130	887
VII. Average fibre	13.0	-	16.0	15.0

*Extractive free o.d. basis

Possessing thickness more than 10mm or more having density 0.3-0.5 g/cm are referred as insulation boards. Properties of fibre boards made from Cymbopogon grass are given in Table 2. Strengthwise the fibre board conforms to I.S.I standards water absorption and thickness swelling is on the higher side which could be drastically brought down by wax coating and by addition of resins. A unit of 5 tpd capacity could be set up at an estimated cost of Rs.10 million with an annual turn over of Rs. 13.0 million.

A small scale straw board/fibre board unit can be set up along with essential oil distillation plant, thereby, utilizing the ligno-cellulosic mare available after the distillation operation. A straw board unit of 3.0 tpd capacity will consume about 5.0 tonnes (bone dry) marc per day. Such a unit is estimated to cost Rs. 2.5 million with a recovery of 55-65% of finished product which is as good as that obtained from conventional agricultural residues. Some of the advantages from such a source of raw material especially for the production of straw boards are:

(i) The ligno cellulosic material coming out of the distillation still can be straight away fed into the rotary pressure digester required for further pulping.

(ii) The digester can be used in full capacity as the material gets compressed to some extent during the distillation process and loading of the digester can also be done in one operation which normally requires 3-4 operations;

Table 2— Fibreboard from cymbopogon grass cooking condition

1.	NaOH w.r.t.o.d. material % 4.0		
2.	Solid: liquid	=	1:7
3.	Cooking temperature ^{0}C	=	135
4.	Time at maximum temperature h	=	3.5
5.	Pulp yield %	=	67
6.	Pulp freeness defibrator seconds	=	67

Properties of fibreboard wax emulsion

	U	T	1.0%	1.5%
1. MOR kg/cm^2	405	500	375	310

2. Tensile strength kg/cm^2	315	382	210	310
3. Water absorption 24 h^0	126	36.0	62	50
4. Thickness swelling 24^1 %	90	28.0	60	44

U= Untreated;T=Heat tempered

(iii) It will economise the consumption of steam and water as the material is sufficiently wet and hot.

(iv) A cooking cycle of 2.0-2.5 hours is sufficient to obtain suitable pulp for straw boards against 3-4 hours given to conventional agricultural residues, as some partial hydrolysis taken place during the distillation process;

(v) It will also save the costs of disposal and the additional space required for shortage of raw material;

(vi) Initial costs on the boiler and overheads will be comparatively less; and

(vii) There will be substantial saving on the cost of procurement of raw material needed for straw board unit.

The only chemical needed is caustic soda to the extent of 4-5% based on bone dry weight of the ligno cellulosic riesidue. Such a type of integrated unit will run more economically than those installed individually.

Small scale material which of 10-15 tpd capacity are also feasible where the raw material is sufficiently ensured. It estimated that a mini paper mill of 15 tpd capacity for the production of white writing and printing paper can be set up at a capital cost of Rs. 60 million and a kraft paper mill at a capital out lay of Rs. 50 million with annual turn over of Rs. 75 million of paper.

MENTHA MARC

This is another material which is also available in large qunatities after the distillation of Mentha arvensis herb. The work on the utilisation of Mentha marc was undertaken for M/s Richardson Hindustan Ltd. Bombay who sponsored a scheme with Regional Research Laboratory, Jammu. The marc is available in large quantities. This too can converted into strow boards in a simila manner as described earlier for Cymbopogon grasses except that the pulp requires some blending with waste paper/corrugated cartons.

Another product that has been developed in this laboratory from Mentha marc is particle board. The residue as it dries up in the air contain 30-40% of leaves and 60-70 of stem portion. Particle boards with elegant surface conforming to standard specifications were prepared from stems of Mentha arvensis marc. Leafportion is undesirable as it forms a fine powder during the process of defibration, thereby, unnecessarily increasing the density of the board. A process of glass fibre surfaced particle board from Mentha marc was also developed. Such boards possess higher strength with superior scratch and moisture resistance than those without it. Physical characteristics of particle boards prepared from Mentha marc are given Table 3.

Particle boards find use as panelling material and in furniture industry. Other uses of particle boards are in flooring and decorative and false ceilings. Plastic surfaced particale boards are as good as laminated decorative panels when the edges are sealed against moisture before use.

Table 3: Physical characteristics of mentha marc

Property	ISI standards	Standards obtained with Mentha particle boards	
		1	2*
Density g/cm^3	0.5-0.9	0.9	1.0
Water absorption he(%)	30	25.0	4.1
Modulus of rupture	90	90-105	123-150

*Surfaced with glass fibre on both sides

Moreover the use of plastic surfaced particle boards require less labour and material for fittings and is thus economical than the paper laminated decorative panels. The main operations involved in the manufacture of particle boards are defibration to get distinct particles shape and size followed by sieving to remove the fines. The particles are treated with synthetic binder converted into a mat and hot pressed. These boards could also be veneered on both sides and can serve as blieck boards.

By this process only 60% of the marc could be utilised which contains the fibres. Rest is all leaves and fines which could be disposed of by burning in the boiler.

A samll scale 3 tpd plant of particle boards is estimated to cost Rs. 7.5 million which include land building plant and machinery and working capitals with annual turnover of Rs. 8.0 million. The plant and machinery for small scale units are indigenously available.

UTILISATION OF WOODY STEMS OF EUCALYPTUS CITRIODORA

The experimental cultivation of this species was undertaken in this laboratory as a source for essential oil. The woody stems after removal of leaves (used for essential oil distillation) are available to the extent of 10 tonnes per ha. This woody material has diameter varying 0.5-25 cm and provides a sufficient quantity for pulping. This material was studied for rayon grade pulp (high alpha cellulose pulp) using prehydrolysis sulphate pulping method. Rayon grade pulp having alpha cellulose of 93.0% and pentosan of 2.1% was obtained against the specification laid down by TAPPI of minimum alpha cellulose 88.0% with maximum limit of pentosan 5.0%. The results from the stems obtained from the harvest of 1.5 year old plant are comparable to 5-6 years old tree of E. citriodora and also to the rayon grade pulp obtained from bamboo (Table 4).

These results indicate the potentiality of the material for the preparation of rayon grade pulp. High alpha rayon grade pulp finds use in various types of industrial products such as rayon yarn cellulose derivatives like carboxymethyl cellulose, cellulose acetate, cellulose acetate butyrate, vulcanized fibre as filler in plastics, etc.

Small scale units based on the ligno cellulosic wastes available from the essential oil industry can play an important role in the development of industry for enhancing the production of items of mass consumption in the country where the resources for bigger units are limited.

Table 4- Comparative properties of rayon grade pulp

	Tappi standards	E.citriodora stems	E.citriodora mature tree	Bamboo
Alpha cellulose[10] (Minimum limit)	88.0	88.3-93.0	88.6-95.5	88.3-93.0
Pentosan(%) (Macimum limit)	5.0	2.10-5.30	2.60-2.80	1.90-12.9
Yield (%) (based on o.d.material)	-	26.8-29.2	28.0-30.3	23.8-30.1

Chapter-16

FRACTIONATION OF ESSENTIAL OILS IN PERFUMERY AND TURPENTINE INDUSTRY

INTRODUCTION

ESSENTIAL oils are obtained from herbs and natural plant materials by steam distillation. They consist of mono and sesquiterpene hydrocarbons their oxygenated compounds and sometimes a smell amount of non volatile material. It is the oxygenated items. Isolation of these oxygenated compounds from the hydrocarbons and their separation without any damage to their odour is an art and is carried out by fractionation.

The histroy of essential oils started with the turpentine oil in America. It is obtained by the steam distillation of oleoresin obtained from pine tree and consists of terpene hydrocarbons only. Its composition vary from species to species. The Indian terpentine obtained from the exudate of Pinus roxburghii Sarg contains a-pinene, b-pinene, carene and small amounts of camphene and longifolene.

Essential oils particularly the perfumery oils are heat sensitive and their fractionation demamd operation of their rectifiers under vacuum with lowest loss of vapour pressure and maximum of separation effect and load capacity.

There are three mian types of fractionating columms used for the purpose. These are (i) Rotary Columms (ii) Plate Columms and (iii) Packed Columms. Their merits and demerits are discussed as under.

ROTARY COLUMNS

These are the most suitable colummns for heat sensitive materials. They have the lowest loss of vapour pressure give maximum separation effect and have highest loading capacity.

These consist of a close fitting rotating shaft which moves in contact with the inner wall of the column wiping the descending refluxed liquid into a thin film and exposing almost each molecule to the heated ascending vapours. This generates maximum amount of vapour to liquid contact. The downward pumping action of the rotor counteracts any flooding tendency and the open spiral path between the band windings provide a continuous vapour path which allows relatively high through put and low pressure drop.

The most efficient column so far made is the Parkin-Elmer Spinning Band column. It is a small Lab scale batch column of 8mm diam 91cm long having 200 theoretical plates. It is capable of separating components having a difference of 0.5^0 C in their boiling points. However it is good for research work only. But such columns are very costly and their separation efficiency falls off quickly with increase in diameter. For example a concentric tube column of 100 mm dia is reported to have only 62 plates per metre height. It falls off sharply to only 6.6 plates per metre in a column of 500 mm dia. Further the repair and maintenance and running cost of such columns is high because of the moving parts involved.

Rotary columns in their modified form such as Rotary spray and thin layer (Luwa of Zurich Switzerland) are available upto 1400 and 850 mm dia respectively. These find application in separating heat sensitive materials under vacuum which include making of pure caprolactum rectification of vitamins and methacrylic acid etc. A typical column is shown in Figure 1.

PLATE AND PACKED COLUMNS

Historically plate columns have been used in petroleum industry whereas packed columns have been widely used in chamical industry the petrochemical industry made use of both the types. However the true selection among these columns for specific systems remained unanswered due to lack of experience and design data.

There are various types of packing and mass transfer trays or plates.

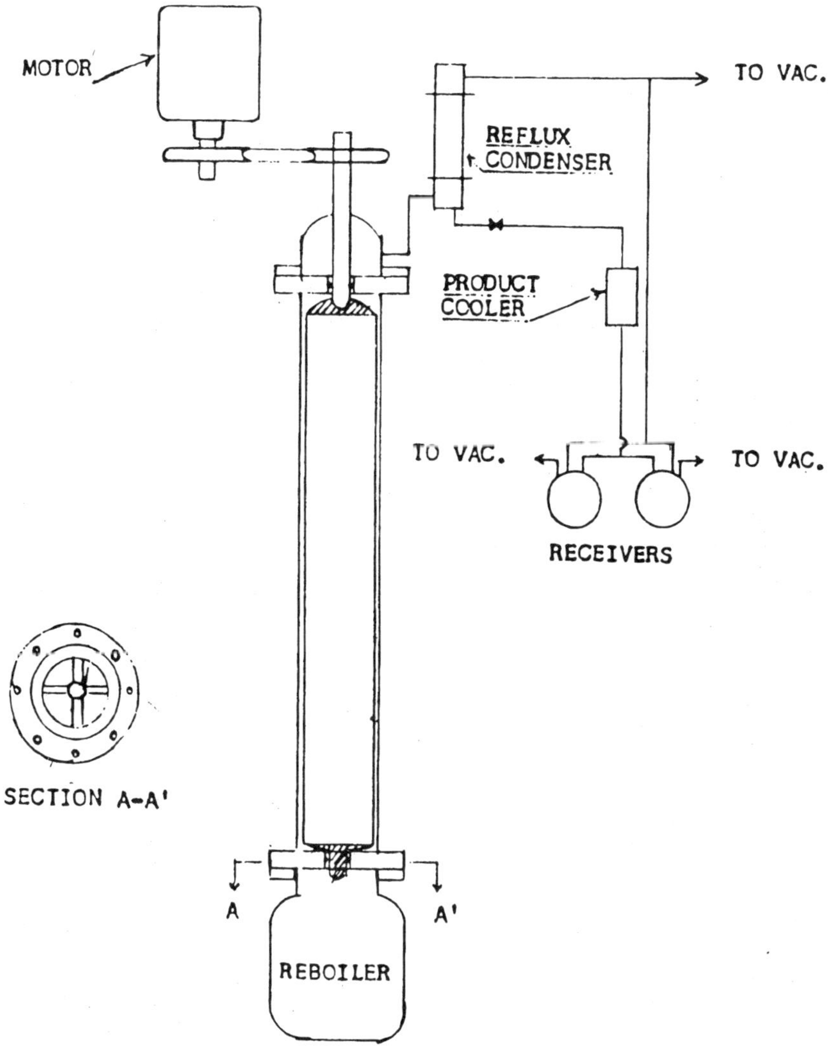

FIG. 1 - CONCETIC TUBE ROTARY COLUMN

Packing usually takes all the avilable space inside the column whereas plates or trays are spaced evenly apart. Though cost is one of the factors in deciding the type of the column but other factors which influence selection are:

1. THE FLUID PHASE

In packed columns liquids are in a dispersed condition and vapours are in turbulent state. These are more suitable for separations where resitance to mass transfer rests in the vapour phase. In case of plate columns the vapour is dispersed while the liquid is in turbulent flow thus making it more suitable for systems where resistance to mass transfer is in the liquid phase.

2. THE TYPE OF FLUID

In case of foaming liquids packed columns are more suitable as the foam collapses more readily in the packing.

However tray columns have advantage where the fluids contain sludges or fats. Valve trays are most suitable in such cases where the moving parts of the valves have self cleaning action which prevent clogging of the openings.

3. MATERIALS OF CONSTRUCTION

Tray columns do not favour construction with non metallic materials such as ceramics, plastic etc which is sometims required for handling corrosive materials. However packed columns can easily accommodate ceramic or plastic packings.

4. EFFICIENCY

Many a times it was thought that large diameter packed columns were less efficient which has been by and by proved otherwise and these are being adopted in more and more industries. Presently packed columns of 11 metre dia or more are in use for rectification.

It was also thought that packed columns were more costly as thay need expensive redistributors and it was difficult to have side steams and feed points in case of continuous columns. This constraint is no more there in the distributors designed by RRL Jammu as the feed and side stream points can be provided in these distributors. These have been successfuly used in columns upto a dia of 750 mm.

Present day paked columns are specially designed and recommended for heat sensitive materials as high efficiency packing materials are avaible which give more number of theoretical plates per unit height with minimum pressure drop and the temperature difference across the column thereby reducing the temperature required in the reboiler. The liquid hold up of such packings is also very low.

Plate columns may be preferred when no extreme demends are made regarding the pressure drop.

BATCH VERSUS CONTINUOUS COLUMNS

In case of multicomponent systems the number of continuous columns required for separating all the components is one less than the number of components present. But the columns can be so designed to have maximum possible purity of each component. The same task of separating all the components can be accomplished by a single batch column but the purity of each component separated will be comparatively low and in less quantity and always followed by middle cuts. Inspite of all this batch columns are preferred where a variety of materials are to be handled in small quantities and at incrvals.

Other advantages of continuous columns are the low residence time of materials under hot conditions lower electric and thermal energy requirement and higher throughputs.

If the columns of same dia and packed height are used for fractionation then in order to get products of same purity:

(i) A batch column requires higher reflux ratio than continuous column.

(ii) A batch column initially gives a product of higher purity, but the purity falls off quickly as more and more product is collected. A continuous column gives a product of constant purity.

(iii) The total quantity of product of certain purity obtained from batch column is less than that obtained from continuous column.

(iv) In batch column the material remains in hot condition (boiling in the reboiler) till the whole product of desired purity is recovered. In case of continuous column there is constant flow of top and bottom products, leaving it under hot conditions only for a short interval of time.

(v) The holding capacity of reboiler in case of continuous column is much less than that in batch column.

A true comparison was arrived at by using the same column as batch as well as continuous one for fractionating turpentine oil of typical composition having 4 components. For using the batch column as continuous one of the distributors was judiciously placed and chosen as feed point to get products of desired composition. A fixed quantity of oil was chosen to process in batch as well as continuous fashion.

(i) In case of batch operation all the components were recovered as products of desired purity in the form of different cuts.

(ii) When operated as continuous column, the feed rate and reflux ratio were so chosen to get top product of desired composition. The bottom product was recycled through the same column at a rate and reflux ratio to get second component in maximum purity as top product. The bottom product of this cycle was again recycled to get the last two components in maximum purity as top and bottom products.

On calculation it was found that.:

1. The quantity of first component of same purity was 35% higher in case of continuous column.

2. The quantity and purity of rest of the components was much better in case of continuous column.

3. The time required to process the same material through continuous column was much less and when computed on annual basis working 300

days a year, it was found possible to process 31.25% more material in continuous column than in batch column.

4. Heat energy saving per annum was found to be 33.63% in case of continuous column.

5. Electric energy saving per annum was found to be 23.8% case of continous column.

It was thus observed that though 3 number of continuous column were required for separating all the 4 components of the oil analysed, but the purpose could be served by using the same continuous column and recycling the bottom products twice to get all the components. This has been possible by using distributors designed by RRL. Jammu and placing them judiciously at a proper height so that the column could take up recycled feed. Not only this it should be possible to design a multipurpose continous column which could use all type of feed giving better results than a batch column thus avoiding the use all type of feed giving better result than a batch column thus avoiding the use of multiple columns for multi component systems.

FRACTIONATION OF PERFUMERY OILS

A perfumer has to handle a variety of highly heat sensitive and costly oils available in limited quantities. A little overheating may cause burning smell in the product. Prolonged boiling in the reboiler may also cause resinification due to polymerisation. Many a time oil components are very close to boiling having a difference of 4 to 5^0 C only in their boiling points. In such cases batch type packed columns packed with most efficient packing are preferred. These columns are operated under vacuum so as to bring down the boiling points of the materials. The operating vacuum (absolute pressure in mm Hg) is so selected that the temperature in reboiler does not approach the decomposition or charring point of the oil which, may result in foul smell. At the same time the column top temperature should be as high as possible so that sufficient temperature difference exists in temperature of vapours and condenser cooling water otherwise the conderser size will go bigger or may even require chilled media circulation for cooling resulting in higher initial and operating cost. Further the higher operating vacuum reduces the column capacity. The loss in capacity being roughly proportional to the square root of the relative decrease in pressure applied.

It is also necessary to keep margin for the rise in temperature dur to pressure drop across the column due to the packed height.

Now a days a variety of highly efficient packings are available. Their action and capacity is generally expressed by a load curve as shown in Figure @ Its saddle curve is typical of many packed columns and is found by experiment only. The corresponding number of theoretical steps n is related to a unit depth of H(M), for a constant liquid / vapour ratio L/V.

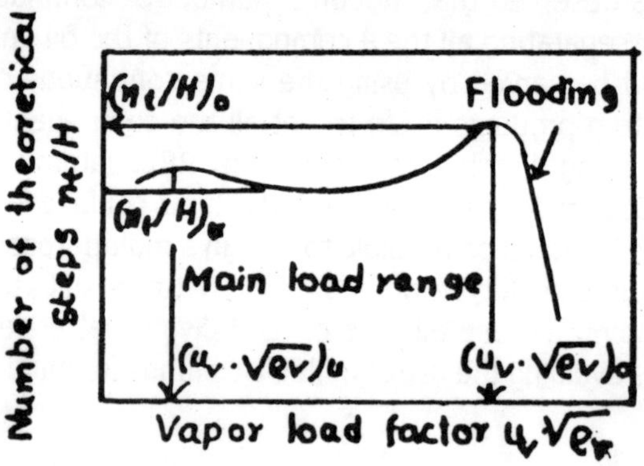

Fig. 2 General separaction versus load curva of a packed column

The function is then plotted. Its curve depends on the physical data of the oil mixture and on the packing used. Thus gives the number of theoretical steps or plates for a packing height of 1 meter. The important part of the curve is the one lying between (n/H)u and (n/H)o corresponding to the load factor and (U pv) and (U pv) The term (U pv) gives the meximum load the column may be put to beyond which the liquid falling would be blocked by the rising vapour causing flooding. At this point the separation efficiency will be impaired. The columns are generally run at 70 to 80% to the flooding point loading for maximum efficiency.

The engineering and commercial evaluation of plate and packed columns is done as per graphs 1 to 8 of Figure 3. These show two different characteristic separations versus load factors. The numbers 1 to 8 on the graphs indicate the sequence of determination/ calculation stages as under.

1. The separation efficiency (E) of mass transfer plate or the equivalent theoretical stages equal to a packing height H(m) n /H (M) is plotted against vapour load factor U pv having vapour velocity based on the free column area and specific weight of the vapour pv (kg/m).

2. The pressure loss of an actual plate p/n (mm water) or the pressure loss per unit height p/H mm (water) for packed column as a function of the vapour load factor.

3. The pressure loss - $\triangle$p/p (mm water) per theoretical stage as a function of the vapour load factor.

4. The specific tower volume as a function of vapour load factor where specific tower volume is the specific volume u/v (m/m s) required per unit of vapour throughput and of separation. For a tower of diameter ds (m) and. The vapour flow through the tower the specific tower volume is given by

For column packing the ratio H/n may be replaced with the reciprocal of the theoretical stages referred to the packing height.

5. The tower cost per m of construction volume C(monetary units/ m) where shell cost is related to column diameter.

6. The specific tower cost

$C_V = V_V\ C$

$C_V = V_V\ C$

is plotted as function of the specific pressure loss p/n in case it is relevant.

7. When pressure loss is not relevant C_V or C_A is plotted as functions of vapour load factor $U_V P_V$.

8. Specific tower cost as a function of tower diameter ds (m). Among the various types of packings available the most suitable for essential oils are Pall rings Interpack Intalox Square grid Fine grid and Wire web packing. Some recent additions and now available in India are modified form of pall rings such as M-pak and Hy-pak rings Hyflux Parlpak S4Y and S2Y which are Similar to sulzar Bx and Mella pak Packings. Some of these packings are shown in Figure 4.

A typical performance of various column packings at 80% of the flooding load and their cost factor Cs for carbon, steel and stainless steel are given in Table 1 & 2.

The reference column with 50mm Pall rings has a specific cost factor of Cs =1, in all cases.

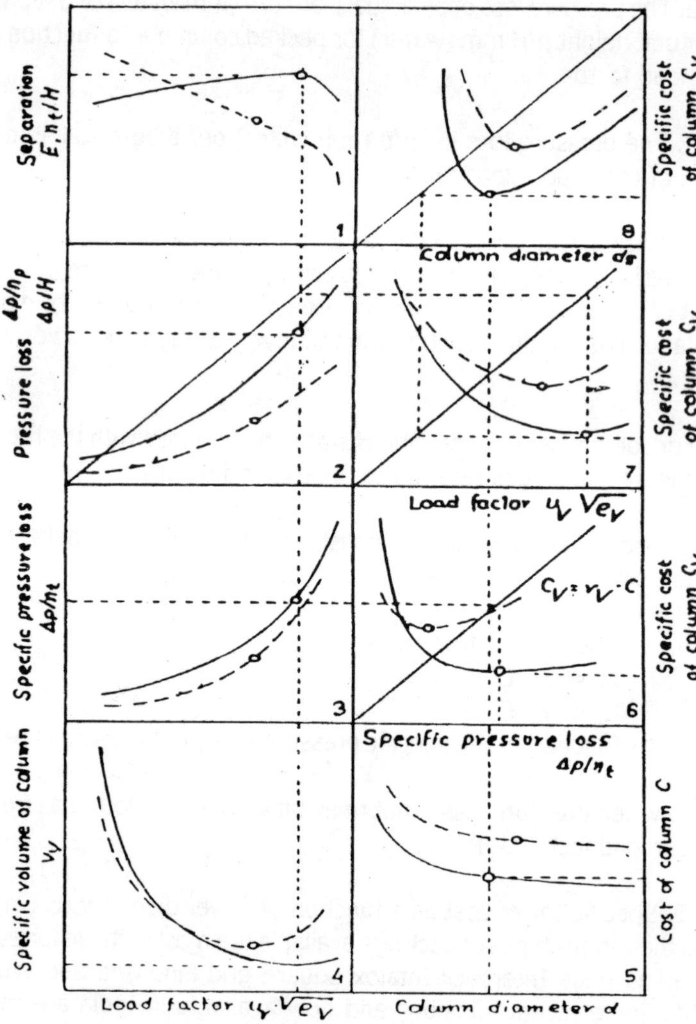

Fig. 3 - Evaluation and optimization of column through steps 1 to 8

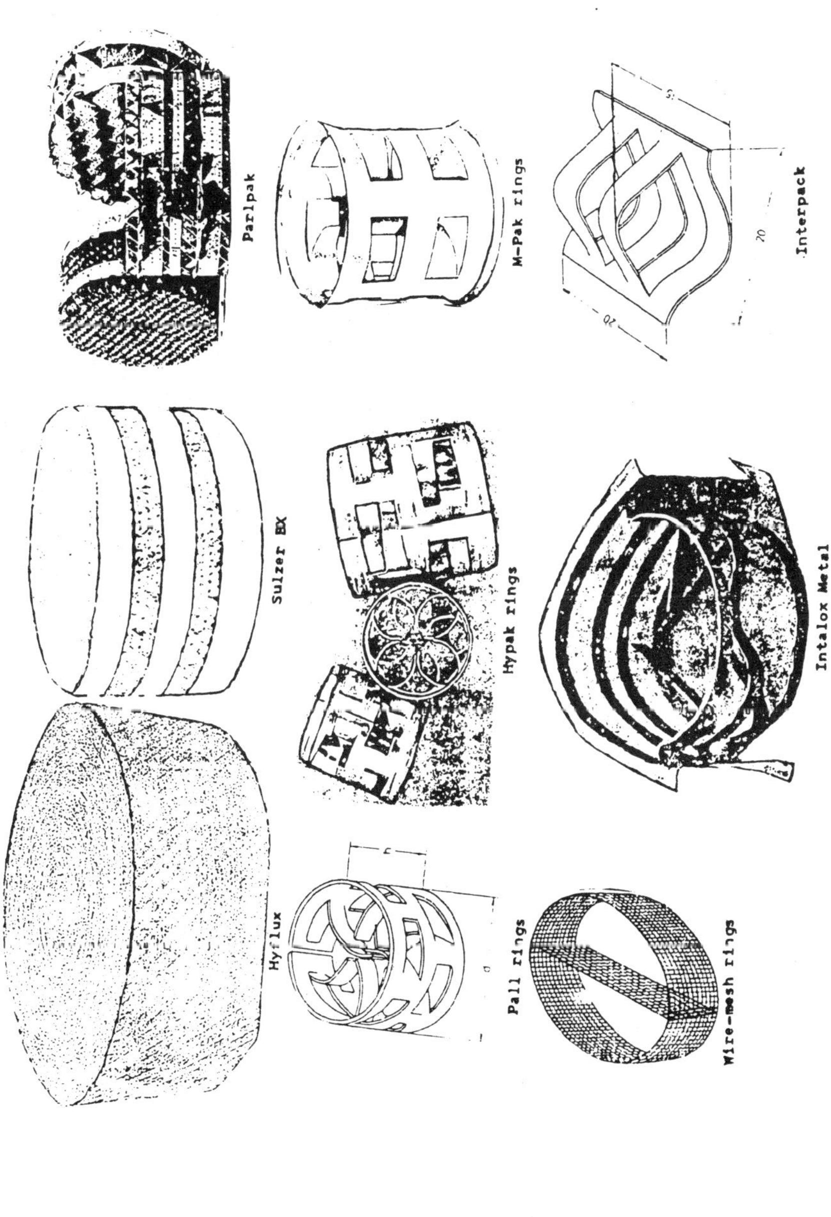

Parlpak
M-Pak rings
Interpack
Sulzer BX
Hypak rings
Intalox Metal
Hyflux
Pall rings
Wire-mesh rings

Characteristics of some selected packings in stainless steel are given in Table 3.

Table 1 - Typical performance of various column packings at 80% of flooding load. ethylbenzene/styrene 100 mm Hg L/V =1.

Column Packing	Uv pv ($m^{-1/2}\ s^{-1}\ Kg^{1/2}$)	n_t/H (1/m)	Δ_p/n_t mmH_2O
1. Wire web	2.82	3.69	14.0
2. Fine grid	2.59	0.71	41.4
3. Square grid	2.38	1.29	17.0
4. Pall rings 15x15x0.4	2.02	3.66	26.9
5. Pall rings 25x25x0.6	2.30	3.02	24.2
6. Pall rings 35x35x0.8	2.40	2.71	25.9
7. Pall rings 50x50x1.0	2.47	2.18	23.8
8. Interpack 20x20x0.4	2.18	2.08	46.1

Table 2— Specific cost factors of various columns made of carbon steel / stainless steel. Ethylbenzene/Styrene 100 mm Hg. L/V = 1 ds (Pall rings 50x50) = 1.5m.

Column packing	Uv pv ($m^{-1/2}\ s^{-1}\ kg^{1/2}$)	Δ_p/n_t ($mm\ H_2O$)	CS Carbon steel	Stainless steel
1. Wire web	3.11	30	-	3.16
2. Fine grid	2.355	..	12.60	3.24
3. Square grid	2.74	..	5.58	2.63
4. Pall rings 15x15x0.4	2.107	..	1.58	1.27
25x25x0.6	2.485	..	1.072	1.251
35x35x0.8	2.586	..	0.899	0.934
50x50x1.0	2.646	..	1.00	1.00
5. Interpack 20x20x0.4	1.88	..	1.55	1.418

$$\text{where CS} = \frac{\text{Cv (Packing + Shell)}}{\text{Cv(50mm pall rings + shell)}}$$

Table 3: Characteristics of some selected S.S.Packings.

Packing	Approximate			% free gas space		F
	Nos/m^3	wt.kg/m^3	Surface area m^2/m^3	Stainless steel	Carbon steel	
Pall rings						
15x15x0.4	2,14,000	603	346	93		97
25x25x0.6	49.600	480	205	94		48
35x35x0.8	13,000	415	130	95		28
50x50x1.0	6,040	385	115	96		20
Hy-Pak						
25x25x=1	29,900	312	177	96		43
35x35x=11/2	9,390	280	125	96		26
50x50x=2	3,670	224	100	97		18
Hy-Pak		S.S.C.S.				
30mm	29,700	187	282	173	97.6	96.1
45mm	9,400	167	190	122	97.9	97.6
Hyflux		432	1930	94.5		
Wire mesh rings						
15x15mm		-	511	96		
Intalox metal =25mm	1,68,425	340		96.7		41
=40mm	50,140	288		97.3		25
=50mm	14,685	186		97.8		16
Inter pack						
20x20x15	2,13,000			95		
PARLPAK S4Y			375	98		
PARLPAK S2Y			250	98		

Where F -- Factor is defined by F=VG p G
Where VG= Vapour velocity, cm/sec.
P_v=Density of vapour g/cm_3

FACTORS AFFECTING THE PERFORMANCE OF PACKED COLUMNS

1. FAULTY DISTRIBUTORS

Distributors form the heart of packed towers. Their proper design is most important. Faulty designs cannot only impair efficiency, but can also reduce the capacity of the column to a great extent. A bad distributor may not give even distribution of liquid over the cross section so that the liquid runs in channels without wetting the whole surface.

2. FAULTY ERECTION

The packed columns should be erected vertically starting from reboiler top to the top of the column. Each and very flange should be levelled with spirit level. A slight tilt from vertical will channelise the reflux towards the wall thereby impairing efficiency. A tilt of 1 % from vertical (of the column) is reported to reduce efficiency to 50- 70% of its normal.

3. TOP CONDENSER

Conventionally horizontal condenser is used for condensing vapours from the top of the column. Then part of the condensate liquid is sent as reflux and rest taken as product. For maximum efficiency the condensate going as reflux should be at its boiling point which is never the case by using horizontal condenser. Secondly to keep the reflux temperatues as high as possible a controlled amount of water is passed through the condenser and a second condenser is placed in series to condense the lefrover vapours. This requires water manipulation for temperature control and more energy is still required water manipulation for temperature control and more energy is still required to being the reflux to its boiling point. This energy is provided by the rising vapours in the column, which otherwise was to be used for condensing higher boiling molecules only. This reduces the column efficiency. This also results in energy loss of around 15 %.

This deficiency can be overme by provding knock back type vertical condenser at the top of the column, so that the reflux comes at its boiling point. Such condensers can be directly placed on the distributors designed by RRL., Jammu. These will no more require any control on water circulation and there is no need for secondary condenser and a separate reflux divider. A general view of such a column is shown in Figure 5.

4. INSULATION

In cars of insufficient on improper insulation, the liquid moves more easily from packing to the wall and vice versa. This is called wall flow effect and happens due to condensation of vapours on the wall because of heat losses.

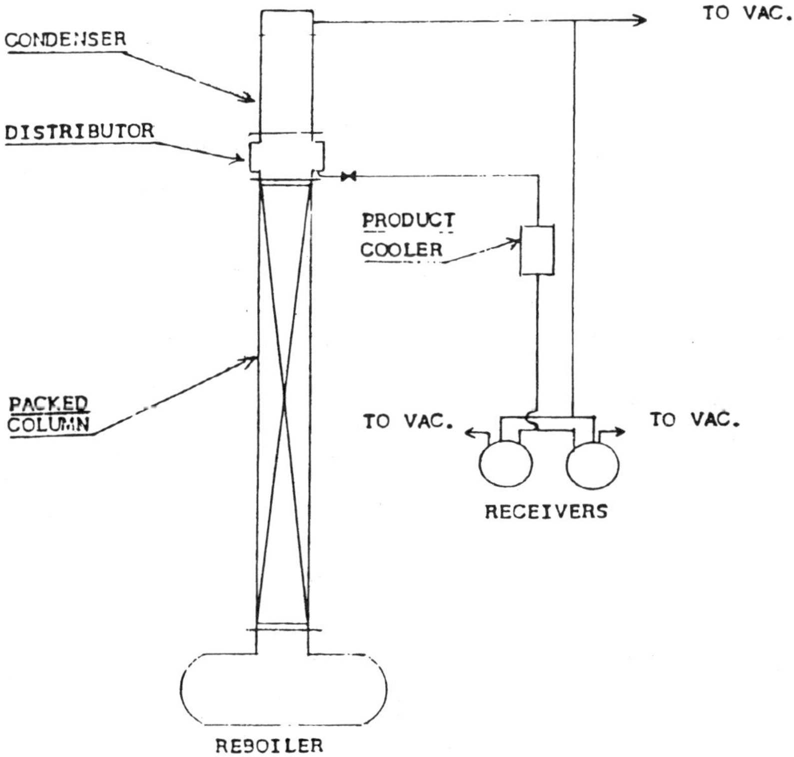

FIG. 5 - BATCH FRACTIONATING COLUMN

RECOMMENDATIONS

FOR PERFUMERY OILS

All S.S. batch type packed column packed with most efficient packing available, such as Wire web 'Hyflux' Sulzar Bx PARLPAK - S4Y, etc. having lowest pressure drop provided with knock back type reflux condenser and well designed distributors are recommended. Reboiler heating with steam is preferred to hot oil circulation as the heat transfer coefficient is much better and for the same surface area the heat transfer rate is higher resulting in lower temperature difference between the heating surface and the reboiler liquid.

FOR TURPENTINE OIL

In case of turpentine oil some time the quantities available are sufficient for processing in continuous columns which are preferred for reasons already discussed. Otherwise batch columns may be used. However in case of feed of constant coposition batch cum continuous column may be preferred in order to have benfits of batch as well as continuons columns. In this case column height and feed point are so chosen that after fractionating the feed for isolating the first component, the bottom product is recycled as feed for isolating the second component. This is repeated if the number of components are more than three.

The turpentine oil does not contain any oxygenated molecules and is thus not so heat sensitive. For this any of the efficient packing like Pall rings, Hy-pak, M-Pak, Mellapak etc.in M.S. may be used in order to reduce the capital investment. Fine packings like Wire web. PARLPAK-S4Y 'Sulzar' Bx are available in S.S. only. Such packings can reduce the packed and thus the total height of the column, though the cost involved is higher. However it may be used case of multipurpose columns which might be sometimes required to fractionate heat sensitive oils like terpineol etc.

Heating may by done through steam or hot oil circulation.

Chapter-17

TAGETES MINUTA (WILD MARIGOLD)

INTRODUCTION

GENUS Tagetes belongs to Asteraceae family. Various species of this genus are native to Mexico Australia South Africa and South America where from these have spread to Europe and other countries and are grown as ornamentals. The plants are annual herbs or shrubs and mostly found growing as wild crop. This genus is known for the presence of essential oil in leaves and flowers. South Africa Brazil and Australia are the main producing countries of Tagetes oil in the world. In India the four important species found are Tagetes minuta Tagetes patula Tageteserecta and Tagetes signata.

Tagetes minuta is considered as the best source of valuable essential oil than other species of the genus[3]. In India, this species finds habitat in Western Himalaya between the altitudes of 1000 to 2500 m. Himachal Pradesh, Jammu and Kashmir and Uttar Pradesh are the main growing regions where it occurs in natural habitat and as a weed in crop fields. It is a highly aromatic annual herb and attains height of 1-2m.

Agronomical morphological and chemial investigations carried out during last six years in this institute have shown this plant as an economic crop for hilly regions. Various parameters for the cultivation, chemical analysis and commercial production of Tagetes oil have been standardized by us. As a result of development and transfer of total technology package by this institute to various entrepreneurs around three tonnes of Tagetes minuta oil is being produced in H.P. for export purpose. The essential oil produced in mid hill regions is found to have a balanced ratio of monoterpene ketones which are responsible for the better olfactory value of the oil than that produced from plain areas of U.P. and Punjab with low olfactory value.

The oil exhibits bronchodilatory tranquilising, hypotensive, spasmolytic and anti inflammatory activities. Saxena and Srivastava reported the Juvenile hormone activity of the oil against Dysdercus koenigii. Photosensitization activity due to the presence of some thiophenes was reported by Downum and Towers. Marandufu et al have reported that 40 ppm of 5E ocimenone isolated from Tagetes minuta oil caused 100% mortality of mosquito Larvae (Aedes aegypti).

CROP MANAGEMENT

Tagetes minuta has been domesticated from wild but till now there has been no systematic effort to develop a specific crop variety because variations in morphological characters of the plant have been observed. It has a wide adaptability to varying soil and climatic conditions. It can easily be cultivated in all types of soils and even under partial shade of other higher vegetations or trees. It germinates in almost all seasons except in extreme cold and hot weather conditions. An increase in temperature beyond 35^0 C and hot weather conditions inhibit the seed germination.

Sporadic germination can also be noticed round the year except in low temperature conditions during the winter period. The main crop periods for the economical production of oil is May to November or July to November depending upon the sowing time. The cultivation of Tagetes minuta is possible invarious parts of the country but in Hinachal Pradesh and other hilly regions have the advantage of producing the quality grade oil because of climatic suitability.

Medium to fine soils free from all weeds are ideal for getting higher herb yields. Compact soil and weed population does not allow the plant to grow well. Direct sowing of seeds is done in the field. Raising of seedlings in the nursery and then transplantation into the field is a little costlier practice but gives assured crop yield. Sufficient soil moisture is required for proper germination at the time of sowing. Around 0.5 kg achenes (seeds) are sufficient for plantation in one hectare of land. The plant spacing (60cm x 45cm) is optimum for transplantation of the crop.

The crop responds well to irrigation during dry period. Spring sown crop requires 3-4 irrigation. There should be sufficient soil moisture at the time of seed germination. However' the crop stands weel in rainfed conditions. Presently the crop is produced mostly under natural conditions. As the plant does not survive under water logged conditions' a good drainage system is essential to remove at excessive ground water particularluy during the rainy season.

Experimental studies have indicated that Tagetes minuta required adequate fertilization. Nitrogen is required to be given in split doses during sowing after two months of seed germination and at flower bud initiation time. The required quantity of phosphorus and potassium is mixed with the soil before seed sowing or at the time of transplantation. Fertilizer doses of 120:60:60 kg/ha of NPK are required for getting maximum yield of thc crop. Tagetes minuta crop competes well with weeds if seed sowing is done in well prepared soil. One or two operations are necessary to remove the major weeds from the field. When initial soil preparation is not done properly crop gets infested with weeds. Thorough weeding is essential for getting maximum oil yields.

In general, marigolds are almost free from diseases and insect pests. Occasionally crop is found to be infected with viruses at the end of rainy season. No specific control measures have so far been developed.

HARVESTING AND DISTILLATION

Essential oil is present in it leaves flowers and seeds while stem is devoid of any oil. The higher ratio of leaves and inflorescence to the stem produces maximum quantity of oil. The age of leaves and flowers affects the oil content and also its quality. Crop should be harvested at full blooming stage for maximum herb yield and for better quality of oil. Right stage of tonnes/ha biomass and 50-60 kg/ha oil yield (0.3%) is obtained when crop is harvested at full bloom stage. A net return of Rs. 30-40 thousands per hactare can be obtained prowided the recommended package of practices are followed.

The essential oil from the crop is obtained by steam distillation. Fresh herb material, harvested at full bloom stage is distilled as fresh or even after 2-3 days of shade drying. However green herb should not be piled in heaps. It should be thoroughly spread on the floor under shade conditions before distillation. Experimantal studies revealed that tha disitillation of fresh herb gives better quality od oil than the sun dried or stored material.

QUALITY EVALUATION

Some preliminary reports on chemical composition of its oil have been published. Recently a detailed chemical composition on Tagetes minuta oil from Himachal Pradesh has been publised by Singh et al reporting 20 constituents in its flower oil. Thappa et al have also reported the chemical composition of the oil from Himachal Pradesh. There is no report on the quality determining constituents of Tagetes minuta oil and' therefore' in this dircection a systelmatic study was made by this institute. Leaves and flowers of Tagetes minuta yield 0.8 and 1.0% oil respectively in laboratory scale on fresh weight basis. The yield on pilot scale distillation of whole plant material varies from 0.20 to 0.35%. The composition of oil from leaves and flowers was separately investigated by us.

The oil contains three monoterpene ketones namely dihydrotagetone tagetone and ocimenone as the major constituents. The variations with respect to composition of these three important constituents was observed and monitored by us periodically from May to November. The results are in good agreement with those of Villiers, who reported changes in the essential oil constituents with the state of development of plant till the fruit ripening stage.

The total composition of oil was studied with respect to the maturity of crop during May to November (vegetative stage to full blooming period). The analysis of fresh oil from whole plant material leaves and flowers was carried out by GC and GCMS. The young crop in vegetative stage contained the major amount of tagetone. It was observed that on maturity of crop the amount of dihydrotagetone increased with the decrease of tagetone and ocimenone contents. At full blooming stage when herb and oil yields are maximum the percentage variation in three monoterpene ketones was found as dihydrotagetone (45 60%) tagetone (15 25%) and ocimenone (20 30%).

In an another experimental study carried out by us the plant growing wild in the hills of Himachal Predesh was collected from six different locations and one sample was collected from plain areas in U.P. The percentage variation of three ketones in the oil samples was monitored by GC. It was found that the ratio of monoterpene ketones in the oil samples of hilly regions was almost same whereas it differed considerably when high percentage for dihydrotagetone and low percentage of ocimenone content was found in the Tegetes oil from plain areas of U.P. The results with respect to variation in major constutuents have been given in Table 2. These variations in the monoterpene ketones of Tagetes oil are attributed to different geographical locations and photoperiodic effects. These variations play an important role in determining the quality of oil. The oil obtained from the mid hill is perferred in the market.

The three ketones tagetone (ZE) dihydrotagetone and ocimenone (ZE) get easily polymerised becuase of their unstable nature and this deteriorates the quality of the oil. However it has been seen that the same compounds prepared synthetically are found to be somewhat stable. The polymerisation of oil occurs to a considerable extent in the course of 3 to 4 months even if the oil is stored in refrigerator. This is explained because of more number of double bonds in three acyclic ketonic constituents which are jointly responsible for the polymerisation of this oil.

It is also presumed that the presence of ocimene also leads to polymerisation of the Tagetes oil and 'therefore' the oil is required to be protected from light after distillation.

Table.1- Constituents of Tagetes minuta oil from whole plant flowers and the leaves

Sl. No.	Name of constituent	Whole plant oil	Flower oil	Leaf oil
1.	2 methyl ethyl butyrate	1.42	1.23	0.57
2.	2,3,5 trimethyl furan	0.81	0.51	0.25
3.	Sabinene	0.41	traces	0.37
4.	Octanol	0.45	0.34	0.27
5.	Dihydrotagetone	44.11	56.02	63.81
6.	1-Octanol	0.40	0.28	0.32
7 .	Piperitone	0.35	0.18	0.35
8.	Tagetone (Z & E)	17.36	9.63	17.85
9.	Ocimenone (Z & E)	30.20	25.48	13.16
10.	Thymol	0.19	traces	0.52
11.	B-Caryophyllene	0.98	0.31	0.42
12.	t-Elemene	0.13	traces	0.19

Table 2 - Percentage variation of monoterpene ketones at full blooming stage of different locations

Constituents	1	2	3	4	5	6
Dihydrotagetone	47.55	41.53	53.09	44.62	55.99	71.69
Tagetone (Z E)	18.59	17.11	20.39	16.98	15.24	13.93
Ocimenone (Z E)	27.55	31.71	15.06	26.30	23.45	7.24

1.Jogindernagar 2.Palampur 3.Solan 4.Mandi 5. Droh 6. Badaun (UP)
(4500 Ft) (4200 Ft) (5000 Ft)(3000 Ft)(3500 Ft)(1000 Ft)

The oil should be stroed in amber coloured bottles or aluminium/ss containers well packed upto brim and kept completely moisture free. The various changes with respect to major constituents which occurs during storage of the oil has been given in the Table. 3.

The analysis of Tagetes oil (leaves flowers and plant) was carried out srparately on Gas Chomatograph Hewlett Packard 5890 seres 11 on capillary column of HP-1 (10m) temperature programme programme 40^0 C for one min. subsequent increasing at 10^0 C/min to 200^0 c. The constituents are reported in Table.- 1.

Table 3- Variation of some constituents on stroage of Tagetes oil

Constituents	Percentage in fresh oil	Variation after 15 days	Variation after 50 days
Dihydrotagetone	42.49	40.89	7.83
Ocimenone (Z E)	17.22	14.61	11.47
Ocimene		2.50	54.99

The variation in the case of tagetone (ZE) is being presently monitored.

USES OF TAGETES OIL

The major use of the Tagetes oil is in perfumery industry. The flower oil and its absolute are used for compounding of high grade perfumes. Higher concentration of three major ketones in the oil be a good source of base material for the synthesis of valuable aroma chemicals through chemical modifications.

RESEARCH NEEDS

Tagetes minuta oil finds a good market in the perfumery world today. The plant material growing in abundance in mid hills of Himachal Pradesh, Uttar Pradesh and Jammu & Kashmir can form a good source of valuable perfumery material. However genetic improvement and selection of high yielding strains is required to be done for further scientific investigations. It is also required to improve the shelf life of Tagetes oil using antioxidants as it starts polymerising after distillation.

The scientific investigations on the technology package of Tagetes minuta carried out by this Institute since last more than six years has brought this weed as an economic plant of immense importance in the perfumery industry. The Tagetes oil worth about Rs. 40-50 lakhs is being produced in the state of Himachal Pradesh with technical know how given to various entrepreneurs by this Institute. More details on this plant are required to be worked out. The Tagetes oil of desired composition can be obtained by harvesting the crop at particular stage of plant growth. The oil has very strong and penetrating odour.

Chapter-18

ESSENTIAL OIL OF HYPTIS SUAVEOLENS POIT

INTRODUCTION

HIGHER plants have been used for centuries to cure human diseases. The essence and perfumery produced by aromatic plants have significant aesthetic value in day to day life. So the scientists have been encouraged to screen these plants for various biological activities. Essential oils and their constituents extracted from aromatic and medicinal plants have also been found to possess medicinal and pharmacological values. It has also been reported that plant products are less toxic more systemic host metadolism stimulatory easily biodegradable ecologically safe and non pollutive. Recently volatiles of some higher plants obtained in the form of essential oils have been successfully tested against a number of storage fungi and insects by various workers. Further it is also heartening that some of these oils have been found more efficacious than some of the prevalent synthetic pesticdes. A report of the chemical and antimicrobial investigations on essential oil of Hyptis suaveolens Poit (Wilayati tulsi) is described here.

(I) ANTIMICROBIAL EFFICACY OF THE ESSENTIAL OIL OF H. SUAVFOLENS

The essential oil of H. suaveolens has been found to possess antimicrobial activity. The alcohol extract of leaves of H. suaveolens showed antifertility activity whereas petroleum ether and water extract did not show any activity. Pharmacological investigations on the unsaponifiable matter from the leaves and floral parts of Hyptis suaveolens have been undertaken by Saluja and Santani. 50 per cent ethanolic extract exhibited hypoghycaemic by action in rats and anticancer acticancer activity against P lymphocytic leukaemia in mice. However the extract did not show any antibacterial antifungal antiprotozoal antifertility and diuretic activilies. The essential oil extracted from Hyptis suaveolens by hydrodistillation technique showed antibacterial and antifungal activities against 15 micro organisms.

The activity of the oil was found to enhance when combined with oils viz. Piper cubeba, Centalla asiatica and Acorus calamus. The oil of Hyptis suaveolens showed antibacterial activity against six potato bacteria viz. B. polymexa Erwinia carotovora var. atroseptica E. carotovora var carotovora Ps putide Ps. solanacenum and Xanth. vasicatoria. Singh[14] have investigated the antiviral activity aginst Potato virus X Peltoboykinolic acid extracted from Hyptis suaveolens roots did not show antifungal activity. The essential oil showed fungitoxicity against Epidermophyton floccosum Microsporum canus and Trichophyton mentagrophytes at a concentration of 1000 ppm. The ethanolic extract also showed antifungal activity against Rhizoctonia solani.

Very recently Singh et al. investigated the fungitoxic activity of the essential oil of Hyptis suaveolens against a broad spectrum of fungi by food poison technique and data is c reported in Table 1. 100% mycelial inhibition was found against C. paradoxa C. falcatum F. moniliforme F. oxysporum' F. udum' H oryzae & P. atropurpurea even at 1000 ppm (Tabla 1). However the oil is also active (75%) at 500 ppm against these micro orgainsms. The oil has also been found to be active against A. sydowii S. parasiticus P. italicum P. oxalicum and P. citrinum at all the tested concentrations (Table 1). The MIC of the oil investigated by the method of Garber & Houston' against A. flavus C. falcatum and F. moniliforme ws found to be 2000 ppm' 1000 ppm and 1000 ppm respectively (Table 2). The fungitoxicity of the oil was found to be thermostable upto 90^0 C and reported to be more potent as compared to synthetic fungicides viz. Bavistin Blitox 50 Dithane M 45 Agrosan GN Tropsil M & Dithane Z 78 (Table 4).

(II) PHYTOTOXIC BEHAVIOUR OF THE OIL

The phytotoxic effect of the oil on seed germination and seedling growth of Vigna radiata, was studied following Tripathi et al and data are reported in Table 5. Thus the oil was found non phytotoxic towards V, radiata at lethal dose towards pathogens.

(III) CHEMICAL CONSTITUENTS OF THE OIL

Bacon in the year 1909 reported menthol as chief constituent of essential oil from plants gathered in Philippines but Nayak and Guha were unable to confirm its presence. On the other hand they reported 31% (-) sebinene 12% (+) limonene 17% azulenic sesquiterpenes and 40% unidentified sesquiterpenes and alcohols. Subsequent chamical investigation using GC/MS on the essential oils extracted from the aerial part of Hyptis suaveolens collected from Venezuela North East Brazil and Malaysia showed considerable difference in composition.

Table 1 - Fungitoxic spectrum of the oil of H. suaveolens

Fungi	per cent mycelial inhibition		
	500ppm	1000ppm	2000ppm
Aspergillus niger	80.7	90.2	100.0
Aspergillus flavus	50.6	70.5	100.0
Aspergillus sydowii	60.0	80.2	97.0
Aspergillus parasiticus	68.2	77.0	90.0
Penicillium italicum	70.0	72.6	80.2
Penicillium oxalicum	50.0	55.2	80.0
Penicillium citrinum	27.5	30.5	57.8
Ceratocystis paradoxa	50.8	100.0	100.0
Collectotrichum falcatum	80.0	100.0	100.0
Collectotrichum gloeosporoides	48.0	69.5	100.0
Curvularia lunata	70.4	91.0	100.0
Curvularia pallescens	62.5	85.2	100.0
Periconia atropurpurea	52.0	100.0	100.0
Fusarium oxysporum	52.5	100.0	100.0
Fusarium udum	70.0	100.0	100.0
Fusarium moniliforme	87.5	100.0	100.0
Rhizoctonia solani	37.0	68.3	100.0
Pythium debaryanum	43.2	59.0	100.0
Pythium aphanidermatum	56.0	68.6	100.0
Sclerotium rolfsii	50.0	67.0	100.0
Alternaria alternata	62.5	80.7	100.0

Table 2 - MIC of the oil

Concentration (ppm)	per cent mucelial inhibition		
	A.flavus	*C.falcatum*	*F.moniliforme*
250	29.5	50.0	44.6
500	80.7	82.0	90.0
1000	90.2	100.0	100.0
2000	100.0	100.0	100.0
4000	100.0	100.0	100.0

Table 3 - Effect of some physical factors on fungitoxicity of the oil at 2000 ppm

Physical		per cent mycelial inhibition		
		A.flavus	*C.falcatum*	*F.moniliforme*
Effect of temp. (^0C)	50	100.0	100.0	100.0
	75	100.0	100.0	100.0
	90	100.0	100.0	100.0
Effect of autoclaving (15 1b/sq inch pressure for 30 min)		100.0	100.0	100.0
Effect of storage (days)	30	100.0	100.0	100.0
	60	100.0	100.0	100.0
	90	100.0	100.0	100.0

Table 4 - Efficacy of oil as compared to synthetic fungicides

Common name of fungicide	Tride name of fungicides	MIC against fungal pathogens *A.flavus*	*C.falcatum*	*F.moniliforme*
Carbendazim	Bavistin	3000	3000	2000
Copper oxychoride	Blitox 50	2000	3000	3000
Mancozeb	Dithane M-45	2000	3000	3000
Organomercurial dust	Agrosan GN	2000	2000	3000
Thiphenate methyl	Tropsil M	4000	3000	4000
Zineb	Dithane Z-78	3000	2000	4000

Hyptis suaveolens oil -	2000	1000	1000

Table 5. Phytotoxicity of oil (200 ppm) on moong bean plant (vigna radiata)

Germination (%)			Shoot length (mm)		
Period (hrs)	Control	Treated	Period (days)	Control	Treated
24	85	80	3	30	33
48	90	82	5	46	54
72	96	89	7	92	110

Pant et al investigated the oil of the aerial parts of Hyptis suaveolens collected from the Kumaon region of India and found that chemical constituents are different from those collected from South America and Malaysia. The main

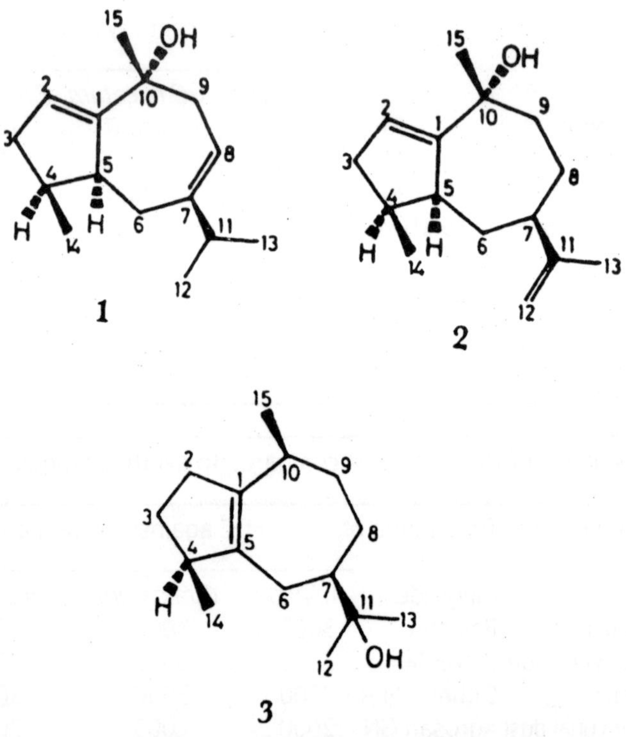

Fig. 1 - Compounds isolated from *H. suaveolens* oil

components were 41.0% sabinene 9.8% B-B-pinene 7.9% caryophyllene 6.8% limonene accompanied by ore than 50% other compouds including Z-a trans bergamotol (2.0%) caryophyllene oxide (5.8%), ar-1 abiet tatriene (4.4%) and ar abiettatrienol (0.4%). Very recently Singh et al investigated the essential oil of Hyptis suaveolens collected from Gorakhpur India and 489 constituents have been identified which are reported in Table 6. It has been found that 29 are monoterpenoids (62.9%) and 19 are sesquiterpenods (24.9%). Significent different in chemical composition of the major components have been observed as compared to oils collected from various regions and reported in literature (Table 7). Three new sesquiterpene alcohola viz. guaia 1(2) 7-dien-10-ol [1] guaia-1(2)′ 11-dien-10-ol [2] and guaia-1 (5) en-11-ol[3] have also been isobated by CC and TLC (preparative) from essential oil of Hyptis suaveolens which are reported in Fig.1. Their structures have been deduced on the basis of spectroscopic analyses and confirmed by comparison with the published informations for the compounds themselves.

Table 6 - Composition of the essential oil of H.suaveolens

Peak No.	Retention time	Kovats index	Compound the	Percentage in oil
1.	9.90	920	A-Thujene	0.64
2.	10.18	929	B-Pinene	1.61
3.	10.66	944	Camphene	0.05
4.	11.58	971	Sabinene	22.51
5.	11.72	974	B-Pinene	5.67
6.	12.16	986	Myrcene	0.67
7.	12.69	1000	A-Phellandrene	0.26
8.	13.00	1011	Car-3-ene	0.35
9.	1317	1016	Terpinene	1.63
10.	13.28	1019	p-Cymene	0.55
11.	13.65	1028	Limonene	5.34
12.	13.86	1035	1.8-Cineole	0.04
13.	13.98	1046	(A)Ocimene	0.10
14.	14.71	1057	Terpinene	3.06
15.	14.87	1061	trans sabinene hydrate	0.36
16.	15.60	1079	Fenchone	0.56
17.	15.85	1080	E-Terpinolene	10.06
18.	15.98	1088	Linalool	0.37
19.	16.22	1093	Cis Sabinene hydrate	0.03

Peak No.	Retention time	Kovats index	Compound the	Percentage in oil
20.	16.53	1101	fenchol	0.13
21.	17.42	1128	Camphor	0.36
22.	17.99	1145	Isobroneol	0.04
23.	18.36	1155	Broneol	0.11
24.	18.82	1168	Terpinen4-01	7.80
25.	19.16	1177	Terpineol	0.28
26.	20.44	1213	Citronellol	0.06
27.	20.62	1219	Nerol	0.10
28.	21.25	1238	Geraniol	0.08
29.	21.51	1246	Piperitone	0.09
30.	25.27	1364	A-Ylangene	0.08
31.	25.69	1377	B-Bourbonene	0.04
32.	26.04	1389	B-Elenene	0.30
33.	27.00	1422	A-Caryophyllene	15.16
34.	27.33	1434	trans Bergamotene	1.60
35.	27.68	1446	Guaiene	0.10
36.	27.89	1454	Humulene	1.57
37.	28.44	1484	Germecene	0.07
38.	28.59	1478	Allo aroma dendrene	0.04
39.	28.77	1484	Salinene	0.94
40.	29.03	1439	B-Salinene	1.71
41.	29.43	1507	B-Bisabolol	0.02
42.	29.58	1513	Cadinene	0.27
43.	29.85	1524	A-Cadinene	0.06
44.	31.00	1567	B-Spatulenol	0.37
45.	31.18	1574	B-Caryophyllene oxide	1.06
46.	32.22	1617	A-Cardinol	0.03
47.	32.93	1641	B-Eudesmol	0.49
48.	33.83	1675	A-Bisabolol	1.06

Table 7—Comparison of major compounds of the essential oil of *H. suaveolens* from various places

Compounds	% of compounds in the oil obtained from various places					
	Malasian[25] oil	Bangalore[22] oil	Venecuelan[23] oil	Brazilian[24] oil	Pantnagar[26] oil	Gorakhpur[27] oil
Sabinene	4.90	31.00	-	-	41.00	22.51
Limonene	-	12.00	-	-	6.80	5.34
β-Caryophyllene	41.10	17.00	8.80	10.37	7.90	15.16
1,8-Cineole	7.90	-	-	30.80	0.60	0.04
Fenchone	traces	-	42.30	traces	-	0.56
Caryophyllene oxide	-	-	-	-	5.60	1.06
α-Terpinolene	-	-	-	1.59	-	10.06
γ-Humulene	-	-	-	2.07	-	1.57
Terpinen-4-ol	-	-	-	0.45	2.90	7.50
α-Guaiene	-	-	-	0.63	0.60	0.10

Conclusions

The volatile oil of H. suaveolens possesses strong antifungal acitivity against various fungi. The fungitoxicity of the oil has been found to be thermostable and remains unchanged even on autoclaving and stroage. The oil was found to be more potent as compared to commercial synthetic fungicides and exhibited no phytotoxicity against Vigna radiata.

Chemical investigations of the oil have proved the presence of 48 constituents out of which 29 are monoterpenoids (62.9%) and 19 sesquiterpenoids (24.9%). Major components are sabinene B-Caryophyllene terpinolene, terpenen 4-ol, pinene Limonene terpinene A-sabinene terpenene A-pinene A-humulene trans- A-bergamotene and Caryophylene oxide. However the percentages of constituents have also been found to change for oils, investigated from different regions. Three sesquiterpene alcohol such as guaia 1 (2) 7 dien 10-ol guia-(2) 11 dien -10-ol and guaia 1-(5) en 11 ol have also been isolated and identified from the oil of H. suaveolens.

Chapter-19

SUPER-CRITICAL FLUID EXTRACTION (SCFE) TECHNOLOGY - FOR SPICE EXTRACTION

ABSTRACT

The basic working principle and advantage of the SCFE process, reasons for use of SC carbon dioxide as an extractant, parameters to be determined in the designing of SCFE plant, such as (i) required rate of production, (ii) mode of operation (continuous or batch-type) (iii) bulk-density of the solids fed (iv) the form (v) consistency and (vi) moisture content of the material (vii) Ratio of solvent mass flow-rate to the mass solids treated (viii) the extraction time, etc, have been briefly discussed, and based on these factors, an illustration of a plant for extraction of pepper (the most important spice of the world and so also, of India) has been provided Later, the R & D work done on some important Spice Essential Oils and Oleoresins and their dominant chemical constituents using SCFE process, is reviewed and briefly discussed. The commercial SCFE plants in use in some of the developed countries like Germany, Canada, Australia, etc. and other commercial SCFE activity areas have also been reviewed. At the end, the future scope of the SCFE process and R & D needs in the area have been highlighted.

INTRODUCTION

Spices, which are consumed mostly in flavouring of innumerable foods, are gaining considerable economic/commercial importance as is evident from world trade (Table) in spices (256,000) tons worth about 1.5 billion $ US (1-3) India is one of the major spice producing and exporting countries of the world as is evident from the exporting countries of the world as is evident from the export earnings of over Rs 600 crores (Rs 6000 millions) during 1994-95 (4-6). Because of the several built-in defects in the use of whole or ground spices in processed foods, such as : (a) Variable flavour strength, (b) presence of polyphenols which could discolour some manufactured food products, (c) slow release of flavour, (d) microbial contamination, etc., Spice Oleoresins, Spice Essential Oils, and other spice extractives are now being used commercially in sophisticated food products in place of gound spices.

India again, is one of the leading countries producing and exporting about a dozen important spice oleoresins (about Rs. 80 crores worth, but these oleoresins are being produced by use of chemical organic solvents, the use of some of which is now prohibited in spice importing countries like UK, USA, Germany, etc. Likewise steam-distillation too adversely affects the basic quality of essential oils, notably the low boiling volatiles. To overcome these built-in defects, Super-Critical Fluid Extraction (SCFE) Process" provides an excellent new and versatile alternative for the extraction of spices as discussed in this book.

1.1 SCOPE OF THIS PRESENTATION

This book presents (a) the basic working principle and advantages of the SCFE process (b) reasons for use of SC carbon dioxide as an extractant and (c) parameters to be determined in the designing of SCFE plant, such as (i) required rate of production, (ii) mode of operation (continuous or batch type) (iii) bulk-density of the solids fed, the form, texture or consistency and moisture content of the material (iv) Ratio of solvent mass flow-rate to the mass of solids treated (v) the extraction time etc., have been discussed and based on these factors, an illustration of a plant for extraction of pepper) has been provided. Later, the recent R & D work done in India and abroad on some important Spice Essential Oils in India and abroad on some important chemical constitents using SCFE process, is highlighted and briefly discussed. The commercial SCFE plants in use in some of the developed countries like Germany, Canada, Australia, France, Austria, etc. and other related commercial SCFE activity areas have also been reviewed. At the end, the future scope of the SCFE process and R & D needs in the area have also been highlighted.

SUPERCRITICAL FLUID EXTRACTION SYSTEM (SCFE)

Supercritical fluid (SCFE) is a versatile separation technology which is receiving increasing attention in view of the selectivity of the extraction from a mixture of components. The pressure -temperature dependent solubility in the solvents with excellent mass transfer characteristics are being utilized in wide range of food processing industries including spice processing. The SCFE technology has received considerable attention as is evident from a number of standard works/books and reviews given at the end of this presentation.

TABLE: WORLD TRADE IN SOME IMPORTANT SPICES

Sr. No.	Spices	'000 tons'
1.	Pepper (black, white, green)	125-130
2.	Capsicums	55-60
3.	Spice seeds (6 Spices)	55-60
4.	Cinnamon/Cassia	33-34
5.	Turmeric	15-20
6.	Ginger	15-16
7.	Nutmeg/Mace	12-15
8.	Cardamon (Small)	9-10
9.	Curry Powder	5-6
10.	Cloves	3-4
11.	Pimento (All Spices)	3-4
12.	Vanilla and	2-3
13.	Saffron (Tons)	3-5

2.1 WORKING PRINCIPLE AND SCFE PROCESS DESCRIPTION

For the extraction of spices or essential oils, the process (Schematic), described in Figure, is generally employed. The spice material loaded in the extractor is brought in contact with the supercritical solvent at a relatively high pressure ranging from 60-300 bar and at temperature of 35°-70°C. The supercritical solvent after getting enriched with the solute, is passed through a micrometer valve or pressure reducing valve, where the pressure on the separator side is around 4-60bar and temperature is lower due to a sudden diabetic expansion of the supercritical solvent. This results in lower solubility of the solute . Once the material separation occurs. the gas is again compressed back to extract the material. Thus, solvent recycling is also possible, by means of the compressor or liquid pump.

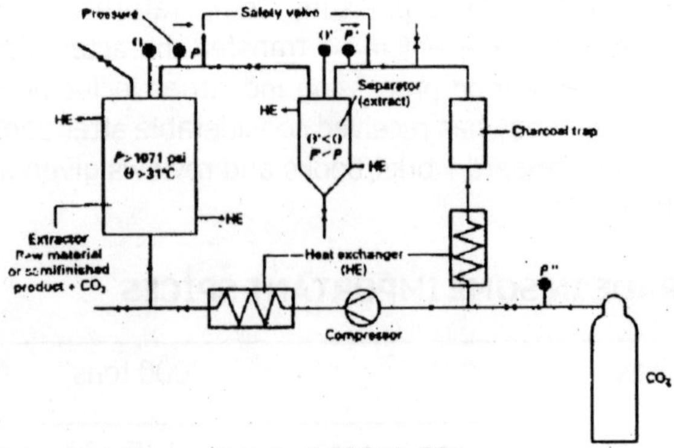

Fig. A typical Super Critrical (SCA) CO_2
Extraction System for Spices and Flavour, etc.

2.2 Carbon Dioxide as SC Solvent - Its Plus Points

SC Carbon dioxide is used as a solvent for extraction of food materials such as spices, coffee, hops, etc., because it is (i) cheap, (ii) abundant in nature, (iii) non-toxic, (iv) non corrosive (v) inert, (vi) non-inflammable, (vii) devoid of environmental contamination, (viii) the boiling point and heat of evaporation are low and hence, it is easy to separate it from solute mixture with less heat energy, (ix) due to lower critical temperature, the extraction of the material can be carried out at near ambient temperature : (x) it can be especially used in extracting thermo-labile compounds, (xi) lesser energies are needed for compression due to its lower critical pressure, (xii) further, separation of the extract can be effected by expanding the carbon dioxide, where the temperature of the separation can be low. The above 12 plus points have made SC carbon dioxide quite popular all over the world.

2.3 ADVANTAGES OF THE SCFE PROCESS

There are several advantages of this process. Some of them are mentioned here (2-3) :

(i) **Low temperature separation :** It produces extracts from natural products where the heat-sensitive components remain undamaged.

(ii) **No Solvent residue :** The extracted solute can be made almost solvent free, i.e. the residual solvent content can be reduced to almost O ppm.

(iii) **Solubility Variation :** The solubility variation of the active constituents can be achieved by simply increasing or lowering the extraction temperature and pressure.

(iv) **Fractionated Extraction and Fractionated Separation :** The different constituents of natural products may be fractionally extracted and the extracted solutes may be fractionally separated.

(v) **Cheap Solvents and their Recycling :** Solvents can be completely recycled and also gases like carbon dioxide which are cheap may be used. This gives lower cost of solvents compared to conventional luquid extraction.

(vi) **Low Energy Process :** The SCFE is a low energy intensive process requiring low utilities consumption.

(vii) **Fast diffusion :-** The diffusivity of supercritical liquids is higher than that of liquids and viscosity is lower than that of liquids and viscosity is lower than that of liquids. This gives higher mass transfer rates.

(viii) **Easy Solvent Recovery :** Due to high volatility of solvents, they can be easily recovered.

(ix) **No Environmental Risks :**

(x) **No Fire Hazards** are there when carbon dioxide is used as the solvent.

3.0 PARAMETERS TO BE DETERMINED IN SCFE PROCESS DESIGN

3.1 NEED FOR BASIC PROCESS DATA

As a basis for selecting dimensions of the plant and of individual items of equipment, a prior knowledge of some basis process data is necessary such as: (i) the required rate of production (ii) mode of operation of the plant (Whether continuous or batch-type), (iii) bulk-density of the solids fed (iv) the form, texture or consistency of the material and its moisture content; (v) ratio of solvent mass flow rate to the mass solids treated, and (vi) the extraction time (3) These parameters must, therefore, be determined during the course of a few preliminary experiments.

Of these parameters, the required rate of production is first specified. Depending upon the rate, the mode of operation i.e.whether batch or continuous type is decided. Bulk-density of solids fed must be determined experimentally. These three parameters enable the volume of the extraction to be calculated.

The quantity of solvent to be introduced into the plant is determined precisely from the required operating temperature and pressure. Then, by knowing the time of extraction, the mass flow rate of solvent can be calculated. Hence, the cross-sections of pipelines can also be calculated accordingly.

Eggers and Tschiersch have given extraction of spices as an illustration of the initial prediction of the order of magnitude of a plant.

Important Parameters of the SCF Extraction Plant for Spices (19).

(i) Producton rate :	(i) 500 tons of the spice p.a.
(ii) Min.no.of working days:	(ii) 200 working days p.a.
(iii)Mode of operation/shifts day:	(iii)Three shifts per day
(iv) Bulk density :	(iv) 500 kg/m^2
(v) Mass flow rate/mass ratio	(v) 20 kg CO_2/hr kg of spice
(vi) Time of extraction :	(vi) 7 hr/batch (inclusive of filling and emptying of the plant

These values indicate a volume of V = 1.67 M^3 for the extraction vessel and nominal diameter of 50 mm for the pipelines in the plant.

4.0 SCF EXTRACTION OF SPICE ESSENTIAL OILS, OLEORESINS AND MAJOR CHEMICAL CONSTITUENTS PRESENT THEREIN

The standardization in the food industry has led to spice extracts or oleoresins to be used in place of ground spices, Extracts of spices such as pepper, nutmeg, and chillies were obtained. The volatile oil of pepper, commonly called pepper oil obtained as the first fraction followed by the oleoresins and piperine. The extraction of ginger was also carried out by using supercritical carbon dioxide. For all oleoresins extractions, the temperature range was 40-55°c and pressure was varied from 200 to 400 bar. The degree of extraction of piperine from black pepper was almost 98% and that of essential oil, 81% . The extract was yellow as compared to the olive green extract with methylene chloride as solvent. Similarly, the extraction of Capsaicin from Chillies was 97%. These results confirm earlier findings.

5.0 SCFE OF PEPPER OIL

A large number of products have been extracted with SC carbon dioxide. Extracts of spices/essential oils or oleoresins are commercially important. Extraction of pepper for pepper oleoresin using SC carbon dioxide of ginger using carbon dioxide has been reported mostly from India.

5.1 SCF CO_2 EXTRACTION VERSUS CONVENTIONAL SOLVENT EXTRACTION

Conventionally, black pepper is powdered and subjected to steam distillation and solvent extraction in a two-stage process. At CFTRI. volatile oil was of pepper was extracted with SCF carbon dioxide without contamination with non-volatile compounds. The oil obtained was of excellent quality and had monoterpene to sesquiterpene ratio much less than that in the steam distilled oil. The recoveries of volatile oil have been higher than those in steam distillation. The essential oil obtained by SCFE had excellent fixative character. This can also be seen from table on higher yields and lower time of extraction by SCFE process than that by steam distillation technique.

Table : Analysis of Pepper, Nutmeg and Chillies-Co-extraction

19 Particulars	Material Before CO^2	After	CO^2 Extracted	Degree of Extraction (%)	Extract commercial (Usually)
					CH, Cl_2
		I	PEPPER BLACK		
Piperine (%)	10.1	0.3	44.0	97.7	41.2
Essential Oil (%)	3.5	0.1	12.7	81.1	15.0
Water (%)	9.3	0.1	12.7	81.1	15.0
Colour of extract			Yellow		Olive Green
		II	NUTMEG		
Essential Oil (%)	7.4	0.1	19.0	99.0	20.0
Hexane - soluble matter (%)	46.0	1.7	100.0	98.0	100.0
Water (%)	4.9	4.4	1.6	0.1	
Colour of extract			Whitish yellow		Yellowish brown
		III	CHILLIES		
CAPSAICIN (%)	0.86	0.03	4.9	97.0	4.7
Water (3)	3.2	1.8	1.3	0.1	
Colour of extract	-	-	red	-	red

Table : Physical and Chemical Characteristics of Paper Oil (26)

Physico. Chemical Characteristics	Steam distillation	SCFE (CO^2) 8 MPa	8MP a	10MPa	10MPa
		40^0C	60^0C	40^0C	60^0C
Yield of Oil (%)	2.42	2.10	2.25	2.83	2.62
Refractive index	1.479	1.483	1.475	1.483	1.483
Specific Gravity	0.8834	0.8844	0.8864	0.8859	0.8759
Optical Ratation	-6.74	+0.76	-1.11	+0.13	+0.35
Total Hydrocarbons	84.32	80.40	87.65	82.70	78.60
Monoterpenes (%)	73.19	58.83	68.82	61.01	51.45
Sesquiterpens (%)	26.7	41.17	31.17	38.99	48.55
Oxygenated Compounds	3.24	7.69	4.02	6.69	7.90
Caryophyllene (%)	16.49	18.53	13.05	15.04	24.01

Table : Physico-chemical Characteristics of Pepper Oleoresin (17)

Physico - Chemical Characteristics	Supercritical Carbon dioxide extracted (SCFE)	Conventional Oleoresins (Solvent Extracted)
Appearance and Odour	Yellow, consisting of upper oily layer and lower crystalline layer	Dark gren, Olive green or olive drab extract: usually consist of an uper oily layer and a lower crystalline layer
Volatile oil content	18-35 ml/100	15-35 ml/100
Optical rotation	-15	-1 to -23
Refractive index	1.4872	1.4790 1.4890
Piperine (Spectro-photometry)	45.55 %	35 - 45 %
Residual solvents	oil	as per FDA

Table : Physico-chemical Characteristics of Ginger Oleoresin

Physico - Chemical Characteristics	Supercritical Carbon dioxide extracted (SCFE)	Conventional Oleoresins (Solvent Extracted)
Appearance and Odourq	A dark yellow to brown viscous liquid with characteristic odour and flavour of ginger	a dark brown viscous to highly viscous liquid with characteristic odour and flavour of ginger
Volatile oil contact	20ml/100 gm	18.35 ml/100 gm
Specific gravity	0.8672	
Refractive index	1.49	1.4880 - 1.4970
Optical rotation	- 54.17	- 30 to - 60
Oleoresin content	22 %	
Residual solvents		neet FDA regulation

Table : CO^2 Extraction of the active Principle (Piperine) from Pepper (19)

Active Principle to be separated	Extracting Agent	Entrainer	Operating Extraction	Conditions of : Spearation
Piperine from Black Pepper	CO_2 N_2O. SF_6 CHF_3SF_2CI CHF_2CI CF_3 $=CH_2C3f_8$	H_2O	$35^0$to 80^0 C 80 to 300 bar	Decrease of of pressure

Table : The Comparative Yield and Extration Times for 11 Spices Extracted by Liquid Carbon dioxide and Prepared by steam Distillation

Material	Liquid carbondioxide		Steam Distillation	
	Yield (% w/w)	Time (Hrs)	Yield (% w/w)	Time (Hrs)
Cardamom	9.4	2.5	9.0	5
Chilli	4.9	2.5	-	-
Clove	20.0	2.0	15.0	6
Cumin	4.5	2.0	2.5	4
Cumin Black	4.5	2.0	1.0	-
Fennel	5.8	2.0	3.0	5
Ginger	3.7	2.5	1.6	6
Mace	18.5	2.5	13.1	-
Parsley	9.8	2.0	2.7	5
Poppy Seed	2.5	2.0	-	-
Turmeric	3.4	2.0	3.5	-

SCFE OF BLACK PEPPER OLEORESIN

Table shows the physico-chemical composition of the oleoresin obtained by conventional extraction and SC carbon dioxide extraction. The Piperine content of carbon dioxide extracted was better.

SCFE OF GINGER OIL

As in the case of Pepper, ginger oil also can be extracted without the contamination of non-volatile Compounds by supercritical fluid extraction. The ginger oil extracted at the institute at 8-10 MPa at temperatures of 40° to 60° C was found to be of excellent quality and had hinger sesquiterpene content than that in steam-distilled oils. The gas chromatograms indicated that the monoterpene content was less than 12% and the content of compounds like zingiberene, curcumene and humulene was greater in SC carbon dioxide extracted oils than in distilled oils. The quality characteristics of the ginger oleoresin obtained by SCF carbon dioxide are presented in table .

SCFE (CO_2) OF PIPERINE PEPPER

Typical data on piperine are presented in table which are self explanatory.

ECONOMICS OF THE SCFE PROCESS

It is estimated that an extractor with volume 1 m^3 may cost about Rs. 7.75 crores, the cost break - up is: the carbon dioxide loop (40-50%), carbon dioxide recovery system (20-25%) and the pressure vessels (25-40 %). The operating cost per shift is around Rs. 50,000-Rs 60,000. The economics of the plant are dictated by a number of factors such as (i) the operating cost per cycle, (ii) the number of cycles per day (iii) the capacity of the cycle and (iv) the unit value added by the product. In case of pepper oleoresin, a plant of 3 tons/day capacity can produce the product at a cost of Rs 450/Kg as against Rs 300-340/Kg of conventional product. Adopting a number of cost reduction steps like (a) power recovery during decompression, (b) reduction in dead time cycle, (c) multistage counter-current extraction, etc., the cost of the product can be reduced substantially - SCFE processes will be viable for production of only high value and stable priced products required for specialized use in food and drug industry. The IIT, New Delhi Scientists and Engineers based on their fabrication experience in SCFE opined that the cost can be reduced to Rs 20-50 lakhs depending upon plant specification and nature of raw materials etc.

COMMERCIAL-SCALE SCFE PLANTS IN U.K. AUSTRIA, GERMANY, AUSTRALIA & FRANCE

SCFE plants working successfully on commercial scale in Germany, U.K., Austria, France, Canada And Australia and the extracts obtained from the liquid and SC carbon dioxide are finding their way into the international market. Hence there is an urgent need for development of design of a cheaper ande efficient indigenously made SCFE plant in a developing country like India.

FACTORS AFFECTING PLANT DESIGNING

The major points to be considered in plant design are : (i) output major capacity, (ii) mode of operation, (iii) bulk density of the raw material, (iv) solvent of material ratio and (v) extraction time. The pressure vessels have to be designed for pressures of 10-30 MPa with an allowance for increasing stress. The steel vessels should be corrosion-resistant and easy to decontaminate. In addition, counter-current extraction for higher efficiencies and multi-tube high pressure heat exchanger for heating the liquid to SC carbon dioxide are essential.

OTHER COMMERCIAL SCFE ACTIVITY AREAS

In addition,. commercial activity or interest has been reported by over 30 companies including some end-users of the technology, equipment suppliers and engineering companies. The activity is generally in the areas of spices extraction, essential oils extraction, oilseeds extraction, flavours extractions, extraction of pharmaceutical materials, extraction of coal, coal tar and crude oil, for the separation of mixtures including separation of isomers, for effluent treatment, and in supercritical fluid chromatrography.

FUTURE SCOPE FOR SCFE PROCESS

SCFE is a capital intensive process requiring high-pressure vessels and pumps. The low cost of carbon dioxide and the low energy cost of separation do not offset the high capital costs. However, where the cost of the products is more than $2.5/kg (Rs75/Kg), the extra cost that supercritical extraction adds to the product, may be acceptable because of the better quality and higher shelf-life of the products. In food industry, the supercritical extraction is likely to be extensively used for products like spices, coffee, tea, etc.

Chapter-20

CITRONELLA OIL PROCESS OF MANUFACTURE

Planting and cultivation : Prior to planting the land must be cleared, plowed and harrowed. Citronella is propagated by means of rooted crown divisions of mature grass the jtime of planting being the rainly season from June to December. For this purpose clumps of mature plants are pulled from the grounds trimmed of all but 5 or 6 inch of their tops and divided into single or double stalked root segments which should be kept wet until planting. The root segments are set out at intervals of 3 ft. in rows 2 ft. apart. The roots of the new plant must be fixed firmly in the ground and well covered with soil. In the first three months i.e. until the grass fills the rows monthly cultivation is necesssary. After the first harves one cultivation will be sufficient. No fertilizers are used. Shortly before each harvest all weeds should be eradicated. Citronella flowers acre a year usually at the end of November in the rainy season each flower grows on separate stalk. Neither the flower not the stalks contains any essential oil.

HARVESTING

In actual practice the grass is harvested before it reached the flowering stage the leaves can usually be cut for the first time six months after planting and subsement harvest may tke place at intervals of four months which permits three harvests per year. The grass should then be permitted to reach the flowering stage. The grass is harvested when the blades reach a height of approximately 3 ft. It is cut by hand with matchets just above the first node and collected in bundles of about 50 lbs. Dry leaves may be hauled to the stills immediately wet leaves should be left in the field for one day to dry partly and to loose excessive moisture.

Distillation : Prior to distillation the leaves are reduced to 4 -inch pieces by meanes of twin power cutters placed opposite each other . The material is then fed by gravity into the still and packed tightly. Live steam of 15 lbs pressure (measured at the steam inlet gauge) is injected but as soon as the first vapours appear at the condenser outlet (usually after 10 minutes) the steam pressure is reduced to 5 lb. When the condensate flows evenly the steam pressure is raised gradually to a maximum of 25 lbs and kept up as long as no vapour appears at the condenser outlet distillation is compeleted when an appreciable amount of oil can no longer be separated from the condensate. The flow of oil may be checked by drawing sampler periodically at the condenser outlet. Depending upon the condition of the leaf material distillation of one charge requires from 3 to 5 hour at the most. The oil collected after hrs. contain very little citronellal, the chief constituent which determines the price of each lot of oil It is therefore, preferable to stop distillation provided, of course, that a normal yield of oil has been obtained. It has been found that the yield of oil is influenced chiefly by two factors the age of the planting and the amount of rainfall. The condensing system consists of a simple copper or aluminium spiral tube immersed in cold water. The spiral tube is connected to the tapering end of the digester (top) and the other end of the tube projects into the receiver which is a copper or aluminium vessel. In the receiving vessel citronella oil takes the top layer and water lower layer. On one side of the receives just above the bottom there is a bent tube which allows of the water of the lower layer to flow out.

The upper layer in the oil is now decanted into the drying unit where an hydrous sodium sulphate is added to the old and mixes. The mixture is now filtered in a small filter. The anhydrous sodium sulphate is added for dehydration of the oil is for removing the moisture from oil.

The dehydrated oil is filled in can or drums and sealed air tight. The oil should not be exposed to light frequently and should be kept in a dark and cool place. Coloured glass, stainless steel or aluminium are preferred to copper container for storage.

DISTILLATON PROCESS ERECTION AND DISTILLATION OF SUITABLE TYPE OF STILL

Even though steam distillation is a harsh treatment, citronella oil is prepared in this way. At present three methods of distillation are practised. They are water distillation, water and steam distillation and steam distillation, water distillation is the crudest method of separating oil from lemon grasses. This is a simple process in which the plant material is placed into the still, water added and the vessel is fire heated. Water and oil distill together. They are condensed in a simple condenser. The oil takes top layer.This process of water distillation has the disadvantage of exposing the delicate extential oil to a prolonged distillation in the presence of water which results in the unnecessary hydrolysis of esters and oxidation and resentification of unsaturated compounds.

The distillation method of water and steam type is better than above described method. Here the stills fitted with a horizontal perforated plate upon which the lemon grass rests. The lower part of the still is filled with water to a level some what below the grid and the charge is subjected to distillation by passing low pressure steam. This avoids direct contact of plant materials with distillation by pasing low pressure steam. This avoids direct contact of plant materials with distillation water below. This method provides lower yields.

Now the modern method practised is steam distillation. This method is suggested for the preparation of citronella oils.

THE ELECTION AND OPERATION OF SUITABLE TYPE OF STILL

Apart from the question of capital cost, the prospective producer of cirtronella oils will be guided by several considerations, both technical and practical, when deciding what type and size of still is to be installed. From technical view point, steam distillation gives the best and quickest result but some people are using water and steam stills also.

Practical considerations are mainly bound up with the question of whether the still is to be portable or a fixed installation. If the crop is cultivated' a fixed steam-heated still should be erected in the area of cultivation, the still being provided with means of rapid charging and discharging to ensure rapid distillation and quick turn-over. Where the crop is not cultivated, but has to be collected from a wide area or "difficult " country, it should be brought to a fixed distillery if transport can be arranged, but if it is not practicable, it will be necessary to use a portable still. It might be possible to mount a small steam-heated still on a lorry or trailer. It is of the atmost importance to have an simple water supply for the condenser, whatever type of still is used. The still should, therefore, be situated near to stream, river or lake , when a piped supply is not available.

WATER AND STEAM STILL:-

These are more expensive than water stills, largely owing to the necessity of providing a steam generator, but are better than water stills for the small producer. The feature of this type of still is that the plant charge does not come into contact with the boiling water; it is, in fact, a step towards the steam still. The distillation rate is much faster and provided and still is well lagged to prevent excessive condensation in the still, the charge does not get excessively wet, more does the charge brun, Consequently, spoilage due to hydrolysis and decomposition is greatly reduced. So that the yield of oil is higher and its quality better than it obtained by water distillation.

Water and steam stills give good results with most types of plant material, than about 2°C (say 5°F) above the temperature of the water entering the condenser. If the condensate does run warm, the rate of distillation should reduce and, if possible a large condenser substituted.

A coil condenser is economical in the use of cooling water, it also allows water to be heated for the next still chage in the case of water distillation. Patent tubular -type condenser have certain merits they occupy little space, and prevent the escape of steam into the open air -but they may be difficult to repair.

Inactive metals should be used in the construction of a condenser tinned copper, stainless steel, pure tin or aluminium. With tinned copper the plating does not last and is not early repaired. Aluminium is suitable for most essential oils, but not those containing appreciable quantities of phenols, which react with the metal. Aluminium is also subject attach by water of certain hardness.

FUEL

As far as possible, the spent charges, after suitable drying in the sun should be used as fuel for subsequent distillation. Those crops of relatively including citronella oil. The charge should be reduced to regular size, but should not not be too finely powdered. It should be packed firmly and evenly, otherwise the steam will not permeate the whole charge but will form channels through the more loosely packed parts, greatly reducing the rate of distillation and increasing the risk of decomposition. The operation

of these stills, except that a basket must not be used, as much of the steam would probably escape round the basket, rather than through the charge. The flatter should be packed directly on the grid above the water. The grid may be fitted with chains so that the entire charge may be lifted out by tackle after distillation.

STEAM STILLS

While the most expensive to install, steam stills gives better result than water-and-steam stills, The rate of distillation is high and the chances of hydrolysis of the end decomposition very small. The charge should not be finely powdered as this leads to "channelling " and firm and even packing of the charge is essential. Whereas in the other two types of stills, the temperature within the still does not exceed 100°C, or the pressure rise above atmospheric pressure, both temperatue and pressure can be varied in steam stills. Hence, they are essential for the distillation of leaves, seeds, roots and wood containing high boiling constituents, they are frequently used in large distillation units for her baccous plants.

The plant material should be placed on a removable grid placed above the steam coil, the grid placed above the steam coil, the grid beijng fitted with chains for use with lifting tackle, the whole charge being lifted out after distillation. A bsket must not be used. It is necessary for the charge to be fairly finely chopped or ground except where it consists of thin walled tissue through which the oil present in the free state and dry out the plant charge. Diffusion will cease and it will be necessary to alternated with, saturated steam in order to maintain the yield of oil. Prolonged distillation with wet steam may cause excessive condensation in the charge, with consequent lumping and "Channelling."

CONDENSER

With all type of stills, condensation should be as rapid and efficient as possible. The distillate should not be allowed to run more low value, will not bear the cost of alternative fuel.

STORAGE OF CITRONELLA OIL

The care taken to produce an essential oil of good quality can be entirely vitiated by subsequent faulty conditions of storages. Under certain conditions, citronella oil detriorate rapidly and it is essential first to free the oil from water and then to transfer it into suitable airtight and light proof containers, stored in a very cool atmosphere.

The oil drawn from the separator, can be cheaply and adequately dried by means of anhydrous sodium sulphate, which can be prinkled on the surface and stirred in for about 15 minutes. This salt absorb as the water associated with the oil, and settles down in a compact layer, leaving the oil clear and bright. It may then be decounted or filtered.

DETERMINATION OF ALDEHYDE AND KETONES

Of the many procedures which have been suggested for the determination of aldehyde and ketones only four general methods have attained practical significance.
These are:-

1) Bisulphite method.
2) Neutral sulphite method.
3) Phenyl hydrazine method.
4) Hydroxylamine method.

(1) Bisulphite method:- The bisulphite method is an absorption process based upon the general reaction.

$$RCHO+NaHSO_2 - RCH\begin{matrix}OH \\ SO_3Na\end{matrix}$$

Upon shaking a measured quanitity of oil with hot aqueous solution of sodium bisulphite, an addition compound forms which is generally water soluble and which dissolves in hot bisulphite solution; the non aldehyde portion of oil separate as an oily layer which can be measured conveniently in the graduated neck of a carria flask. The bisulphite method is per haps the most convenient and simple of the four general methods. As such it is frequently use us the trade because it requires no standard solution, analytical balance, or special skill.

Procedure:- We will introduce 75cc of a freshly prepared saturated, aqueous solution of sodium besulphite into a 150 cc flask, Having a thin

PROCESS FLOW SHEET

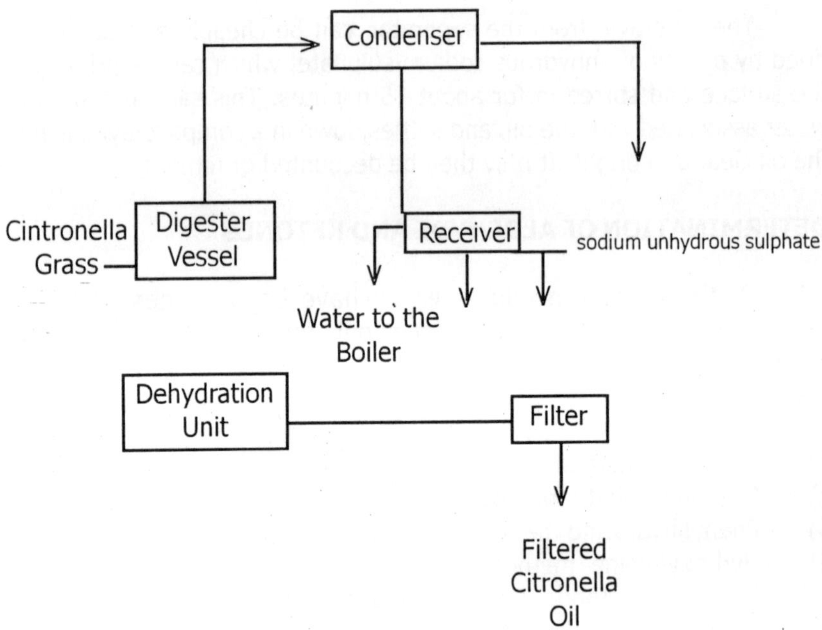

neck iraduated in 0.1 cc divisions. Then droping 10 cc of the oil into the flask by the use of tripetle. Upon through shaking a semi solid mass frequently will results.

After this immersing the flask in a beaker of boiling water and occassionally shake until the solid addition compound has gone completely into a solution. A further addition of 25 cc of bisulphite solution is made, and the flask is again repeatedly shaken. After standing undistur bed in the beaker of boiling water for 10 minutes to per unit the unreacted oil to rise to the surface, adding sufficient sodium bisulphite solution to force the unreacted oil into the neck of the flask. Any drophts of oil into the neck of the flask. Any drophts of oil adhering to the sides are made to rise into the neck by gently tapping the flask, and by rotating rapidly between the palms and the hands. After cooking the flask to room temperature, measure the amount of unreacted oil. The aldehyde content may then be calculated by means of following formula:-

Percentage of aldehyde = 10 (10-No. of c.c of unreacted oil)

2) **Neutral Sulphite Method:-**

This is also an absorption method using a neutral sulphite solution, sodium hydroxide is liberated as the reaction proceeds.

Procedure:- Introducing 75 cc of freshly prepare, aqueous solution of sodium sulphite into a 150 cc flask, having a thin neck graduated in 0.1 cc division. Then adding few drops of a 1% alcoholic phenolphthalein solution and neutalise the free alkali with a 50% aqueous solution of acetic acid solution. Then pippetting exactly 10 cc of the oil into the flask and shake thoroughly. Immerse the flask in a beaker of boiling water and shake repeatedly. Neutralizing the mixture from time to time 50% acetic acid. Continuing this procedure until no further pink colour appears upon the addition of a few more drops of phenol phthalein solution. Permitting the flask to remain in the boiling water for an additional 15 minutes to assure complete reaction. Then adding sufficient neutralized sodium sulphite solution to raise the lower limit of the only layer within the graduated portion of the neck. Any droplets of the oil adhering to the sides are made to rise the neck by gently tapping the flask and ley rotating it rapidly between the palm of the hands. After cooling the flask to room temp. measure the amount of unreacted oil the aldehyde content may be then calculated by means of the formula given under bisulphite method.

PLANT ECONOMICS OF CITRONELLA OIL

Rated Plant Capacity = 90.00 Mt

LAND & BUILDING

1.	Land 1000 area (illsideforest)	Rs.	55,10,000.00

PLANT & MACHINERY

1. Dozing excanator and tiller equipment
2. Earth digging grass cutting and plaining equipments
3. Steam distillation still with condensers and oil separators
4. Disintigrator
5. Centrifugal filtration unit
6. Air conditioner for storage of oil
7. Boiler vertical coal fired smoke tube
8. Lab testing equipments

9. Depolluting equipments
10. Electrification and installation

FIXED CAPITAL

1.	LAND & BUILDING	Rs.	55,10,000.00
2.	PLANT & MACHINERY	Rs.	11,70,000.00
3.	OTHER FIXED ASSETS	Rs.	1,85,000.00
	TOTAL	Rs.	68,65,000.00

RAW MATERIALS

1. Citronella grass
2. Manures & irrigation
3. Miscellaneous chemicals

TOTAL CAPITAL INVESTMENT

TOTAL FIXED CAPITAL	Rs.	68,65,000.00
TOTAL WORKING CAPITAL FOR 3 MONTHS	Rs.	3,15,847.50
TOTAL	Rs.	71,80,847.50

TURN OVER/ANNUM

Return by sale of 27000 kgs citronella oil pure	Rs.	54,00,000.00

PROFIT SALES RATIO = Profit / Sales x 100 = 46.70 %

RATE OF RETURN = Operating profit / T.C.I x 100 = 35.12 %

BREAK EVEN POINT (B.E.P) = 44.77 %

Chapter-21

CLOVE OIL

PROCESS OF MANUFACTURE

Oil of clove is the valuable oil obtained by steam distillation of dried flower buds , dried leaves or dried stems respectively of clove tree botanically known as eugenia caryopuyllus.

This process of obtaining clove oil from aromatic plant is a batch process, but specific condition such as temperature pressure length of the cycle and amount of pretreatment of plant meterial are the most important factor.

Firstly all the plant materials must be broken up to some extent before they are changed to the still. This process called communition exposes some of the plants oil glands, and reduces the thickness of material to be handled in the still . The overall effect is to greatly increase speed of vaporization and distillation of the oil during steam distillation three things happen at once : oil and hot water diffuse through the plant membrance, some components of the oils hydrolyze, put of the oil is decomposed by heat. The ideal distillation, there is one in which diffusion rate is as high as possible while hydrolysis and thermal decomposition are kept to a minimum. During distillation some part of the oil dissolves in the water present within the plant cell, this solution is carried by osmosis through the cell membrance, and at the surface the oil is vapourized by passing steam. The rate at which the oil becomes available for distillation is related to its solubility in water. For this reason, the higher boiling but more water soluble oil component occasionally distill over lover before the lower boiling , less soluble parts.

When steam passes through the still containing the plant material, the clove oil is carried over with the steam into a shell and to be condenser mounted horizontally. The condenced oil and steam flow into an oil separator where they are separated by means of the diference in sp. gravity between the two liquids. Since large amounts of water are collected in proportion to the amount of clove oil , the water is recycled to the still along with fresh steam.

The usual distillation takes about 24 hours . From a charge of about 4,000 lb of clove spice yields about 600 lbs of clove oil.

PLANT ECONOMICS OF CLOVE OIL

Rated Plant Capacity = 300.00 KGS/day

LAND & BUILDING

1. Land required 1500 sq. mt.	Rs.	10,60,000.00

PLANT & MACHINERY

1. Steam distillation unit.
2. Shell and tube condenser.
3. Receiver.
4. Separator.
5. Baby boiler.
6. Storage tanks.
7. Filling and Bottling.

FIXED CAPITAL

1. LAND & BUILDING	Rs.	10,60,000.00
2. PLANT & MACHINERY	Rs.	6,30,000.00
3. OTHER FIXED ASSETS	Rs.	3,00,000.00
TOTAL	Rs.	19,90,000.00

RAW MATERIALS

1. Cloves
2. Packing material.

TOTAL CAPITAL INVESTMENT

TOTAL FIXED CAPITAL	Rs.	19,90,000.00
TOTAL WORKING CAPITAL FOR 3 MONTHS	Rs.	58,40,910.00
TOTAL	Rs.	78,30,910.00

TURN OVER/ANNUM

By Selling 90000 kg/annum. of Clove Oil.	Rs.	3,15,00,000.00

PROFIT SALES RATIO = Profit / Sales x 100 = 21.04 %

RATE OF RETURN = Operating profit / T.C.I x 100 = 84.63 %

BREAK EVEN POINT (B.E.P) = 22.95 %

Chapter-22

EXTRACTION OF ESSENTIAL OILS BY SUPER CRITICAL FLUID (CARBON DIOXIDE) METHOD FROM FLOWERS, HERBS AND SPICES

MANUFACTURING PROCESS FOR EXTRACTION OF ESSENTIAL OILS FROM FLOWERS, HERBS, SPICES BY SUPER CRITICAL FLUID (CARBON DIOXIDE)

A. Extraction of Essential Oil from Flowers:-

Solvent Extraction Process using super critical Fluid (CO_2):-

Extraction using super critical fluid instead of solvents viz. hexane, benzene etc. is a much beneficial.

FROM FLOWERS:-

Extraction of Essential oils from flowers by super critical fluids (SCF) is first carried out in an extraction unit with jacketed reactor convected with condenser system. In the jacket steam is passed impart requisite temperature to the contents in the jacketed vessel, containing the charge comprising of various flowers viz. Jasmine, lavender, etc. using SCF and the vaporization of the essential oils is conducted out under vacuum separately from individual flavers based on their boiling points. These essential oils in the form of vapors rise from the main distillation unit and get condensed in the reflux condenser from which they are taken to their respective storage tanks, packed in suitable containers and despatched for marketing.

The super critical fluid used in the above operation is carbon dioxide. This super critical carbon dioxide at temperatures and pressures above the critical point of 31.06°C and 7.38 m pa (73.8 bar) may be employed.

After the extraction of essential oils, which are volatile oils, the remaining soft is withdrawn and transferred to the solvent extraction unit fitted with heating system using oleum ether for extraction of oleoresins.

In the extraction unit the stuff is well stirred which the solvent is introduced into the system. When the extraction is complete, the solution is filtered and the solvent distilled off. In more upto date equipment, counter-current extraction may be affected through a series of percolators which are fitted, with trays packed with the remaining floral stuff. The solvent after passing through the plant material passes to a vacuum still (vacuum distillation system with condenser, etc.), where it is distilled of and returned for fresh extraction i.e. the recycle of the solvent is accomplished. The relatively less volatile perfume oils remain in the still. The product is usually a solid mass and consists of a mixture of oleoresins plant waxes, pigments, etc. which is known as concrete on treatment with alcohol the insoluble plant waxes can be filtered off, removal of alcohol from the solution yields obsolete.

There are two types of extractors i.e stationary & rotory extractors. The former consists or vertical cylinders provided with perforated metal goods arranged horizontally around a vertical shaft. The floral stuff is well changed on grids extraction is affected by successive washings whereby each batch of floral stuff is brought into contact with the solvent three times. The final extract is distilled to recover the solvent.

The rotory extractor consists of a tinned iron-drum rotating on a horizontal axis. The interior is divided into four compartments (loalding flowers) by means of perforated metal partitions. The solvent remains at the lowest part of the extractor and when one compartement is lifted in the course of the movement of the drum the liquid seeps through the perforations and drips back to the bottom. Each batch of flowers receive three washings. The extract pumped to a vacuum still and the solvent distilled of at a temperature below 60° 90-95% of the solvent is recovered. The concrete is cooled filtered and further concentrated in vacuo. The floral concrete so obtained contains the odoriferous principles and a considerable amount of plant waxes and pigments. For preparing the absolute the concrete is exhausted with warm alcohol and insoluble wax separated. The clear solution is cooled to -20° to -25° when more wax separates out.

PROCESS FLOW DIAGRAM
FOR EXTRACTION OF ESSENTIAL OILS FROM FLOWERS USING SUPER CRITICAL FLUID METHOD

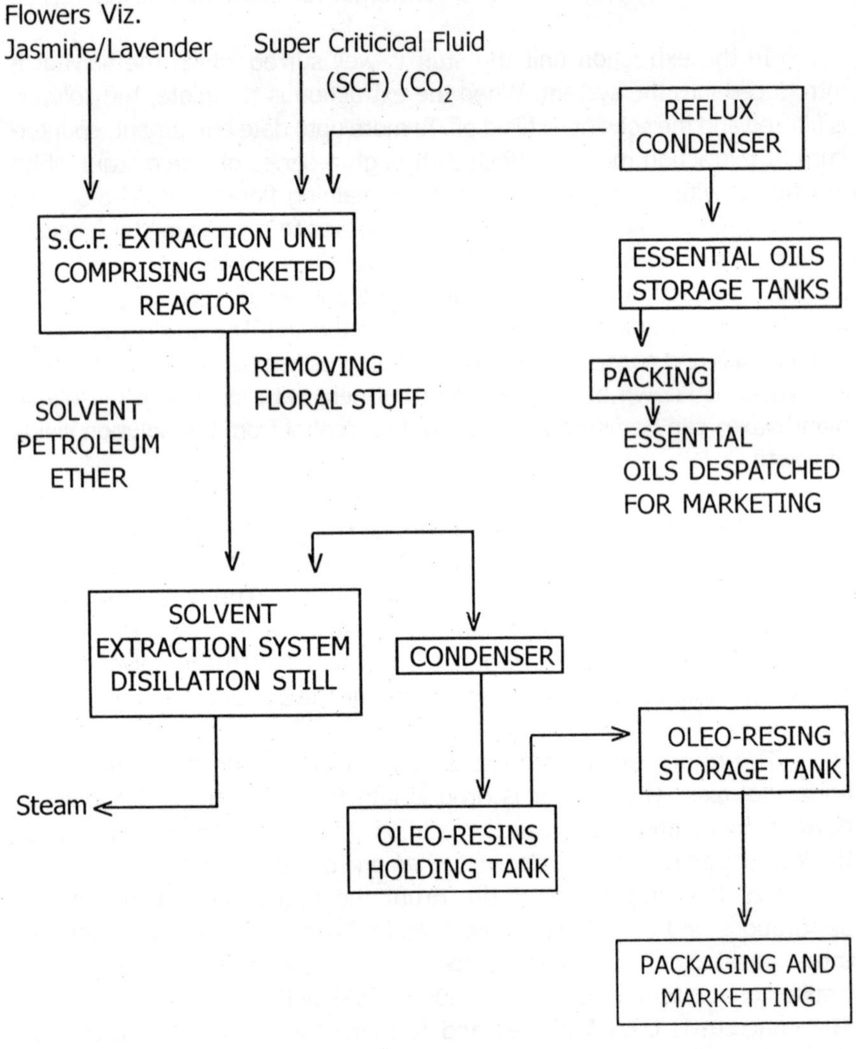

B. FROM HERBS

(Spikenard (Jatamansi)/Cinnamon/Zeodary (Kachur)

The process of extraction of respective essential oils from Herbs comprises the following steps:-

1. Cleaning of the Herb Rhizome,
2. Washing,
3. Drying,
4. Disintegration into small chips,
5. SCF Extraction for Essential Oils using super critical Fluid (CO_2),
6. Condensing of Essential oils,
7. Bottling of Essential Oils & despatch,
8. Solvent Extraction using petroleum ether for extraction of oleo-resins,
9. Bottling of oleoresins & despatch.

1. CLEANING:-

Individually the respective herbs viz. spikenard (Jatamansi)/Zeodary (kachur) etc. of rhizomes are cleared off the adhering soil.

2. WASHING:-

The herbs rhizones are then washed with water to wash off the remaining adhering dust or any other impurities.

3. DRYING:-

Then these rhizomes from which the respective essential oil is to be extracted, are dried.

This process of drying of Herbs rhizomes is carried out in the sun for economical reasons.

However, precautions are to be observed that the place where these items are kept for drying in the sum should be such that dust or dirt and any other foreign matter shouldn't get contaminated with them during drying.

PROCESS FLOW DIAGRAM FOR EXTRACTION OF ESSENTIAL FLUID METHOD

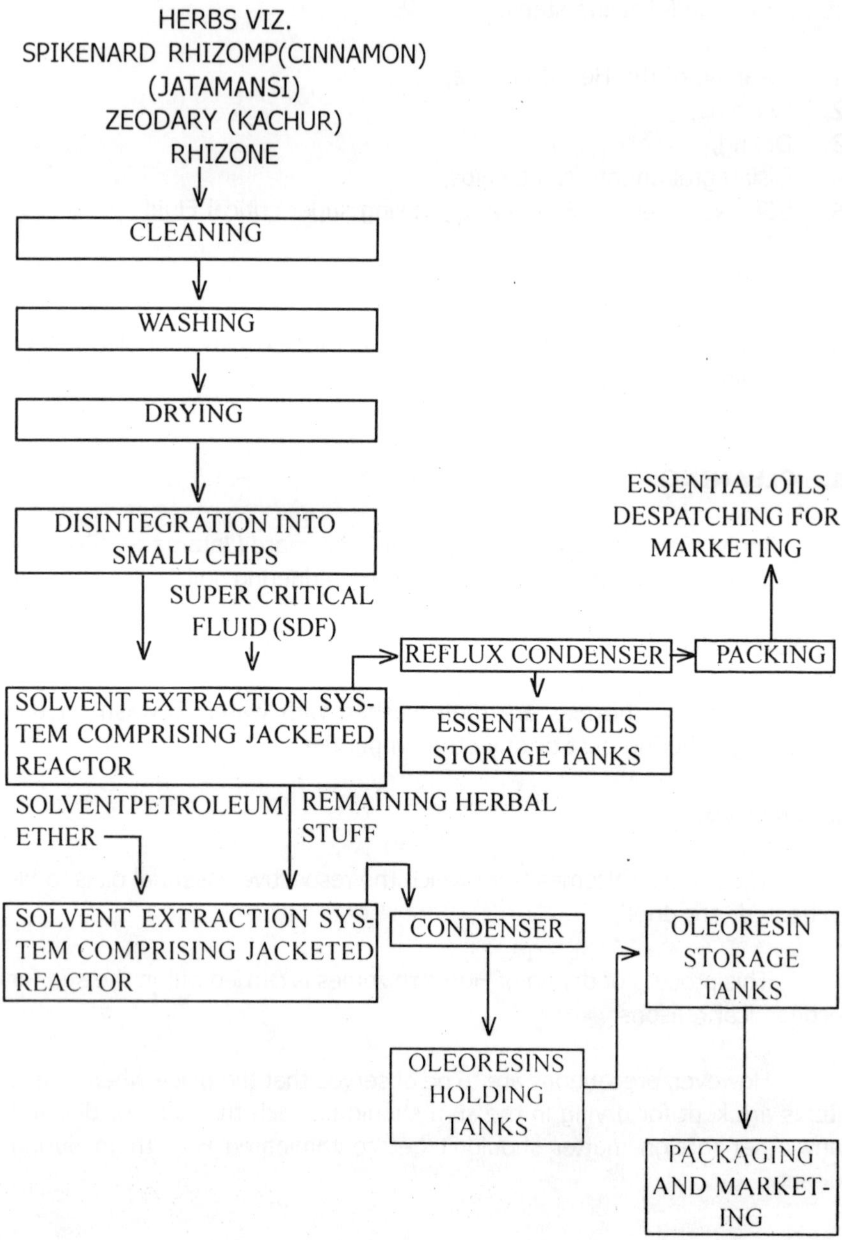

4. Disintegration into small chip:-

Prior to the SCF extraction of essential fluid, the cleared and dried rhizomes are disintegrated into small chips, rather caushed to coarse powder.

5. Rest of the process is similar to that described under section (A) for extraction of essential oils from flowers.

6. FROM SPICES:-

Viz. Coriender, Cumin, Aniseed, Ajowan, Ginger, etc.

The process of extraction of essential oil from spices using super critical fluid involves the following major step.

1. Cleaning of spices,
2. Cutting the item into small pieces/pulverising,
3. Loading of the still of SCF Extraction Unit,
4. Extraction of Essential oils from respective spices,
5. Bottling of Essential oils,
6. Solvent Extraction using petroleum ether for extraction of oleoresins,
7. Bottling of oleo-resins and despatch.

1. CLEANING:-

Individually, the respective spices viz. coriender, cumin, Aniseed, Ajowan, ginger, etc. are cleared off the adhering soil of impurities.

2. DRYING:-

The item whose oil is to be extract is dried. This process is proposed to be carried out in sun, for economic reasons. The place where these items are kept for drying in sun should be detected such that the dust and dirt water or any other foreign matter shouldn't get contaminated during drying. One most suitable place is the roof of the working shed. The side walls of the roof should be of sufficient height.

3. CUTTING INTO PIECES:-

The items like Cardamom, Cumin seeds and King's Cumin are not need to be cut into pieces for they are naturally present in small size. But for Ginger, it is need to be cut into small pieces.

PROCESS FLOW DIAGRAM FOR EXTRACTION OF ESSENTIAL OILS FROM SPICES USING SUPER CRITICAL FLUID (SCF) METHOD

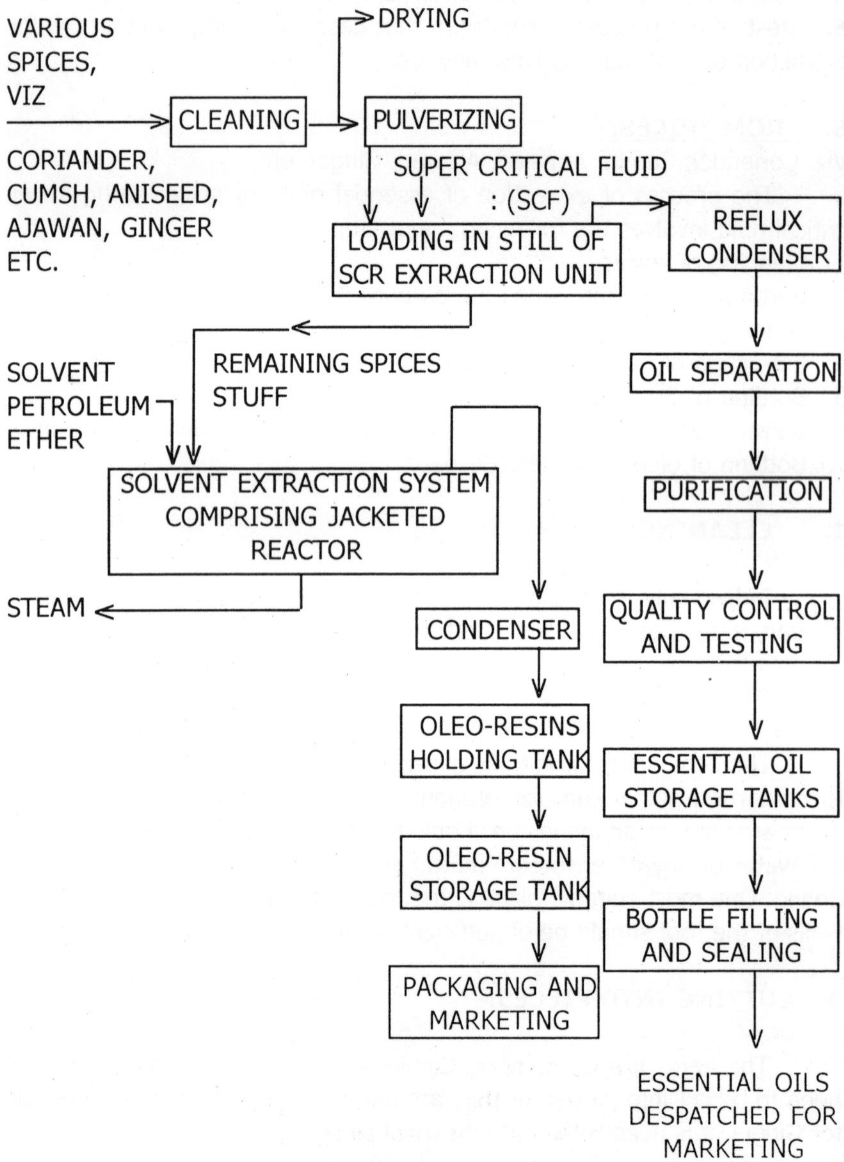

PLANT ECONOMICS

LAND & BUILDING

Total land area 3000 sq.mtrs.	Rs.	44,75,000.00

PLANT & MACHINERY

1. Extraction Unit, using Super Critical Fluid(SCF) Jacketed Reactor for condenser,
3. Solvent Extraction system with complete accessories and heating system
4. Vacuum distillation system with condenser
5. Automatic washing machine
6. Cabinet dryer electric operated
7. Disintegrator complete with motor
8. Automatic sieving machine
9. Pulverizer
10. Centrifugal Separator
11. Bottle filling and sealing machine
12. Boiler steam generating
13. Carton sealing machine
14. Storage tanks,
15. Storage tank for SCF & solvent
16. Instrumentation and process control
17. Lab. equipments

FIXED CAPITAL

1. LAND & BUILDING	Rs.	44,75,000.00
2. PLANT & MACHINERY	Rs.	1,84,10,000.01
3. OTHER FIXED ASSETS	Rs.	40,90,000.00
TOTAL	Rs.	2,69,75,000.01

RAW MATERIALS

1. Flowers Jasmine/Lavender/etc.
2. Herbs spikenard(Jatamansi)/cinnamon zeodary (kachur),
3. FOR SPICES :- Coriander

4. Cumin (Jeera/Seeds)
5. Aniseed
6. Ajowan (Bishop seeds)
7. Ginger (Green)
8. Eucalyptus leaves
9. Garlic
10. Neem leaves
11. Taj patta
12. Turmeric
13. Orange Peel (Dried)
14. Super Critical Fluid (SCF) (Carbon dioxide)
15. Petroleum Ether Solvent

TOTAL CAPITAL INVESTMENT

TOTAL FIXED CAPITAL	RS.	2,69,75,000.01
TOTAL WORKING CAPITAL FOR 3 MONTHS	Rs.	2,66,30,475.00
TOTAL	Rs.	5,36,05,475.01

TURN OVER/ANNUM

1. BY SALE OF: (A) Essential oils from Jasmine/Lavender/etc. Flowers
2. (B)Essential Oils from Herbs Spike nard (Jatamansi)/Cinnamon/ Zeodary (Kachur)
3. (C) ESSENTIAL OILS FROM SPICES :- Coriander Oil
4. Cumin Oil
5. Aniseed Oil
6. Ajavan Oil
7. Ginger Oil
8. Eucalyptus Oil
9. Garlic Oil
10. Neem Oil
11. Tej Patta Oil
12. Turmeric Oil
13. Orange Peel Oil
14. II.(A) Oleoresins from Flowers Jas-mine/Lavender
15. (B)Oleo-Resins from Herbs(Spikenard (Jatamansi/Cinnamon/Zeodary(kachur)

16. (C) OLEO-RESINS FROM SPICES:-
    Oleoresins from Coriander
17. Oleoresins from Cumin
18. Oleoresins from Aniseed
19. Oleoresins from Ajawan
20. Oleoresins from Ginger
21. Oleoresins from Encalyptns
22. Oleoresins from Garlic
23. Oleoresins from Neem
24. Oleoresins from Tejpatta
25. Oleoresins from Turmeric
26. Oleoresins from Orange Peel Rs. 14,49,67,200.01

PROFIT SALES RATIO = Profit / Sales x 100 = 16.52 %
RATE OF RETURN = Operating profit / T.C.I x 100 = 44.68 %
BREAK EVEN POINT (B.E.P) = 39.65 %

Chapter-23

EUCALYPTUS OIL

PROCESS OF MANUFACTURE

Eucalyptus oil is obtained in India by the distillation of leaves and terminal branches of E.globulus (Blue Gum Tree), which grows on Niligiri, Ammamale and Plain Hills

The leaves are collected from trees filled in fuedl to the towns hills. Nature leaves from trees of 15 years or above are preferred. They are dried in shade for 3 days and subjected for distillation in stills. The crude oil is separated distillation in stills. The crude oil is separated from the distillation in stills. The crude oil is separated from the distillated, filtered and then refined from the distillation, filtered and then refined by distillation after adding caustic potash. The refined oil is filtered and then bottled for marketing. Hydrogen peroxide is used for decolouring the oil. The oil can be marketed as

I. Double distilled (pale yellow colour)

II. Double distilled & extra refined (colourless)

DISTILLATION

Even though distillation is a harsh treatment a great many oils are produced in this way. In these cases, the perfume bearing part of the plant is cut down or picked up and taken to the distillation unit where it is distilled to separate the perfumery material from the plant part.

These methods of distillation are in use viz water distillation, water and steam distillation and live steam distillation. Water distillation is the crudest method of separating oils from plant parts. This is the simple process in which the plant material is placed into the still, water added and the vessel is fire heated. Water and oil distill together. They are condensed. The oil and water layers are separated subsequently. The process of water distillation has the disadvantage of exposing the delicate essential oil to a prolonged distillation in the presence of water, which results in the unnecessary hydrolyres of esterlic. The tendency now is to use more modern distillation equipments of the water and steam and type in where the still fitted with a horizontal perforated plate upon which the product material rests. The one material rests. The lower part of the still is fitted with water to a level somewhat below the grid and charge is subjected to distillation by passing low pressure steam. This avoids direct passing low pressure steam. This avoid direct contact of plant material into the distillation water below. The water beneath the perforated grid is described after the completion of distillation and replaced with fresh water.

Steam distillation method differs from the water and steam distillation method because no water is kept in the bottom of this-still. Live steam at 40-000 lbs/sq.in is injected through steam coils below the charge, the pressure within the vessel is controlled according to the nature of material handled. A modern distillation unit may also incorporate other refinements such as solvent extraction of the water distillation waters. This enables the water soluble portions of the essential oil to be recovered. The oils separated by distillation are sometimes rectified or factioned by hydro distillation at a low pressure for improved colour and odour. The odours and objectionable impurities are removed in the folreruns and late-runs during rectification.

DISTILLATION PROCESSES:

In the batch distillation a batch of material is charged to the still. Heat is applied and the vapours are removed continuously with no partial condensation of the vapours or refluxing of the condenser. It is chiefly confined to small scale operations which are intermittent and in which efficiency of operation and heat is sacrificed for simplicity. In the continuous distillation process, the efficiency is better but the cost of operation. In this type of distillation, the still is fitted with a fractionation column and reflux condensus. In this cases still may be heated wither by steam or electricity.

OPERATION:

The method of working is to place sufficient quantity of water in each still and to pack the leaves tightly upon the grid supported upon the bottom. Before the lid is put in position a thick mixture of mud or clay is placed along the ilange. On top of this is placed a strip of horrian or similar packing material and second layer of clay is applied. The lid is then lowered on the flange and fastered by meand of cross timbers, wooden wedges and iron stirrups, which are attached to the tank. The still is built upon a support of bricks or stones and a wood fire is placed beneath. When the water boils the steam passing up through the leaves separates the oil from the plant allows and carries it over, in a caporous state into a condenser where oil and water condenser and flow out into a suitable receptacle where the oil floats upon the surface of the water and is ultimately separated. The time of distillation variety from 3-18 hr. according to the species.

REFINING:

Crude medicinal grade Eucalyptus oil is subjected to redistillation. Small quantities of water, objectionable volatile aldehydes (principal isovaleric aldehyde) and some prene, are removed is this way. The main or middle fraction, constituting about 85 to 90% of the oil and containing not less than 70% cineole, is marketed as a rectified eucalyptus oil. The residue in the still, consisting of x-terpineol, sesquiterpenes, sesquiterpene alcohols, p-isopropyl phenol, cumminal or phellondral, cryprone etc. is used as a source of these substances, in the manufacture of commercial disinfectant. The phenolic, aldehydic and ketonic substances passes marked germicidal properties.

Yield:- The oil yield depend on

1. Type and ageof Leaf, Randomless of sample, composition of sample is objective leaf selection etc.

2. Storage of Samples: Changes in oil central and constitution during storage, Moisture content of sample preventions of sweating etc.
3. Steam distillation technique: Technique & Time of distillation etc.

LOCATION CONDITIONS:

This plant is based mainly on the agricultural product. So the economics of the plant will much depend on the location of the plant. The factor influencing the plant site selection and economics are discussed below:

RAW MATERIALS

Raw materials for the product is only eucalyptus leaves which is a natural product and hence plant will be seasoned. In order to avoid this dependency sufficient stock of leaves should be done. It is advisable that the plant should be located near the raw material source.

MARKET:

Market is the second major point which affects the economics of the plant very much. So the plant should be located adjacent to the market as well.

WATER POSITION:

Water is used in huge quantities in this plant. In order to meet the requirement of water, sufficient water should be available on the selected site. If water, arrangement is not available, then it is better to more own tube well.

TRANSPORTATION FACILITIES:

Transportation is used in all the industries at two stages. One is for transporting raw material to the factory site and other is for transporting the finished product to the market. So it should be carefully studied that the selected site is connected to the desired placed by roads and rails well.

LABOUR:

Labour required for this units is very less. Hence it does not affect the economists very much. But still the labour availability is kept in view whilte selected the site.

POWER AND FUEL

There is not much need of electrical powder for this industry. Only fuel is used in bulk quantity Furnace Oil is the best fuel. It is easily available everywhere in India. Therefore this does controll the production and economics.

All the above factors are studied carefully while selecting the site. Few factors are contradictory and therefore a compromise is made sometimes.

PROCESS FLOW SHEET

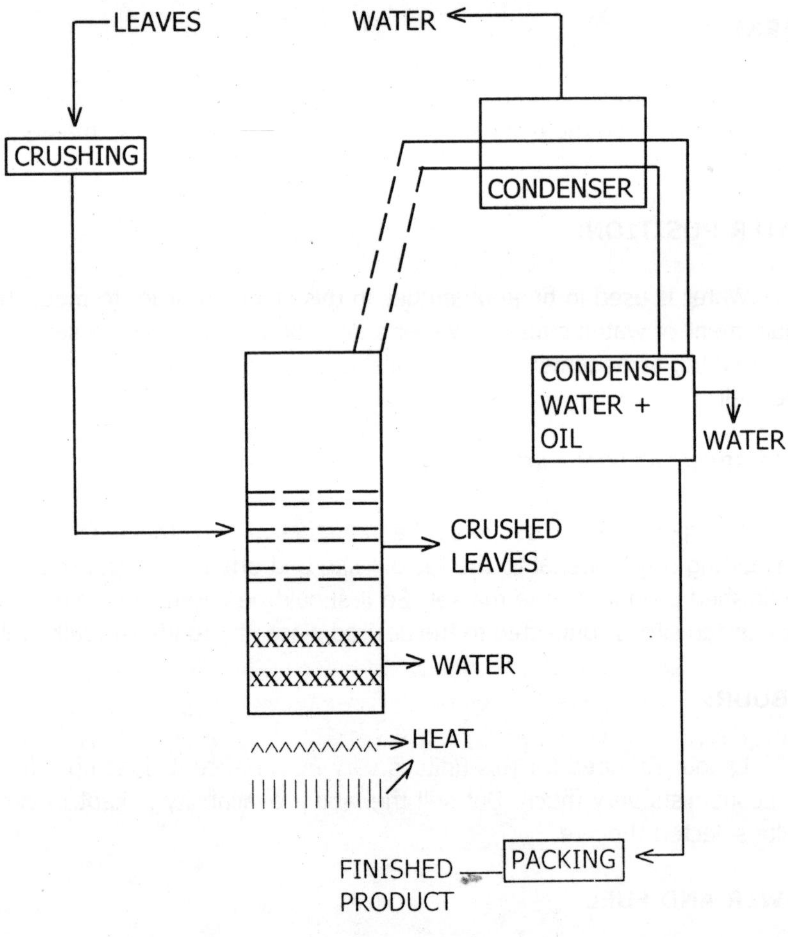

PLANT ECONOMICS OF EUCALYPTUS OIL

Rated Plant Capacity = 100.00 KG/day

LAND & BUILDING

1. Land area 2 acre	Rs.	1,50,000.00

PLANT & MACHINERY

1. Distillation (mild steel) equipped with grill etc.
2. Crushing Machine
3. Condenser/Condensring column
4. Separator
5. Rectifying column
6. Filter Press
7. Motor, Pumps
8. Boiler
9. Storage Tank
10. Cost of electrifications piping

FIXED CAPITAL

1. LAND & BUILDING	Rs.	12,37,500.00
2. PLANT & MACHINERY	Rs.	6,07,000.00
3. OTHER FIXED ASSETS	Rs.	12,000.00
TOTAL	Rs.	18,56,500.00

RAW MATERIALS

1. Eucalyptus leaves
2. Containers steel, glass bottles

TOTAL CAPITAL INVESTMENT

TOTAL FIXED CAPITAL	Rs.	18,56,500.00
TOTAL WORKING CAPITAL FOR 3 MONTHS	Rs.	7,36,125.00
TOTAL	Rs.	25,92,625.00

TURN OVER/ANNUM

1. Receipt from the sale of 30000 kg. Eucalyptus oil	Rs.	45,00,000.00

PROFIT SALES RATIO = Profit / Sales x 100 = 16.90 %

RATE OF RETURN = Operating profit / T.C.I x 100 = 29.34 %

BREAK EVEN POINT (B.E.P) = 63.52 %

Chapter-24

GINGER OI

MANUFACTURING PROCESS
PREPARATION OF RAW MATERIAL

Distillation of ginger oil on an industrial scale does differ some what from distillation of essential oils in general.

CLEANING

Prior to any combination, the spice must be freed from extraneous matters, such as dust, dirt, pebbles and metallic objects. For this purpose salting machine with a magnetic screen and screens of different diameters are used.

MILLING

For the grinding of ginger, mills of different type are used, some are equipped with rotating tooth disk, some are hammer mills and for some special purposes, triple- roller mills are used . Both the rotating tooth disk mills and the hammer mills have a considerable airflow, which causes a certain loss of volatile oil from the ground ginger.

The rotating disk mill may be adjusted to the desired grain size of the milled product, but frictioned heat develops during grinding and therefore they are with a cooling device. Hammer mills are not practicable when the material is small and contains a relatively high percentage of fats. For such case crushing in triple roller mills, which rotates at different velocities and have ribbed rollers is the appropriate method of comminution.

SOAKING

Ames and Mathews mention the desirability of soaking of some plant material for instance, cinnamon bank and also of grinding the spice prior to distillation.

LOADING OR CHARGING

Ground ginger must be loaded into the still and distilled without any delays otherwise, losses of Essential oil and deterioration through oxidation are inevitable. The oil distiller must realize that this valuable product will some day be used in food without any further preliminary purification. Contamination of essential oil with rust, dirt, salt of copper or water can not be tolerated. Therefore, the distillation apparatus should preferably be made of stainless steel. As a minimum requirement the lid of the still, the gooseneck, the condenser and the flerentine flask or oil receiver should be made of this material.

BLEACHING OF GINGER

The peeled ginger hands are washed in water and kept steeped in plain water for 2 to 3 hours. Thereafter, they are takenout and steeped in about 1.5 to 200% lime (Cao) Solution for about 6 hours. They are then drained and sun dried on mats, barbecues, or a clean cement floor. This liming or bleaching of ginger not only improves its colours but also helps to preserve it better. Care should be taken to use the best quality slaked lime in order to get better whiteness.

Application of these chemicals requires proper control especially in the bleaching of ginger.

DISTILLATION

Ginger Oil is obtained by the steam distillation of the dried ginger. The best raw material is African ginger. It is not only lower priced than other qualities but also gives a higher yield of oil. In general the yield varies from 1.5 to 3 percent of volatile oil. averaging 2%. Prior to distillation the dry material should be comminuted, then charged into the stills immediately. Care must be taken to distribute the mass evenly on several trays. Within the still Distillation is Carried out with direct steam depending upon the charge in the still and the steam depending upon the charge in the still and the steam pressure applied, distillation of one charge may require up to 20 hour. The distillation water may require cohobation.

Peeling and shaving of the rhizomes constitute an excellent material for distillation, giving a good yield of oil, provided distillation is carried out immediately after peeling.

PRACTICE OF DISTILLATION

STEAM DISTILLATION

Recovering of the Oil dissolved or suspended in the distillation water consists in saturating latter first with salt and then extracting the solution with volatile solvents - as highly purified petroleum there or Benzene. This is usually done twice. The drawn off and united solvent solutions are there concentrated in still by driving off the solvent first at atmospheric pressure and later in vacuo, until every trace of solvent is eliminated from the oil.

FLOW DIAGRAM FOR GINGER OIL

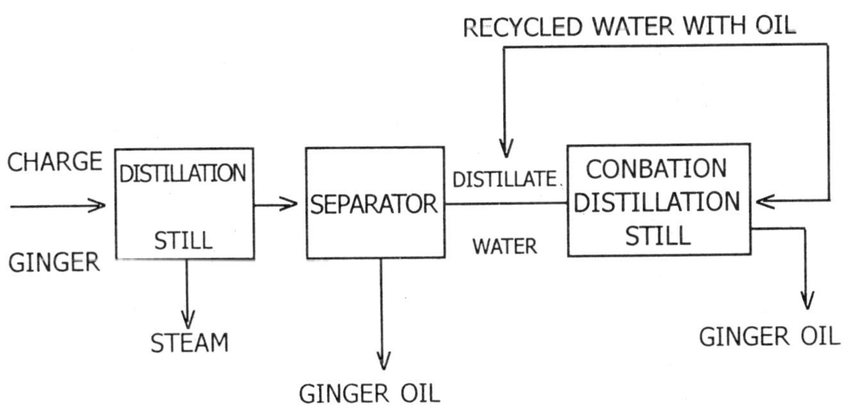

PLANT ECONOMICS OF GINGER OIL

Rated Plant Capacity = 200.00 Kgs/day

LAND & BUILDING

1. Land area required 1400 sq.mt	Rs.	7,35,000.00

PLANT & MACHINERY

1. Boiler
2. Distillation Still
3. Condenser
4. Storage tank
5. Piping system etc.
6. Accumulator
7. Pulveriser
8. Pumps
9. Electricity Installation erection & commissioning
10. Weighing & Testing equipments

FIXED CAPITAL

1. LAND & BUILDING		Rs.	30,10,000.00
2. PLANT & MACHINERY		Rs.	6,50,000.00
3. OTHER FIXED ASSETS		Rs.	37,500.00
	TOTAL	Rs.	36,97,500.00

RAW MATERIALS

1. Ginger
2. Lime
3. Nacl

TOTAL CAPITAL INVESTMENT

TOTAL FIXED CAPITAL	Rs.	36,97,500.00
TOTAL WORKING CAPITAL FOR 3 MONTHS	Rs.	16,24,695.00
TOTAL	Rs.	53,22,195.00

TURN OVER/ANNUM

1. By sale of 6000 kg Rs. 1,02,00,000.00

PROFIT SALES RATIO = Profit / Sales x 100 = 21.72 %

RATE OF RETURN = Operating profit / T.C.I x 100 = 41.63 %

BREAK EVEN POINT (B.E.P) – 50.48 %

Chapter-25

JASMINE ROSE & LILY OIL EXTRACTION PLANT

MANUFACTURING PROCESS

There are two modern methods used for manufacturing flower oil which are delicate in nature which are thermally unstable and chiefly separated by either solvent extraction using volatile solvents. Another method used for extraction of flower oil is supercritical fluid extraction method.

(i) SOLVENT EXTRACTION METHOD:

Delicate oils which are thermally unstable are chiefly separated by solvent extraction using volatile solvents. Solvents are generally selected according to the plant materials and their constituents. Leaves, fruits, roots, moss, resins are extracted with benzene with or without admixture of acetone or petroleum ether. Flowers are advantagenously extracted with petroleum ether. Excellent extraction results have been reported with liquified gas butane which is reported with liquified gas butane which is known under the trade name of Butaflor.

Extraction temperature plays very important role in controlling the solvent selectivity and solvent power. Therefore, solvent extraction is conducted at suitable temperature depending upon solute and solvent solubility behaviour.

Stationary and rotatory type of extractors are generally employed for extraction of active principles from plant materials. Low solvent inventory and high essential oil yield are observed in case of rotatory extractor in comparison to stationary extractor.

In the process of solvent extraction solvents penetrate the cells of the vegetable and dissolv the essential oil but they also dissolve waxes, colours etc. Semlsolid concretes obtained after removal of solvent under reduced pressure is further extracted with highly pure alcohol. In order to remove wax the extract is then filtered after precipitation at low temperature. Absolute is thus produced from wax free alcohol extact after removal of alcohol under vacuum.

SELECTION CRITERIA OF SOLVENT:

Following factors require careful consideration while selecting a solvent for extraction.

(i) Solvent should completely and quickly dissolve the odouriferous principles of the plant materials.

(ii) It should not dissolve inert matter like waxes, pigments and albuminous compounds.

(iii) Solvent should have low boiling point so that it can be easily removed without affecting the aroma of oil at low temperature. But, boiling point should not be too low as it may increase solvent loss by evaporation in warm climate.

(iv) The solvent should not dissolve water as water present flowers would dissolve and accumulate in the solvent.

(v) Solvent must be chemically inert, i.e. no reaction with constituents of flower oil.

(vi) The solvent must have uniform b.p. and must be free from high b.p. constituents.

(vii) It should be low-priced and nonflammable. if possible.
Use of mixed solvent is quite active field of research and it should be attempted in extraction of active principles from various plant materials of economic importance.

(ii) SUPER CRITICAL FLUID EXTRACTION METHOD

Supercritical fluid extraction is emerging as a versatile and important tool to separate components that are susceptible to separate components that are susceptible to thermal degradation. It is analogous to liquid extraction and distillation as both solubility and volatility effects are utilized. Temperature and pressure gradients are two major driving forces in the process. When solvent and feed mixture are brought into intimate contact. soluble components are extracted from the feed mixture. After extraction raffinate and extract phases are separated. Solvent is separated from extract phase by varying the operating conditions and is recycled back after make-up.

The region near the critical point is of great importance. Normal values of reduced temperature and reduced pressure lie between 0.9 to 1.2 and 1.0-3.0 respectively. In this region, small variation in density. In case of solvent having low critical pressure, it is easier to get required density and solvent power. Density and solvent power in SCF are like those of liquid whereas transport properties and compressuibility are like those of gas.

Recent studies show that SCFE is products, carbondioxide is preferred solvent because it is cheap, nontoxic, non-corrosive, non-flammable, easier to handle and requires mild processing conditions during extraction and good solvent power for aldehydes, ketones, esters and alcohols.

Isolation studies of essential oils from natural substances have clearly shown that liquid carbondioxide extraction is superior and faster to steam distillation.

ADVANTAGES:

(i) Solvent power of supercritical fluid can be easily controlled according to the requirement.

(ii) Extraction conditions can be adjusted easily to separate different constituents selectively.

(iii) Supercritical fluids have higher diffusivities and lower viscosities than those of normal liquids resulting in better penetration into substrates and quicker attainment of equilibrium.

(iv) Supercitical fluids present no surface tension and wetting properties.

(v) SCFE can be easily adopted to isolate components that are highly susceptible to thermal decomposition.

(vi) The energy cost is lower than that of conventional process because product can be made solvent free by variation in operating conditions without any difficulty.

EXTRACTION WITH SOLVENT:-
CONSTRUCTION OF APPARATUS:-

Until some years ago the extractors and stills were constructed of copper, because this metal retains its value after rapping the apparatus, and the pliable copper can be hammered and retires are easily made. Lately, however, the extractors are constructed more often of heavily tinned sheet iron which is much cheaper and, therefore offerts the advantage of fower investment and quicker amortization.

The apparatus must be of solid construction to stand wear and tear; all extractor pipes and valves should be within easy to save time and exclude mistakes on the part of the operators. Pipes and valves must be sufficiently wide to prevent formation of pressure by air and petroleum ether apors, one of the principal causes for loss of the solvent and solutions to and from the apparatus, and considerably speed up operation. Pumping of solvents and solutes is done by air pressure created by air compressors.

The extractors are mounted on elevated metal platforms along the inside walls of the building. The platform runs even with the ground outside of the building, so that arriving flower material may be charged directly into the extractors and the exhausted flowers discharged with equal ease.

Loss of solvent during the operation presents one of the most serious problems. These losses are usually caused by incomplete distillation of the solvent from the exhausted flowers, by insufficient condensation in the contensers, or by too narrow pipes and valves creating pressure and blowing off a mixture of air and solvent vapour. To avoid this as much as possible the whole system of extractors, evaporators and solvent tanks is arranged as a closed circle, with only one outlet where escaping solvent vapours can be condensed. The Societe Carbonisation et Charbons Actifs some years ago developed an efficient, rather small sized apparatus in which solvent vapors are absorbed by activated carbon and recovered by blowing live steam through the saturated carbon. A current of hot air then reactivates the carbon. The apparatus is simple and permits considerable economy in factories where large amounts of solvent are in circulation.

Description of Extraction Batteries.- A battery consists of three or four extractors, four or five metal tanks holding solvent and solutions, and an evaporator for concentrating the flower oil solutions. There exist two types of extractors-viz., the stationary and the rotatory types. Some factories employ both, but only one type can be used in the same battery.

The stationary extractors usually have a capacity of 1,200 liters, holding about 135 kg. of jasmine flowers, or 180 kg. of rose flowers. From 400 to 450 liters of solvent are required for extracting 100 kg. of flowers. Losses of petroleum ether may range from 12 to 14 liters for 100 kg. of flowres treated, but the loss can be considerably reduced with the solvent recovery apparatus described above.

The stationary extractors are cylindrical, standing vertical. In the interior they should be provided with several perforated metal grids arranged horizontally arounda vertical central support shaft. The flowers are charged upon these grids, thus spreading loosely over a larger surface and preventing lumpin. The solvent can thus penetrate the mass freely and uniformaly. After the flowers have been charged into the extractor, the metal cover on top is closed tightly with clamps.

Extraction is carried out methodically by successive washings where by each batch of flowers is treated three times with solvent. A third washing is used as second washing for the next flower batch, then as first washing, and is finally pumped into the evaporator for concentration. The solvent distilled off is used as fresh solvent for a third washing which serves again as second of the next flower batch, etc. A fourth extraction, in most cases, yields at best only small quantities of waxes and other inter substances. The actual flower oil is contained in the first and second washing, while the third one serves merely to wash down parts of the second washing still adhering to the flower material. There exist, however, cases of emergenecy, especially during the height of the harvest, when great quantities of flowers arrive and must be worked up quickly in order to avoid fermentation. In such cases the third washing is often eliminated altogether, in order to save time. Just how to proceed requires experience and good judgement on the part of the factory manager.

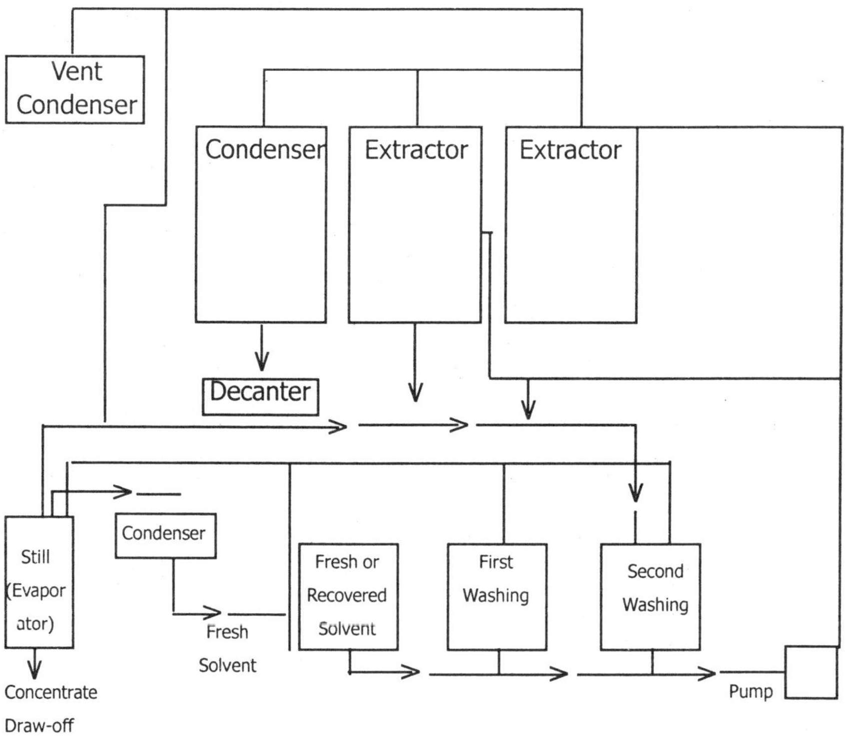

Fig. 3.24 Schematic diagram of an extraction system.

After the third washing the flowers are parctically exhausted, and can be discharged. However, they still contain a considerable amount of adhering solvent which, before discharging the flowers from the extractor, must be recovered by steam distillation, i.e., by simply blowing live steam through the mass. Water and solvent, after condensation, separate automatically in a specially constructed Florentine flask.

The first washing requires about 45 min., the second 35 min., the third 25 min. For drawing off the solutions and pumping in the next washing , 5 to 10 min. must be allowed for each operation. Including 90 min. of steam distillation for recovering the solvent still adhering to the exhausted flowers, complete extraction of one batch of flowers requires about 4 1/2 to 5 hr. However, no striet rules can be laid down, as every flower type requires a different method of working , and every manufacturer follows his own ideas.

Rotatory Extractors:- Year ago, Charles Garnier invented a rotatory extraction apparatus which was adopted by many factories. In modified and improved form the apparatus represents a simple, solid and moderately priced piece of machinery.

The latest model consists of a heavily tinned iron drum rotating around a horizontal axle. Four perforated metal partitions, rectangularly and horizontally arranged around the central axle, divide the interior into four compartments into which the flowers are charged through four manholes. While the whole system rotates slowly, the flower material moves, tumbles and disp into the solvent lying on the bottom of the extractor. The liquid seeps through the perforations and drips back to the bottom when one compartment is lifted out of the solvent in the continuous movement of the whole frum. Thus, the solvent does not fill the extractor but only the lowest part, the flowers dipping slowly and continuously into the solvent and rising again in the rotatory movement.

Three successive washings are usually made, carried out similarly to the systematic extraction method described under stationalry apparatus. The first, i.e., the most saturatede washing, is then pumped into the evaporator and concentrated by distilling offf the solvent. After the third washing has been drawn off the exhausted flower material, live steam is blown into the extractor to distill over and recover the petroleum ether still adhering to the extracted flowers.

The advantages of the rotatory extractors as compared with stationary apparatus are evident. Through the movement of the flower material in the solvent, its action becomes more penetrating and more effective, resulting in a somewhat higher yield. Figured as concrete, it is about 8 per cent higher in the case of the rotatory apparatus. Since the solvent covers only the bottom drum and not the whole flower material, as in the stationary apparatus, much less solvent is in circulation and , therefore, evaporation losses are reduced. Only 160 to 170 liters are required in the rotatory apparatus to extract 100 kg. of flowers. The loss of solvent for 100 kg. of flowers is less than in stationary extractors ; it may be 8 to 12 liters but can be reduced by using the previously described solvent recovery apparatus.

One rotatory extractor does the work of three or four stationary extractors arranged in one battery. Although superior in many ways the rotatory extractors suffer from several disadvantages and cannot altogether replace the stationary type; for example, the latter is better adapted to voluminous plant material, such as lavender, which cannot be so easily charged and discharged through the manholes of the rotating drum.

Concentration of Solutions:- The first, i.e., the most concentrated, washing is filtered through a fine screen and pumped into the so-called evaporator in which the greater part of the solvent is driven (distilled) off. These evaporators are of varying construction, representing basically a modified water or steam bath. In other words, the heating is done by indirect steam blown into a steam jacket beneath the still. The solvent, however, should not be completely driven off in this operation. Most manufacturers stop operation when the temperature in the still (evaporator) reaches about 60°, because any higher temperature at atmospheric pressure would be harmful to the delicate flower perfume. The first washing contains, of course, only a small percentage of flower oil. Therefore, concentrating of this washing in the evaporator means driving off 90-95 per cent of the solvent. (The recovered solvent serves as fresh solvent for a third washing.) The concentrated solution remaining in the evaporators is permitted to cool, is filtered, then transferred into a special, smaller vacuum still, and there completely concentrated in vacuo.

Final Concentration:- Vacuum stills of small capacity (50 to 100 liters) serve for this purpose. The final concentration represents a most delicate operation and requires much experience and constant attention on the part of the operator. The concentrating has to be done at as low a temperature as possible, yet any trace of solvent must be eliminated. Every manufacturer has his own, often secret, methods of purification. The completely concentrated and purified products represent the so-called floral concretes, which contain the odoriferous principles of the natural flower perfume, plus a considerable amount of plant waxes, albuminous material and color pigments. The concretes are, therefore, usually of solid consisteney and only partly soluble in 95 per cent alcohol.

Concrete Flower Oils:- Although these insoluble concretes are more difficult to work with, some perfumers prefer them to the alcohol soluble absolutes, which are obtained by precipitating and eliminating the insoluble waxes with strong alcohol, and concentrating the filtered alcoholic solutions. Distilling off the alcohol from the solutions when making these absolutes undoubtedly entails the loss of some of the most volatile and delicate constituents of the natural flower oil. It is ofter claimed that an alcoholic washing of a concrete is superior and more true to nature than a simple alcoholic solution os th ecorresponding absolute. On the other hand, the processing of concretes requires special equipment and considerable tiem; therefore, the absolutes represent a more convenient form of flower oils than the concretes.

Conversion of Concretes into Absolutes.__ The alcohol soluble absolutes are prepared from the concretes by the following general method:

The concrete is either thoroughly rubbed down in a large mortar with a quantity of high-proof alcohol or, as some manufacturers prefer, melted and dissolved in warm alcohol. Subsequently eight to ten times the amount of alcohol is added and the mass stirred for a prolonged period in batteuses, as described under enfleurage. Usually five to six washings of the concrete are made in a systematie way, i.e., a third washing serves as a second one for a following batch of concrete; the second is used as first for a batch of new concrete, the first washing consequently representing the most concentrated solution. After standing and drawing offf the clear solution from the alcohol insoluble waxes, the first washing is then thoroughly cooled in a refrigerator or in a special room, at temperatures ranging from -20° to -25°, when more wax precipitates and is filtered off in the cold. The resulting clear solution can be used as such in alcoholic perfumes.

Most perfume houses have neither the time nor the facilities to carry out their own washing of concretes, and prefer using alcohol soluble floral oils. For those, the manufacturers in Grasse offer the so-called liquid absolutes as the most concentrated form of natural flower oils. These liquid absolutes of extraction are obtained by carefully concentrating the first alcoholic washing of the corresponding concrete at low temperature in a good vacuum still. This process of concentrating involves a loss of several liters of alcohol per kilogram of absolute.

The absolutes are usually viscous oils with a more or less pronounced colur, according to the degree of final purification (for which each manufacture employs his own process). The absolutes are soluble in high-proof alcohol, and represent the most concentrated form of natural flower oils used in practical perfume work. However, they must not be confused with actual volatile flower oil in the scientific sense. The absolutes usually contain from 50 to 80 per cent of alcohol soluble waxes, and only 20 to 25 per cent volatile oil, which can be isolated from the absolute by steam distillation. However, these volatile oils from the absolutes are not offered on the market because of their excessively high price, and because they completely lack the high fixation value of an absolute, which is due to the presence of alcohol soluble natural waxes, etc., in the absolute.

PROCESS FLOWSHEET

Preparation of Jasmine and Lily flower oil.

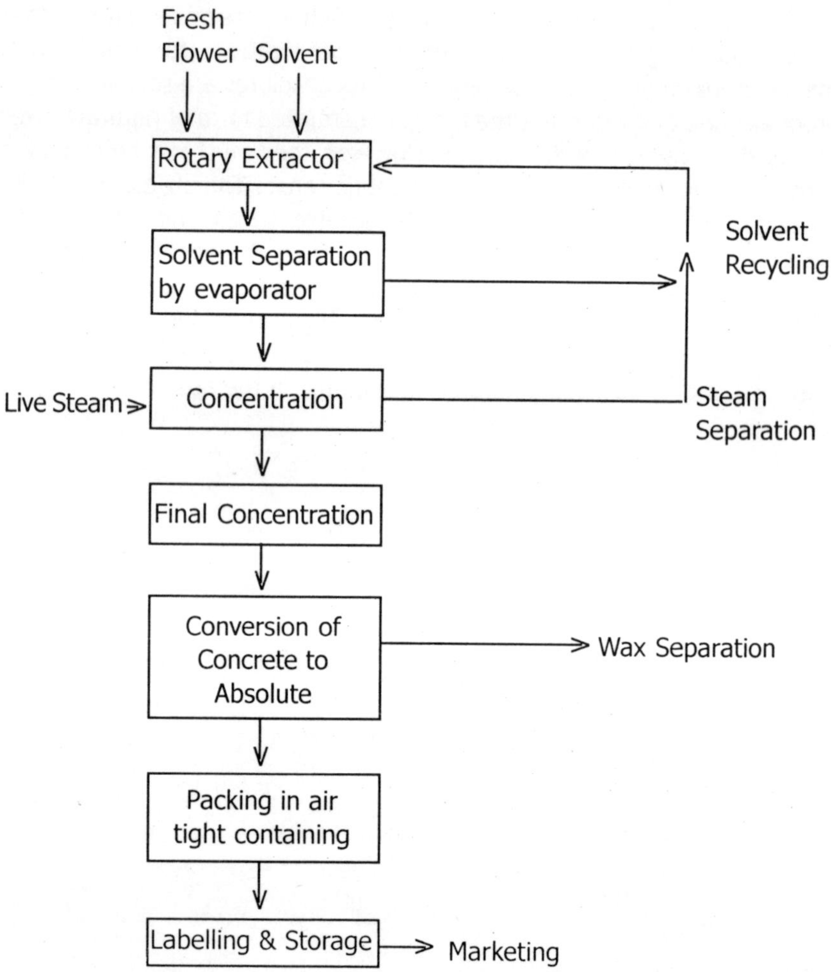

MANUFACTURING PROCESS

Various methods are employed for obtaining rose oil apart from distillation expression. Distillation with water or steam is most widely used method and gives satisfactory results with considerable variety of plant materials. Distillation as applied to the production of essential oils is a means of separating the essential oil from mass of plant material which is not volatile. Reduced to its simple form it consists of mixture of finely divided material with water fed into still which is then heated until the contents boil and the resultings vapour are led to a condenser where they are cooled and converted back into the liquid form. This liquid consists of water containing a small quantity of essential oils which forms a separate layer usually floating on the surface of water. This process is based on the fact that when two volatile liquids which are not mutually soluble are heated together the mixture will boil at a lower temperature than would either of the constituent liquids if heated above.

The individual compounds of essential oils differ considerable in volatility and their boiling points. Very generally within the range 150°c to 300°c. At these temperatures however such reactions as decomposition, oxidation resinification are greately accelerated and would lead to more or less deterioration in the odour and flavour of any essential oil heated to such temperatures. Distillation in the presence of water ensures that the oil will volatilise at a temperature a little below that of boiling water and the spoilage due to the above effects will be reduced to a negligible quantity. When the plant material is finally ground before distillation it may be assumed that practically all the essential oil has been set free from the enclosing tissues. On distillation the lowest boiling that is the most volatile constitutents will at first predominate in the distillate but as the distillation proceeds they will be volatilise by the higher boiling constitutents in order to volatility. In general, it is necessary to prolong the distillation sufficiently to obtain all constituents of the oil. If the time required for complete distillation is reduced, an oil of different composition will be obtained.

In some cases the high boiling constitutents may have little or no perfuming value and it is then advantageous to shorten the time of distillation thus obtaining an oil of higher quality and reducing the cost of labour and fuel.

THEORY OF DISTILLATION

As already specified rose oil consists of the mixtures of volatile solids and liquids which vary considerably in volatility and boiling point. Any susbstance evolves a vapour which exerts a definite pressure at a given temperatures in exactly the same way as the atmosphere does. This pressure is known as the vapour pressure -of the substance and varies with temperature. Vapour pressures are usually measured in mm of Hg. Different substances have different vapour pressure and different rate of variation of vapour pressure of a liquid is increased by heating until it equals the pressure of the atmosphere. The liquid boils if the atmospheric pressure is reduced it follows that the temperature at which the liquid boils will also be reduced.

Distillation can be used to separate two liquids of different vapour pressure.

DISTILLATION OF HOMOGENOUS LIQUIDS:

When the constitutents of a mixture of liquids are all soluble in each other they form a single homogenous liquid and its vapour is a mixture of the vapours of all the constitutents in the proportions in which they are present in the liquid. Its vapour pressure is therefore dependent on the composition of the liquid. An essential oil is a homogenous mixture of those type and in distillation the lower boiling constitutents distill off first, the boiling point gradually rising to that of the highest boiling constitutents. This type of distillation is used in the purification and fractionisation of essential oil and these operations are rarely carried out by the primary producer.

DISTILLATION OF HETROGENOUS LIQUIDS:

A hetrogenous liquid is a mixture of two liquids which are not soluble in each other and which therefore form separate layers when left undisturbed. In such a case each liquid continues to exert the same vapour pressure as it would if present above. The total vapour pressure of the mixture is therefore equal to the sum of the vapour pressure of the individual constitutents of the mixture (provided they do not react chemically) and is not affected by the actual or relative amounts of the constitutents present in the mixture. It follows from this rule that the boiling point of the mixture will be lower than that of any are constituent when heated above. It is for this reason that the boiling point of the mixture will be lower than that a single constituent.

The vapour contains all the constituents of the mixture in volumes proportional to their vapour pressure at the boiling temperatures. This temperature will rise a little as each volatile constituent is completely removed. But not until the whole of the essential oils has distilled over will it reach that of the means liquid left in the still overheating of the essential oil in this avoided.

METHOD OF DISTILLATION:

Most of the industrial stills employed today are directly fired and are of 1000 to 2000 litres capacity requiring no steam generator. They offer the advantage of low initial capital investment and simplicity of operation important features in the primitive valley of roses. The stills are made of copper or aluminium and are of cylinderical shape insulated with bricks or some other suitable material permits even distribution and retention of heat inside of retort. The still top is provided with man hole through which the flowers can be charged. A grid, a few inches above the bottom of the retort to prevents contact of the with the directly fired bottom. On the side, and level with the grid is another manhole through which the exhausted flowers and the residual water can be quickly discharged after the distillation is over. The still is also equipped with a pipe and valve beneath the grid which permits drawing off the residual water when the still is used for cohobation.

Generally the retorts are charged with flower upto about 10" below the still head. The quantity of roses charged depends upon their condition, fresh flower taking up much more space then those stored in the distillery for a few hours. Retorts of 1200 m to 1500 litres capacity -the most popular of the type are charged with 250 to 300 kg of rose petal and 1200 litres of water are added. The whole mass is stirred thoroughly.

Then the manhole in the still is closed and the fire started. After about 1.5 hour actual distillation starts this last another 1.5 hour. The entire operation thus requiring 3 hours.

At the begining great care must be excercised to keep the fire low, so that the actual distillation starts slowly. Otherwise the warm expanding air will blow through the condensers with great velocity carry along the most volatile material along with it. During the operation the inlet for the cooling water in the condensers must be regulated so that the condensate flows at a temperature of 35° to 40°c. At lower temperatures the oil which contain a good deal stearoptene will solidify in the condenser tubes and no oil will appear in the florentine flask (oil separator)

Distillation of the flowers after a slow start should proceed at a lively pace is completed when about 140 litres of water per 250 kg. of flower charged have distilled over. The very small quantity of greenish oil separating with oil separator is called the direct oil. This is drawn off with a pipette and poured in a glass bottle when the oil has been decanted the 140 litres of distillation water are pumped into a storage tank and bucked with first waters, freed from the separated oil of other operations. As soon as first water accumulated they are redistilled as explained below. The exhausted flavour together with the water in the retort are thrown away.

The yield of direct oil obtained by the distillation of flower is very low since much of the oil might have dissolved in the first water. To isolate the dissolved oil the first water has to be redistilled again. For this purpose 1200 litres are pumped into a retort of 1800 litres capacity and 140 litres are slowly and carefully distilled off for 2.5 hours. The water oil is drawn off with a pipette and added to the direct oil. Combined the above two will constitute the rose oil. The oil thus obtained is poured and kept in glass container in Sun light for several hours. This helps the impurities to precipitate and water to separate . The clear oil is then carefully decanted and filtered and stored in tinned copper containers. The oil thus obtained will consist of 25 % direct oil and 75 % water oil. The water in the retort left after this distillation of 140 litres of water is used as the water for first distillation.

1 Kg Rose oil is yielded from 4000 Kgs of pink rosa damascena (rose) flower.

PROCESS FLOW SHEET

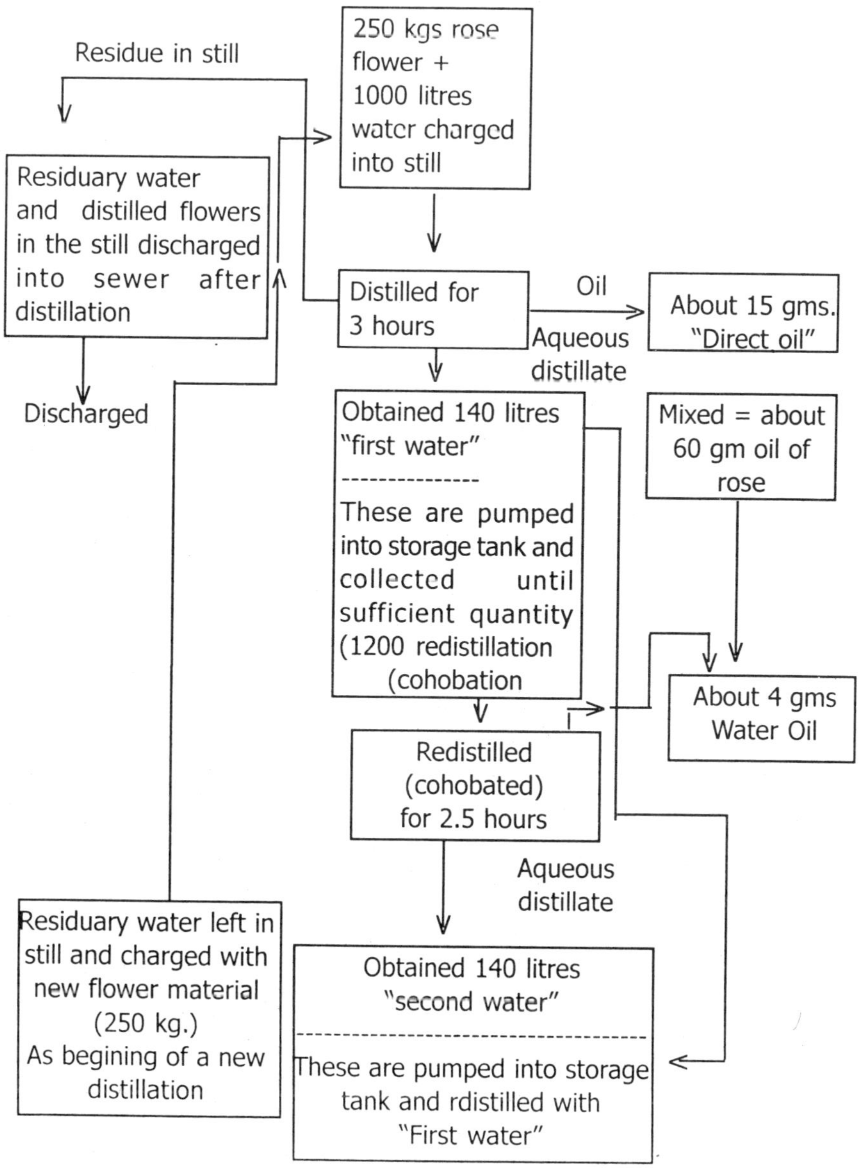

PLANT ECONOMICS OF JASMINE AND LILY FLOWER OIL

Rated Plant Capacity = 10.00 KGS/day

LAND & BUILDING

1.	Land Required 1000 Sqmts.	Rs.	2,00,000.00

PLANT & MACHINERY

1. Feeding Hopper with Bucket elevator
2. Rotary Extractor to extract flower oil,
3. S.S. Jacketed evaporation tank with vacuum system
4. Condenser
5. Vacuum still (SS) for final Concentration
6. Solvent Storage tank (SS)
7. Baby Boiler
8. Pipes, fittings, vacuum pumps, valves, motor
9. Solvent Recycling Unit.
10. Laboratory testing Equipments and Instruments

FIXED CAPITAL

1.	LAND & BUILDING	Rs.	9,30,000.00
2.	PLANT & MACHINERY	Rs.	6,50,000.00
3.	OTHER FIXED ASSETS	Rs.	1,55,000.00
	TOTAL	Rs.	17,35,000.00

RAW MATERIALS

1. Flower Fresh (Jasmine, Lily)
2. Solvent Petroleum ether
3. Glass bottles & Lablcs.
4. Carton made of Cardboard

TOTAL CAPITAL INVESTMENT

TOTAL FIXED CAPITAL	Rs.	17,35,000.00
TOTAL WORKING CAPITAL FOR 3 MONTHS	Rs.	43,16,062.50
TOTAL	Rs.	60,51,062.50

TURN OVER/ANNUM

By Sale of 3000 Kg. flower oil Rs. 2,40,00,000.00

BREAK EVEN POINT (B.E.P) = 29.80 %

PROFIT SALES RATIO = Profit / Sales x 100 = 21.60 %

RATE OF RETURN = Operating profit / T.C.I x 100 = 85.68 %

Chapter-26

JASMINE FLOWER OIL

MANUFACTURING PROCESS

There are two modern methods used for manufacturing of Jasmine & other flower oil which are delicate in nature which are thermally unstable and chiefly separated by either solvent extraction using volatile solvents. Another method used for extraction of flower oil is super critical fluid extraction method.

EXTRACTION WITH SOLVENT:-
CONSTRUCTION OF APPARATUS:-

Until some years ago the extractors and stills were constructed of copper, because this metal retains its value after rapping the apparatus, and the pliable copper can be hammered and retirs are easily made. Lately, however, the extractors are constructed are often of heavily tinned sheet iron which is much cheaper and, therefore offers the advantage flower investment and quicker amortization.

The apparatus must be of solid construction to stand wear and tear; all extractor pipes and valves should be within easy to save time and exclude mistakes on the part of the operators. Pipes and valves must be sufficiently wide to prevent formation of pressure by air and petroleum ether apors, one of the principal causes for loss of the solvent and solutions to and from the apparatus, and considerably speed up operation. Pumping of solvents and solutes is done by air pressure created by air compressors.

The extractors are mounted on elevated metal platforms along the inside walls of the building. The platform runs even with the ground outside of the building, so that arriving flower material may be charged directly into the extractors and the exhausted flowers discharged with equal ease.

Loss of solvent during the operation presents one of the most serious problems. These losses are usually caused by incomplete distillation of the solvent from the exhausted flowers, by insufficient condensation in the contensers, or by too narrow pipes and valves creating pressure and blowing off a mixture of air and solvent vapour. To avoid this as much as possible the whole system of extractors, evaporators and solvent tanks is arranged as a closed circle, with only one outlet where escaping solvent vapours can be condensed. The Societe Carbonisation et Charbons Actifs some years ago developed an efficient, rather small sized apparatus in which solvent vapors are absorbed by activated carbon and recovered by blowing live steam through the saturated carbon. A current of hot air then reactivates the carbon. The apparatus is simple and permits considerable economy in factories where large amounts of solvent are in circulation.

The latest model consists of a heavily tinned iron drum rotating around a horizontal axle. Four perforated metal partitions, rectangularly and horizontally arranged around the central axle, divide the interior into four compartments into which the flowers are charged through four manholes. While the whole system rotates slowly, the flower material moves, tumbles and disp into the solvent lying on the bottom of the extractor. The liquid seeps through the perforations and drips back to the bottom when one compartment is lifted out of the solvent in the continuous movement of the whole frum. Thus, the solvent does not fill the extractor but only the lowest part, the flowers dipping slowly and continuously into the solvent and rising again in the rotatory movement.

Three successive washings are usually made, carried out similarly to the systematic extraction method described under stationary apparatus. The first, i.e., the most saturated washing, is then pumped into the evaporator and concentrated by distilling of the solvent. After the third washing has been drawn off the exhausted flower material, live steam is blown into the extractor to distill over and recover the petroleum ether still adhering to the extracted flowers.

The advantages of the rotatory extractors as compared with stationary apparatus are evident. Through the movement of the flower material in the solvent, its action becomes more penetrating and more effective, resulting in a somewhat higher yield. Figured as concrete, it is about 8 per cent higher in the case of the rotatory apparatus. Since the solvent covers only the bottom drum and not the whole flower material, as in the stationry apparatus, much less solvent is in circulation and , therefore, evaporation losses are reduced. Only 160 to 170 liters are required in the rotatory apparatus to extract 100 kg. of flowers. The loss of solvent for 100 kg. of flowers is less than in stationary extractors ; it may be 8 to 12 liters but can be reduced by using the previously described solvent recovery apparatus.

One rotatory extractor does the work of three or four stationary extractors arranged in one battery. Although superior in many ways the rotatory extractors suffer from several disadvantages and cannot altogether replace the stationary type; for example, the latter is better adapted to voluminous plant material, such as lavender, which cannot be so easily charged and discharged through the manholes of the rotating drum.

Concentration of Solutions:- The first, i.e., the most concentrated, washing is filtered through a fine screen and pumped into the so-called evaporator in which the greater part of the solvent is driven (distilled) off. These evaporators are of varying construction, representing basically a modified water or steam bath. In other words, the heating is done by indirect steam blown into a steam jacket beneath the still. The solvent, however, should not be completely driven off in this operation. Most manufacturers stop operation when the temperature in the still (evaporator) reaches about 60°, because any higher temperature at atmospheric pressure would be harmful to the delicate flower perfume. The first washing contains, of course, only a small percentage of flower oil. Therefore, concentrating of this washing in the evaporator means driving off 90-95 per cent of the solvent. (The recovered solvent serves as fresh solvent for a third washing) The concentrated solution remaining in the evaporators is permitted to cool, is filtered, then transferred into a special, smaller vacuum still, and there completely concentrated in vacuo.

Final Concentration. ___ Vacuum stills of small capacity (50 to 100 liters) serve for this purpose. The final concentration represents a most delicate operation and requires much experience and constant attention on the part of the operator. The concentrating has to be done at as low a temperature as possible, yet any trace of solvent must be eliminated. Every manufacturer has his own, often secret, methods of purification. The completely concentrated and purified products represent the so-called floral concretes, which contain the odoriferous principles of the natural flower perfume, plus a considerable amount of plant waxes, albuminous material and color pigments. The concretes are, therefore, usually of solid consistency and only partly soluble in 95 per cent alcohol.

Concrete Flower Oils:- Although these insoluble concretes are more difficult to work with, some perfumers prefer them to the alcohol soluble absolutes, which are obtained by precipitating and eliminating the insoluble waxes with strong alcohol, and concentrating the filtered alcoholic solutions. Distilling off the alcohol from the solutions when making these absolutes undoubtedly entails the loss of some of the most volatile and délicate constituents of the natural flower oil. It is often claimed that an alcoholic washing of a concrete is superior and more true to nature than a simple alcoholic solution of the ecorresponding absolute. On the other hand, the processing of concretes requires special equipment and considerable tiem; therefore, the absolutes represent a more convenient form of flower oils than the concretes.

Conversion of Concretes into Absolutes:- The alcohol soluble absolutes are prepared from the concretes by the following general method:

The concrete is either thoroughly rubbed down in a large mortar with a quantity of high-proof alcohol or, as some manufacturers prefer, melted and dissolved in warm alcohol. Subsequently eight to ten times the amount of alcohol is added and the mass stirred for a prolonged period in batteuses, as described under enfleurage. Usually five to six washings of the concrete are made in a systematic way, i.e., a third washing serves as a second one for a following batch of concrete; the second is used as first for a batch of new concrete, the first washing consequently representing the most concentrated solution. After standing and drawing offf the clear solution from the alcohol insoluble waxes, the first washing is then thoroughly cooled in a refrigerator or in a special room, at temperatures ranging from -20° to -25°, when more wax precipitates and is filtered off in the cold. This resulting clear solution ca be used as such in alcoholic perfumes.

Most perfume houses have neither the time nor the facilities to carry out their own washing of concretes, and prefer using alcohol soluble floral oils. For those, the manufacturers in Grasse offer the so-called liquid absolutes as the most concentrated form of natural flower oils. These liquid absolutes of extraction are obtained by carefully concentrating the first alcoholic washing of the corresponding concrete at low temperature in a good vacuum still. This process of concentrating involves a loss of several liters of alcohol per kilogram of absolute.

The absolutes are usually viscous oils with a more or less pronounced color, according to the degree of final purification (for which each manufacture employs his own process). The absolutes are soluble in high-proof alcohol, and represent the most concentrated form of natural flower oils used in practical perfume work. However, they must not be confused with actual volatile flower oil in the scientific sense. The absolutes usually contain from 50 to 80 per cent of alcohol soluble waxes, and only 20 to 25 per cent volatile oil, which can be isolated from the absolute by steam distillation. However, these volatile oils from the absolutes are not offered on the market because of their excessively high price, and because they completely lack the high fixation value of an absolute, which is due to the presence of alcohol soluble natural waxes, etc., in the absolute.

PLANT ECONOMICS OF JASMINE FLOWER OIL

Rated Plant Capacity = 10.00 KGS/Day

LAND & BUILDING

Land required 1000 sq. mts. Rs. 4,00,000.00

PLANT & MACHINERY

1. Feeding Hopper with Bucket elevator
2. Rotary Extractor to extract, Jasmine flower oil,
3. S.S. Jacketed evaporation tank with vacuum system.
4. Condenser

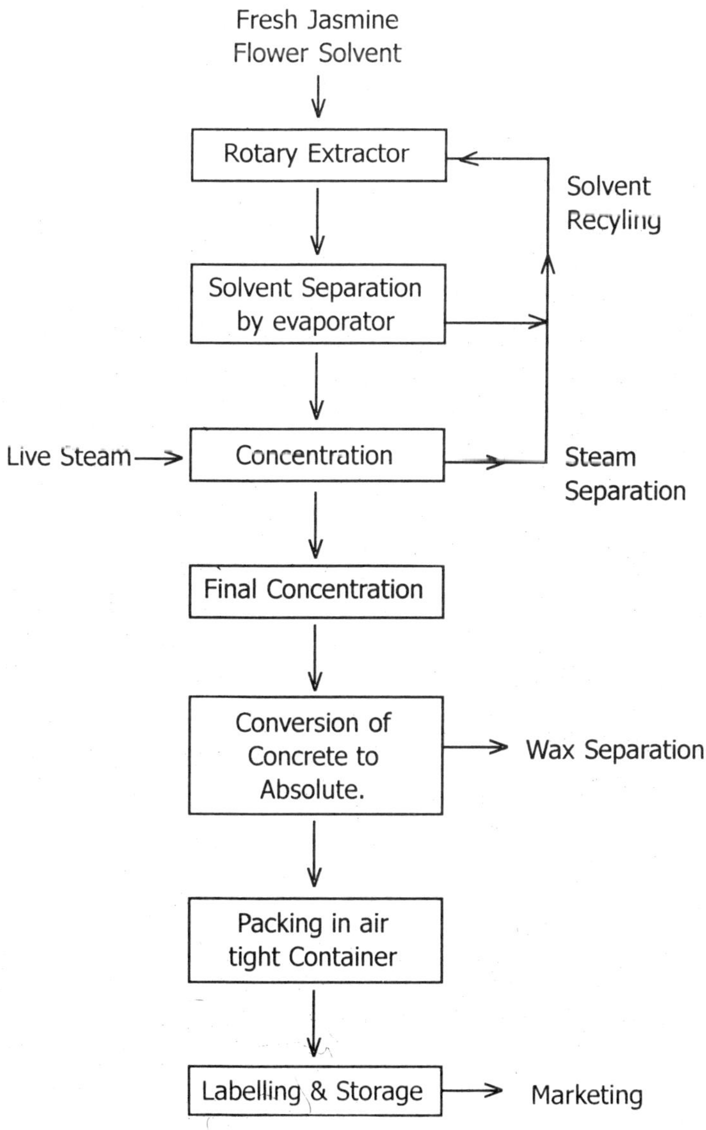

Fresh Jasmine
Flower Solvent
Rotary Extractor
Solvent
Recyling
Solvent Separation
by evaporator
Live Steam
Concentration
Steam
Separation
Final Concentration
Conversion of
Concrete to
Absolute.
Wax Separation
Packing in air
tight Container
Labelling & Storage
Marketing

5. Vacuum still (SS) for final concentration
6. Solvent Storage Tank (SS)
7. Baby Boiler,
8. Pipes, fittings, vacuum pumps, valves, motor
9. Solvent Recycing Unit.
10. Laboratory testing equipments and instruments

FIXED CAPITAL

1. LAND & BUILDING		Rs.	15,00,000.00
2. PLANT & MACHINERY		Rs.	13,45,000.00
3. OTHER FIXED ASSETS		Rs.	2,65,000.00
	TOTAL	Rs.	31,10,000.00

RAW MATERIALS

1. Flower fresh (Jasmine),
2. Solvent petroleum ether
3. Glass bottles & lables
4. Carton made of cardboard

TOTAL CAPITAL INVESTMENT

TOTAL FIXED CAPITAL		Rs.	31,10,000.00
TOTAL WORKING CAPITAL FOR 3 MONTHS		Rs.	58,11,300.00
	TOTAL	Rs.	89,21,300.00

TURN OVER/ANNUM

By sale of 3000 Kg. Jasmine flower oil Rs. 3,00,00,000.00

PROFIT SALES RATIO = Profit / Sales x 100 = 15.47 %

RATE OF RETURN = Operating profit / T.C.I x 100 = 52.03 %

BREAK EVEN POINT (B.E.P) = 40.04 %

Chapter-27

Production Technology Of Jasmine For Essential Oil

The delightful fragrant essential oil of Jasminum grandiflorum is appreciated all over the world. It is an export oriented agro industry in Morocco, France, Egypt, Tunisia, Italy, Sicily, Algeria, India and China. In India there are 16 jasmine essential oil agro industry units located in Tamilnadu, Karnataka and to some extent in Andhra Pradesh & Maharastra. Looking up its significant commercial importance, Indian Institute of Horticultural Research, Bangalore has developed its production technology. It is presented here.

Jasmine may be grown in wide range of soils, but the land must be well drained. Duraction of flowering is longer and yield is higher in sunny warm humid weather of Southern India. Flower picking needs many labourers, hence availability of cheap labour is an important consideration taking up its plantation.

Commercial varieties of Jaji are CO-I Pitchi and Arka Surabhi. Arka Surabhi is a superior strain having 0.35 percent concrete with a potential yield of 35 kg concrete / ha in Karnataka.

Planting material is raised in mist chamber from shoot tip cutting treated with 4000 ppm IBA. Recently a low cost and water saving method i.e. Closed Media Sachet Technique has been devised by the Laboratory of aromatic crops, IIHR, Bangalore, which eliminate need of power operated mist chamber. It saves large amount of water.

A month before planting, pits measuring 45cm x 45 cm x 45 cm should be dug at spacing of 2m x 1.8m. The pits should be filled-up with

2:1 mixture of soil and Farm Yard Manure. Planting is done in the beginning of monsoon. With proper management the plantation remain productive for above 12 years.

For good yield irrigation is required once in 10 to 20 days depending upon season. However the crop has remarkable quality of drought resistance. An experiment at Indian Institute of Horticultural Research, Bangalore, revealed that despite elimination of irrigation for as long as three years, the plants remained healthy. Ofcourse yield was less by about 50 percent.

Regarding nutritional requirement, the recommendation per grown up bush is 100 gm N, 150 gm 2 P_2O_5 and 100 gm K_2 O in 3 slipt doses. Research on use of growth regulations doses. Research on use of growth regulators have indicated that CCC and B-Nine (1000 ppm) induce early flowering and extend blooming period.

Pruning is necessary to get high yields and to keep the bushes to manageable size. It should be done during mid December. Nine to eleven well spread branches should be retained and pruned at 90 cm height. Chemical defoliants such as penta chlorophenol 3000 ppm, potassium iodide 4000 ppm also have been reported to be effective alternatives.

Flower yield/ha from Jaji (Var. Arka Surabhi) is about 500 kg in 1st year, about 5000 kg in 2nd year and 10 tonnes from 3rd year. For extraction purpose flowers are harvested before sunrise. Therefore, proper light should be provided in the field. Instead of flowers, fully matured buds may be harvested and spread up in specially made trays. The buds bloom by 8 pm and then extracted.

EXTRACTION OF JASMINE CONCRETE AND ITS ECONOMIC PROSPECT

Solvent extraction method is most common. Flowers are placed in extractor and dipped in the food grade hexane. The extractor is operated first for 30 minutes, second and third time for 20 minutes. The solvent is drained each time. The first miscella is distilled directly while second and third miscella are combined and used for the extraction of the next batch of flowers. The solvent is removed by distillation and reused. To remove the last traces of solvent, the concentrator is finally connected with a vacuum pump.

The residue left after the removal of solvent is known as 'concrete'. It has semisolid consistency with yellowish brown colour and fragrance of fresh jasmine flowers. It may be stored at 10 to 15^{0}C for over one year. Price of Jasmine concrete ranges from Rs. 14,000/- to Rs. 18,000/- per kg. For use in perfume industry, the concrete is further processed by treating with pure alchohol at 0^{0}C. Final product is called "Absolute". It is viscous, clear, yellow-brown liquid, soluble in 95 percent alcohol. Price of Jasmine absolute is more than double of concrete. It indicate bright economic prospect of this agro industry.

Besides Jaji Jasmine, now a days Jasminum sambac and Jasminum auriculatum flowers are also used to produce essential oil. Hence research work is also underway on these species.

For further details contact :
Director
INDIAN INSTITUTE OF HORTICULTURAL RESEARCH
Hessaraghatta, Banglore - 560 089.
India

Chapter-28

LEMON GRASS OIL

MANUFACTURING PROCESS

Though steam distillation has been considered as an heat treatment for extracting some thing but still lemongrass oil is extracted from steam distillation. At present three methods of distillation are practiced. They are water distillation, water and steam distillation and live steam distillation. Water and steam distillation is the oldest method of separating oil from lemongrass. This process is simple in which the plant material is placed into the still water added and the used is fire heated. Water and oil distill together. They are condensed in a simple condenser. The oil takes top layer. The process of water distillation has the disadvantage of explosing the delicate essential oil to a prolonged distillation in the presence of water, which results in the unnecessary hydrolysis of esters.

The distillation method of water and steam type is better than the one described. Here the still is fitted with a horizontal perforated plate upon which the lemon grass reacts. The lower part of the still is fitted with water to a level somewhat below the grid and the charge is subjected to distillation by passing low pressure steam. The avoids direct contact of plant materials with the distillation water below. This method provides lower yield.

Now the modern method is steam distillation. This method is suggested for the preparation of lemon grass oil.

Here lemongrass harvested is chopped into sizes of 1/4". It is now charged into the digesting vessel. Live steam at a pressure 40 to 100 psig from the boiler units,is directly injected through steam coils below the charge. The pressure within the digester is controlled. Due to the pressure and the heating lemon grass oil distills out. The distillate containing lemon grass oil and steam are withdrawn through a pipe, copper or aluminium and is condensed.

The condensing system consists of a simple copper or aluminium spiral tube immersed in cold water. The spiral tube is connected to the tapering end of the Digestor (top) and the other end of the tube projects with the receiver which is a copper or aluminium vessel. In the receiving vessel lemon grass oil takes the top layer and water the lower layer.

On one side of the receiver just above the bottom there is a bent tube which allows only the water of the lower layer to flow out.

The upper layer i.e. the oil is now decanted into the drying unit where anhydrous sodium sulphate is added to the oil and mixed. The mixture is now filtered in a small filter. The anhydrous sodium sulphate is added for dehydration of the oil i.e. for removing the moisture from oil.

The dehydrated oil is filled in cans or drums and sealed airtight. The oil should not be exposed to light frequently and kept in a dark and cool place. Coloured glass, stainless steel or aluminium are preferred to copper containers for storage.

PROCESS FLOW DIAGRAM

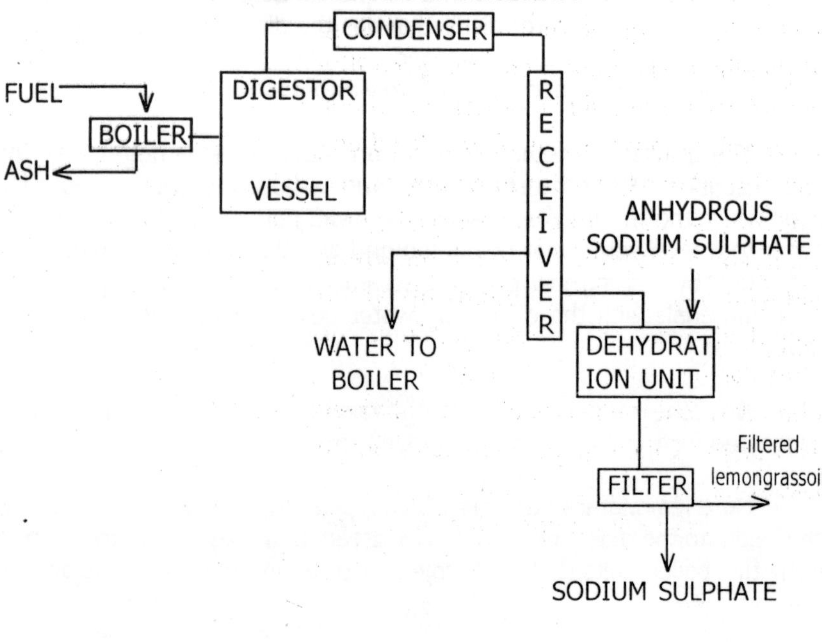

RAW MATERIAL POSITION

The raw material is lemon grass. It is grown in Tirunelveli in Tamil Nadu and in Kerala state. The main lemon grass growing areas in the latter states are Thioderphazha, Muvatupuzha,Meenachil and kumathanad Trichur District in Central Kerala and Kozhikode, Tellichery, Morvantwadi, Nilambut, sranad, peravoor etc. in North Kerala. Besides, the grass is grown in sourthern districts of kottayam, Trivandrum in Kerala state, Kanyakumari and Nilagiris in Tamil Nadu state and coorg and south kerala in Mysore state.

There are two types of lemon grass in Kerala differing in appearance and readily distinguishable by the colour of the stem. The so called red grass leaves yields the normal East Indian Lemon grass oil containing 75% or more of aldehydes (chiefly citral). The bulk of Indian lemon grass oil is produced from the red grass.

The ochar variety, the white grass, is produced in small quantities. The oil derived from the plant has a low aldehyde content. The area under lemon grass cultivation was estimated to be 69000 acres in 1956 out of which 66000 acres are in kerala state, 1000 acres in Tamil Nadu and 2000 acres in Mysore state.

The other chemicals needed for production of lemon grass oil is anhydrous sodium sulphate. It is indigeniously available in abundance.

MANUFACTURERS OF LEMON GRASS OIL

1. M/s Wynad Essential Oils India Ltd. Bangalore

2. M/s. Mysore Government Sandal Oil Factory,

Mysore other units are in small scale.

PLANT ECONOMICS OF LEMON GRASS OIL

Rated Plant Capacity = 4.00 KGS/Day

LAND & BUILDING

1. Land required 200 sq.mt.	Rs.	30,000.00

PLANT & MACHINERY

1. Boiler
2. Digesting vessel, condenser, receiving vessel, condensing vessel, dehydration vessel .
3. Small filter

FIXED CAPITAL

1. LAND & BUILDING	Rs.	1,40,000.00
2. PLANT & MACHINERY	Rs.	1,65,000.00
3. OTHER FIXED ASSETS	Rs.	20,000.00
TOTAL	Rs.	3,25,000.00

RAW MATERIALS

1. Flenuosus grass
2. Anhydrous sodium sulphate

TOTAL CAPITAL INVESTMENT

TOTAL FIXED CAPITAL	Rs.	3,25,000.00
TOTAL WORKING CAPITAL	Rs.	71,940.00
TOTAL	Rs.	3,96,940.00

TURN OVER/ANNUM

By the sale of 1200 kgs Lemon Grass Oil	Rs.	6,12,000.00

PROFIT SALES RATIO = Profit / Sales x 100 = 30.64 %

RATE OF RETURN = Operating profit / T.C.I x 100 = 47.24 %

BREAK EVEN POINT (B.E.P) = 52.64 %

Chapter-29

MENTHA OIL

MANUFACTURING PROCESS

Put pudina herbs on dry basis in distillation plants. Added to it around double amount of of water in the distillation plant, heat the distillation plant at 100°C initial 2 hours. Then cool down and heat the contents to 80-95°C about six hours.

At this time mentha oil will be distilled away through the jacket, on cooling of the mentha vapour to produce piperment oil and collect in the receiver. Then oil and woder mixture will be cooled down and after leaving for some hours it will be separated into two layers. Mentha oil can be separated and packed in plastic bottles or cans.

STEAM DISTILLATION:

Steam or hydrodistillation is the prefered method for producing essential oil, employing either water, met steam or dry steam.

In wet steam distillation the ground otanical herbs is placed on a grid in the still. There may be water below the grid in the still. There may be water below the grid or it may accumulate during process. Steam is introduced from oiler ito the still. Initially sufficient water condenses in the cool charge to wet it slightly. External heat may be applied to limit the buildup of water and wetting of the charge steam distillation is a reasonaby raid method and can be used for most oils with the exceptions.

In dry dream distillation, the ground botanical herbs is placed on a grid in the still. Direct steam is applied and outside heat suppied by a steam acket, is maintained at a temperature sufficient to prevent any water condensation.

But in case of Mentha oil the wet steam distillation is passed through the semidried mentha arvensis present in the distillation still.

PROCESS FLOW SHEET

```
(MASI)
Pudina                          Distillation                         Mentha
herbs ---------------------->   Vessel  ---------------------->      Oil   +
           steared it

                                                            Spent Hay
                                                            (By Products)
```

MENTHOL BOLD CRYSTALS

MANUFACTURING PROCESS:-

Menthol crystals are manufactured from mint oil by refining crystallization and centrifuging.

Mint oil is obtained by steam distillation of mentha leaves in a distillation still the vapours. A mixture of water and mint oil is condensed oil separated to get crude mint oil.

Crude mint oil is refined by vacuum filtration and then chilled in refrigerated chambers to temperatures ranging from 15 to 30°C. Where menthol crystallizes out. The mint oil is kept in the refrigation unit for 90-120 hr., The chilled pieces are taken out and chipped into smaller bits by knives and rilled in a synthetic fibre bag and put into the centrifuge.

The liquid percolates the rembrance during centrifuging and is drained off the centrifuge and the crystals are taken out from the bag and are sent for packing.

The liquor from the centrifuge is recycled to the chilling unit and the same process is repeated three times. Average yields of 15-20% are obtained by the first chilling. The second and third chillings yield 10 to 14% and 5 to 10% respectively depending upon the quality of the mint oil initially used.

Since chilling takes time and the operation is required a number of times, the refrigeration unit must be big enough to provide space for an adequate amount of oil required for an uninterrupted operation of the plant. The average yield of 30-40% depending upon the quality of the mint is obtained by repeated chilling in varying temperatures and centrifuging. The agent oil commonly known as dementholised oil has approximately the following composition.

Free menthol	30-35%
Methyl auatate	30-32%
Menthones	15%
Terpenese	18-25%

The dementholised thus obtained is subjected to chemical treatment for extracting the menthol further. This is accomplished by saponification with sodium hydroxide and subsequent esterification by boric acid. The white crystalline borate esters are formed which are separated and decomposed by steam after washing. A mixture of various isoness of menthol separates out by decomposition with steam. The menthol is recovered by subsequent chilling and centrifuging.

The residual oil is subjected to fractional distillation under reduced pressure in a fractionating column packed with rasching rings. The menthol recovered by distillation is rouged to refrigeration unit for chilling and subsequent centrifuging .

The residual oil after fractionating contains some amount of menthol, but it is not economical to is late it further. However this oil has a food resolve value and is easily marketed.

An additional yield of 10-20% of menthol can be obtained by this additional processing. Thus the total yield of the process ranges between 40-55%. The final yield is basically dependent upon the quality of the peper mint oil used.

Bold crystals can either be made from small crystals or by doing minor changes in manufacturing process. For making bold crystal from ordinary crystals, the hopes are melted in a vessel and required amount of mint oil is added and stirred well. The liquid is cooled in a pan and crushed to desired size.

Bold crystals can also be manufactured by making minor adjustments in manufacturing process. The menthone contained in peppermint oil can be catalytically hydrogenated to menthol, there by enriching the oil with menthol. Regardly the process also out 30 C C of oil were hydrogenated for five hours at water bath temperature with hydrogen with a velocity of 8 to 10 litre per hour and with 2-3% of nickel oxide as catalyst.

After hydrogenation, the oil is cooled under the same conditions as given before during freezing. It is very important to rate that gradual and slow cooling permits the formation of larger and more regular crystals. The freezing plant proper consists of three tanks cooled with bromine solution or of numerous cells, such as used for malcing of ice blocks commersed into three tanks and which cold bromine solution of different temp. circulates.

FLOW SHEET DIAGRAM

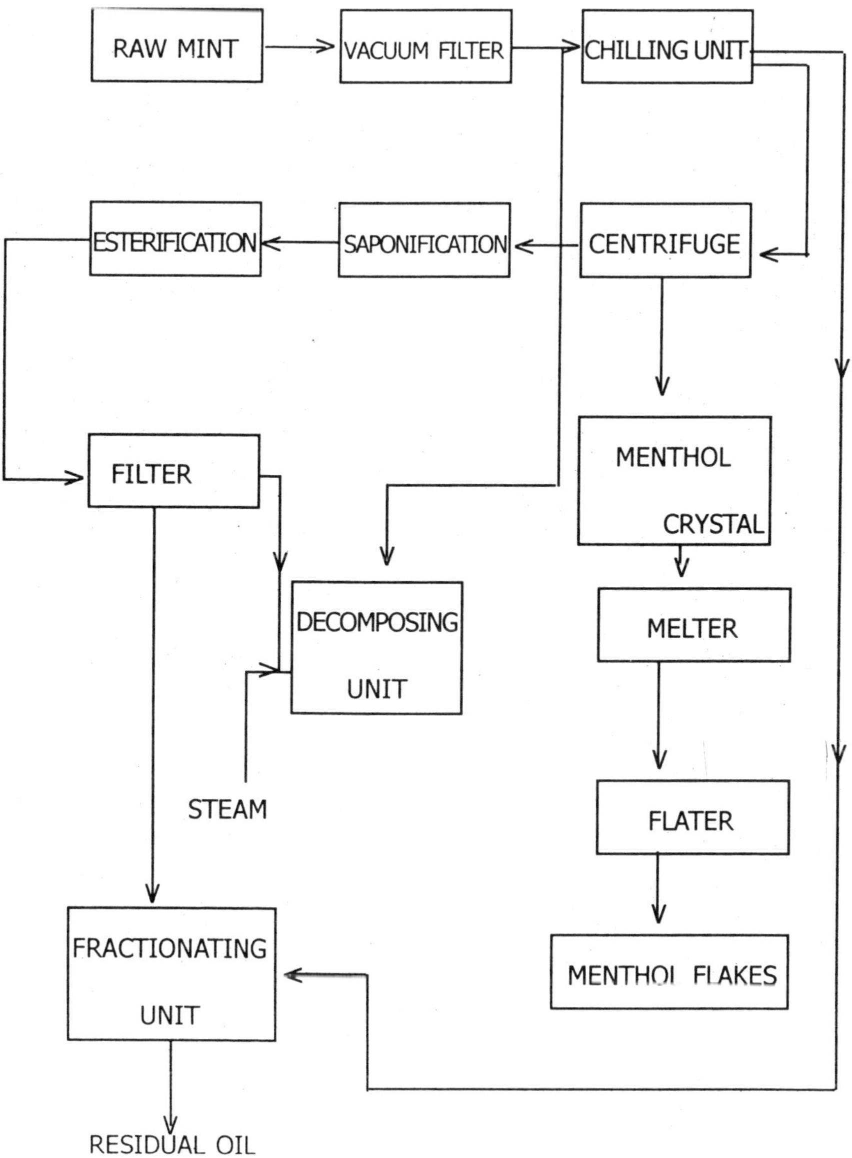

PLANT ECONOMICS OF MENTHOL CRYSTALS

Rated Plant Capacity = 70.00 Kgs/Day (Average)

LAND & BUILDING

1. Total area required 14.8 X 30 METER	Rs.	1,99,800.00

PLANT & MACHINERY

1. Mixing tank (SS)
2. Jacketted Vessel (closed top-SS)
3. Distillation (Fraction column)
4. S.S. tank with S.S. filter to separate out crystals.
5. Motor
6. Brine solution tank (PVC)
7. Water chiller
8. Manual packaging machine

FIXED CAPITAL

1. LAND & BUILDING	Rs.	7,37,300.00
2. PLANT & MACHINERY	Rs.	3,00,000.00
3. OTHER FIXED ASSETS	Rs.	29,500.00
TOTAL	Rs.	10,66,800.00

RAW MATERIALS

1. Mentha oil (Crude)
2. Chemicals, Caustic soda, Boric acid salts
3. Polyethene packets

TURN OVER/ANNUM

1. By sale of Menthol Crystal
2. Dementholied oil

TOTAL Rs. 1,48,80,000.00

PROFIT SALES RATIO = Profit / Sales x 100 = 8.51 %
RATE OF RETURN = Operating profit / T.C.I x 100 = 58.86 %
BREAK EVEN POINT (B.E.P) = 35.57 %

Chapter-30

PAN MASALA (GUTKHA)

MANUFACTURING PROCESS WITH FORMULATIONS

GENERAL FORMULA FOR PAN MASALA

1.	Sandal Wood	26.00%
2.	Kapur Kachri	10.00%
3.	Cloves	1.20%
4.	Cinnamon	5.80%
5.	Dried Rose petals	11.80%
6.	Liquorice powder	25.60%
7.	Cardamom minor	3.50%
8.	Mace	2.40%
9.	Sugar	11.73%
10.	Saffron genuine	0.25%
11.	Peppermint	0.50%
12.	Attar Rose	0.50%
13.	Attar Panri	0.58%
14.	Attar Koda	0.50%
15.	Saccharine	0.08%
16.	Musk Perfumes	0.25%

SAADA (PLAIN) PAN MASALA

Formula : As per 100 parts

Katha	50 parts by weight
Lime12 parts by weight	
Betal Nuts25 parts by weight	
Cardomom minor	2 parts by weight
Cardamom major 3 parts by weight	
PIppermint	1 parts by weight
Sandalwood oil	5 parts by weight
Saffron genuine	0.25 parts by weight
Attar Rose0.25 parts by weight	
Atter Panri	0.25 parts by weight
Atter Keoda	0.25 parts by weight
Saccharine	0.50 parts by weight
Musk perfumes	0.50 parts by weight

MEETHA (SWEET) PAN MASALA

Sandalwood flour	1,000 parts
Rose Patels, dried	500 parts
Cinnamon	200 parts
Kapur Kachri	500 parts
Liquorice (Powdered)	1,000 parts
Sugar	500 parts
Cloves	100 parts
Seeds of cardamom (minor)	100 parts
Pippermint	20 parts
Saccharine	1 part
Perfume	10 parts

PERFUME FOR PAN MASALA (SWEET)

1.	Attar Rose	20 parts
2.	Attar Panri	20 parts
3.	Attar Keoda	30 parts
4.	Musk Perfume	10 parts

PAN MASALA (ZARDA)

FORMULA

It consist of three sections

1.	Tobacco Leaves	70 parts
	Catechu (black variety)	4 parts
	Lime	4 parts
	Black pepper	4 parts
	Taj	2 parts
2.	Cloves	10 parts
	Cardamom (Major)	15 parts
	Cardamom (Minor)	10 parts
	Mace	10 parts
	Cinnamom	15 parts
	Nagar Motha	10 parts
	Tejpat	5 parts
	Sugandhbala	10 parts
	Charils	5 parts
	White sandal wood (Powdered)	10 parts
3.	Attar Rose	30 parts
	Attar Henna	30 parts
	Attar Kewada	30 parts
	Rooh Panri	10 parts
	Attar Motia	4 parts

It is crushed and pulverized in dried form. The powder should pass through 50 microns or like so.

2. LIME

The quick lime available from the market is in the form of lumps. It is first slaked with water to form hydrated or slacked lime. Care should be taken while adding the water as excess of water will make the lime in paste form. Otherwise a powdered lime will be added as requirement. To make a fine powder it may be further ground and pulverised.

3. BETAL NUTS

The betal nuts are first crushed or cut into small pieces. It is wetted in water in a tank over night so that the piece become quite soft.

4. CARDAMOM

Cardamom is peeled off its shell and the seeds are taken out. These seeds are then grounded and pulverised into a fine mesh size.

5. ATTAR & PERFUMES

Attar & perfumes are then mixed and blended well before adding to the main mixture.

PROCESS - (PLAIN & SWEET PAN MASALA)

Pulverise the solid or dry ingredients to convert them into fine powder, then sieve through a fine mesh sieve.

Now, in a stone mortar put the liquid ingredients, add perfume and work with pestle to form a uniform liquid. Add this liquid mixture, to the powder of dry and solid ingredients and rub well until they are mixed well. Pan masala in powder form is now ready to pack into pouches.

ZARDA PAN MASALA

Zarda making process is completed in four different steps, which are.

i. Tobacco leaves are dried in the sun & chipped which arc dyed with various harmless food colours & granuled as discussed later.

ii. A thick extract which is technically called "Kimam" is prepared of tobacco leaves

iii. Powdered spices and tobacco extract is coated on the granule. This process is called 'spice coating'.

iv. Incorporation of perfumes. The details of the above four steps is given below :-

a. Making granules and their dying. It is the first step to make zarda. For this purpose a good formula is given earlier.

Spread the tobacco leaves on a cemented or smooth & clean floor in the sun light and let them dry. These dried leaves broken up into small pieces by pressing them in hands. All the leaves are broken by hands. Then these broken leaves are shifted through 150 mesh sieve to separate fine dust.

Breaking the tobacco leaves and sieving is done continuously till the midribs and large veins of leaves are left. These are separated by sorting and used in making Kimam. By this method tobacco leaves are reduced to almost uniform sized small granules (chura).

Black pepper and 'Taj' are reduced to a fine powder. Catechu is dissolved in some water, boiled for a few minutes and strained through fine cloth. Lime is also dissolved in some water and some strained when cold. Now black pepper, 'Taj' catachu extract & lime water are dissolved in about 20 litre of water and again strained through fine cloth.

This blackish water is sprinkled over tobacco 'chura' and rubbed between hands till all the water is consumed and the 'chura' gets a blackish tint. Now whole of the chura is made into a heep and left undisturbed overnight. It should be kept covered with a thick cloth or gunny bag. The next morning, this coloured 'chura' is spread on the flour in the sunlight to dry.

B. PREPARING TOBACCO EXTRACT

Take tobacco dust, veins and mid-ribs, cigarette cuttings from cigarette fineness and leaves and soak in water. Keep for 3-4 days, stirring occasionally within this time all the nicotine of tobacco will be dissolved in water, which will become of brownish colour. This water is now strained through a fine cloth and powdered gum acacia and sugar is mixed in it. This extract is now bailed over at a mild temperature till its consistency becomes as that of honey and of blackish brownish colour.

c. Coating colour and dried chura with spices

For coating the coloured and dried chura with spices, an extract of selected spices is used. The composition is given earlier. Pulverised all the above ingredient to a very fine powder and dissolve in water. Now add gum acacia and already prepared 'thick tobacco extract'. Mix thoroughly. Coating solution is ready. It is sprinkled over the coloured and dried chura then rubbed within both hands till all the solution is consumed. Now cover it with a cloth for 4 to 5 hours. Then again dried in the sunlight and rubbed over seive, so that granules are made. These granules should be of the size of mustard seeds.

D. ADDITION OF PERFUME

The last step is to add the perfume. The composition of perfume is given earlier. Above prepared Zarda granules are spread in the sunlight to warm them a bit. When these granules have become somewhat, sprinkle the perfume mixture over them & rub the granules in both hands so that perfume is thoroughly and evenly distributed. The whole preparation is immediately put into an airtight pouches and packed.

The information subscribed on the packing is as below :-

1. Name & place of manufacture
2. Trade name of product, if any.
3. Net contents, when packed
4. Date and batch no. of production
5. Price excluding local taxes.
6. I.S.I. Mark, if any
7. Speciality of the product, if any

POUCH FILLING

In the pouch filling machine where it is filled with pan masala according to the capacity. Finally it is pressed and packed.

In India, now we have multi-coloured printed laminates and stand up pouches available with complete system for automatic and semi automatic filling of the same.

The different synthetic films and combination for the manufacture of pouches are :-

1. 200 gauge high density polyethylene (HDPE).
2. Laminate of 12 micron metallised polyester/150 gauge low density polyethylene (LDPE)
3. Laminate of 60 gms maplitho paper/0.04 mm foil /150 gauge low density polyethylene.
4. 250 gauge polypropylene (PP)
5. 250 gauge polypropylene and further sealed in a pouch made from a

laminate of 12 micron metalised polyester/150 gauge low density polyethylene.

6. Laminate of 12 micron polyester/0/012 mm Aluminium foil/40 micron high molecular weight high density polyethylene (HMHDPE).

PROCESS FLOW DIAGRAM FOR MANUFACTURING OF PAN MASALA

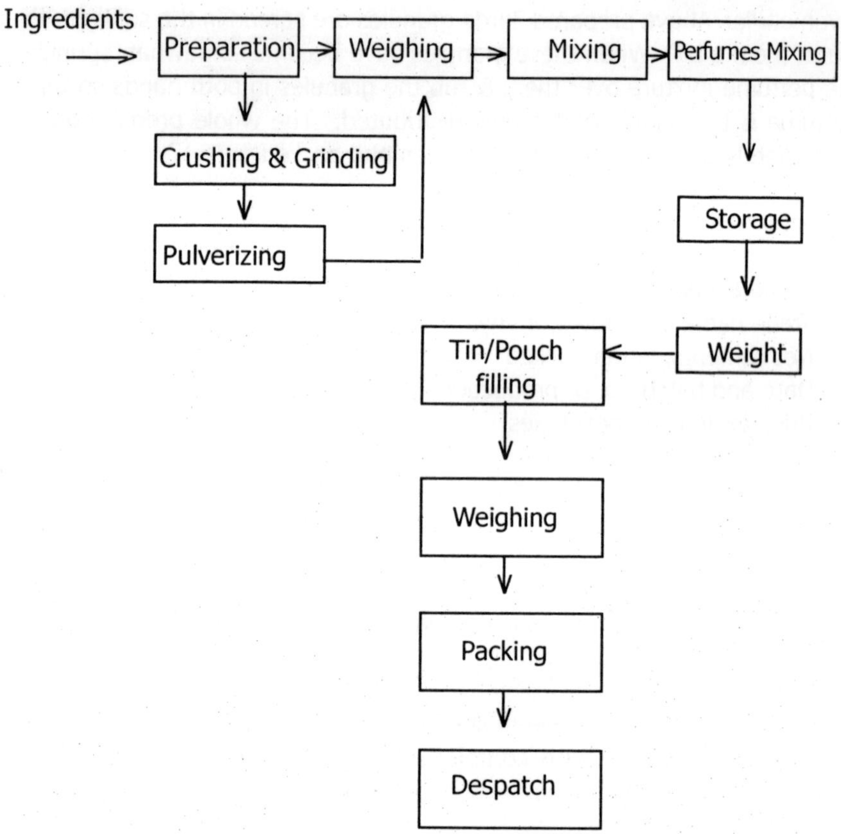

PAN MASALA (PLANT ECONOMICS)

Rated Plant Capacity = 200.00 Kgs/Day

LAND & BUILDING

1.	Land Area 350 sq.mt.	Rs.	1,75,000.00

PLANT & MACHINERY

1. Feeding and self sealing m/c
2. Coarse pulveriser
3. Betal nut cutter
4. Ribbon blend mixer
5. Automatic weigh balance
6. Weigh Balance
7. Tin filling & sealing machine

FIXED CAPITAL

1.	LAND & BUILDING	Rs.	5,55,000.00
2.	PLANT & MACHINERY	Rs.	3,03,000.00
3.	OTHER FIXED ASSETS	Rs.	1,21,000.00
	TOTAL	Rs.	9,79,000.00

RAW MATERIALS

1. Kutha
2. Lime
3. Betal nut
4. Cardamom minor
5. Sandal wood flour
6. Cardamom major
7. Cloves
8. Cinamom
9. Sugar
10. Saccarine
11. Peppermint
12. Perfumes

13. Pouches
14. Tin pack

TOTAL CAPITAL INVESTMENT

TOTAL FIXED CAPITAL		Rs.	9,79,000.00
TOTAL WORKING CAPITAL		Rs.	5,72,088.00
	TOTAL	Rs.	15,51,088.00

TURN OVER/ANNUM

By selling of 60000 Kgs of Pan Masala	Rs.	90,00,000.00

PROFIT SALES RATIO = Profit / Sales x 100 = 18.83 %

RATE OF RETURN = Operating profit / T.C.I x 100 =108.98 %

BREAK EVEN POINT (B.E.P) = 38.17 %

Chapter-31

PALM OIL CRUSHING UNIT

MANUFACTURING PROCESS

The palm oil is produced by extraction from the reddish to orange pulps of the oval shaped fruits which grow on stalks in fresh fruit bunches (FFB) on the oil palms. Pure oil and kernel are the main final product besides minor quantities of solids which are used for animal feed and fertilizer shell and dry fibres are used neither the palm oil processing line for fuelling the steam boiler.

TECHNOLOGY AND PROCESS DESCRIPTION

1. RECEPTION OF RAW MATERIAL : -

The fresh fruit bunches are brought from the field to the mill by means of trailors or trucks which pass through weigh bridge (for quality control for the in coming FFB and the out going product as well).

After weighing the bunches are dumped on the storage area which is either a concrete floor or a raised unloading ramps in (small scale plant). Depending upon the type of sterilizer and the capacity of the plant filling of sterlizer baskets or cages is carried out by hand or by suitable system (gravity, loader's etc.) In large plants unloading hopper or specially designed reception system are applied.

2. STERLIZING

In this section the fruit bunches are submitted to direct steam at a pressure of approx 3 bar over a period in the range of 3-60 minuted depending on the weight/size of the bunches.

Setrilization is carried out with the following objective in view :

- Prevention of any further rise in FFA (free fatty acid content) due to enzyme action by inactivation of these lipolytie

- Facilitation of mechanical stripping Toloosen the fruits from the bunches, sufficient most heat must penetrate to the point of attachment of the fruit to the stalk.

- Modification of the colloids of the pericap and stalk in a way that deoiling of the fruit solids is favoured in the following pressing phase. This applies both to the fibre solids and to the solid in crude oil which are deoiled in the clarification.

- Pre-conditioning the nuts to minimize Kernel breakage during both pressing and nut cracking

- Adequate sterilization permits sufficient heat penetration to cause a high percentage of the kernel to become detached from the shell. The process of loosening the kernels is continued in the nut silos and must be completed before the nuts are cracked if "split nuts" are to be avoided.

- Vertical type sterilizer used in small plant are with a limited volume while for large scale plants ster;lizer employed are big and of horizontal type and in continuous sterilization process.

3. STRIPPING :-

After sterilization of the complete FFB, the fruits are separated from the bunch stalks in the stripping station no palm oil is contained in the colyx leave and the stalks of the FFB, but during sterilizing and stripping some oil is absorbed by them. As for as calyx leave are concerned the absorbed quantity is unimportant since they will be pressed along with the fruits.

They could be screened off before, however, their presence have been found helpful to improve the press fibre de-oiling. The bunch stalks.

On the other hand, cannot be pressed and it is important, therefore, to keep the amount of oil transferred to them to a minimum and to care that no significant quantity of residual fruit remain attached.

4. DIGESTING :-

After the bunches have been stripped the sterilized friuts are reheated together with the accompanying calyx leave and these the pericarp is loosened from the nut and prepared for pressing. This is achieved in steam heated vessel (digester) provided with a rotating shaft to which stirring arm's are attached.

5. PRESSING / OIL EXTRACTION :-

Pressing is the most usual method of extracting erude palm oil from digested palm fruit other methods are centrifuging and the wet process. Modern types of Presses with highest efficient are continuously operating double screw presses, in which two parallel screws are running siole by side in a common perforated press cage.

The position of a double cone is controlled by drautically in order achieve constant cone pressure applied to the fruits. Such presses can be rated for different through puts at different screw speeds depending upon the various type of fruits. During the pressing operation, the press cylinder will be flushed with hot water the rate of which is determined by the vate of crude oil usually the water to oil ratio in 1:1

6. CLARIFICATION AND STORAGE:-

The crude oil obtained by pressing centrifuging or by the wet process contain varying amount of water together with empurities cosisting of vegetable matter which is partly dissolved in the water and partly form's insoluble solids. Oil is now pumped through direct steam heater to a settling tank water contents are reduced to 0.2% and then oil moves to pure oil storage tank simultaneously the kirnel recovery is carried out by various steps such as

Nut drying Nut cracking Kernel separation drying.

* The suggested capacity of the plant for producing palm oil is crushing 24 tonne of FFB per (8 hour) shift which is ideal one for extracting

palm oil.

The yield of pure plam oil in 21% and kernel 4%

PROCESS FLOW SHEET FOR PALM OIL

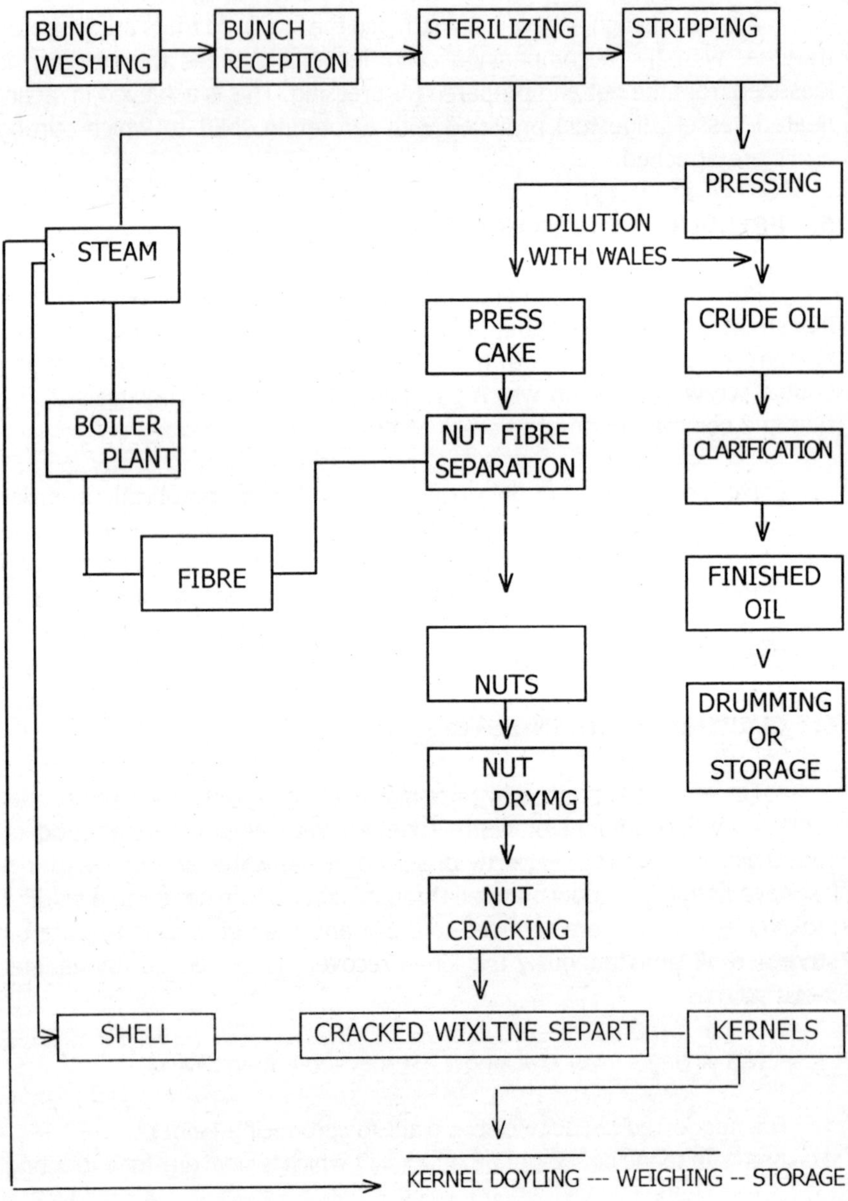

Rated Plant Capacity = 24.00 TON (F.F.B.)/Day

LAND & BUILDING

1.	Land Area reqd. 5000 Sq.mts.	Rs.	10,00,000.00

PLANT & MACHINERY

1. Fruit bunch Elevator
2. Sterilizing Plant
3. Stripping plant including stalk in cinerator
4. Extracting Station including digester & screw press
5. Clarification plant including settling tank and reheater
6. Oil storage tanks with drum and lorry filling equipment
7. Weight Bridge
8. Kernel plant with equipment for nut/fibre separation
9. Steam Boiler
11. Oil filling machine

FIXED CAPITAL

1.	LAND & BUILDING	Rs.	37,70,000.00
2.	PLANT & MACHINERY	Rs.	1,00,00,000.00
3.	OTHER FIXED ASSETS	Rs.	25,00,000.00
	TOTAL	Rs.	1,62,70,000.00

RAW MATERIALS

1. Fresh fruit bunches of Palm tree
2. Packing material mild steel drum

TOTAL CAPITAL INVESTMENT

TOTAL FIXED CAPITAL	Rs.	1,62,70,000.00
TOTAL WORKING CAPITAL FOR 3 MONTHS	Rs.	1,09,98,375.00
TOTAL	Rs.	2,72,68,375.00

TURN OVER/ANNUM

1. Sale of Palm oil (Pure) 1512 Ton — Rs. 4,83,84,000.00
2. Sale of palm kernel 288 ton — Rs. 1,29,60,000.00

PROFIT SALES RATIO = Profit / Sales x 100 = 15.82 %

RATE OF RETURN = Operating profit / T.C.I x 100 = 35.58 %

BREAK EVEN POINT (B.E.P) = 55.24 %

Chapter-32

ROSE PLANTATION & ROSE OIL EXTRACTION

MANUFACTURING PROCESS

Various methods are employed for obtaining rose oil apart from distillation expression. Distillation with water or steam is most widely used method and gives satisfactory results with considerable variety of plant materials. Distillation as applied to the production of essential oils is a means of separating the essential oil from mass of plant material which is not volatile. Reduced to its simple form it consists of mixture of finely divided material with water fed into still which is then heated until the contents boil and the resultings vapour are led to a condenser where they are cooled and converted back into the liquid form. This liquid consists of water containing a small quantity of essential oils which forms a separate layer usually floating on the surface of water. This process is based on the fact that when two volatile liquids which are not mutually soluble are heated together the mixture will boil at a lower temperature than would either of the constitutent liquids if heated above.

The individual compounds of essential oils differ considerable in volatility and their boiling points. Very generally within the range 150°c to 300°c. At these temperatures however such reactions as decomposition, oxidation resinification are greately accelerated and would lead to more or less deterioration in the odour and flavour of any essentialoil heated to such temperatures. Distillation in the presence of water ensures that the oil will volatilise at a temperature a littile below that of boiling water and the spoilage due to the above effects will be reduced to a negligible quantity. When the plant material is finally ground before distillation it may be assumed that practically all the essential oil has been set free from the enclosing tissues. On distillation the lowest boiling that is the most volatile constitutents will at first predominate in the distillate but as the distillation proceeds they will be volatilise by the higher boiling constitutents in order to volatility. In general, it is necessary to prolong the distillation sufficiently to obtain all constituents of the oil. If the time required for complete distillation is reduced, an oil of different composition will be obtained.

In some cases the high boiling constitutents may have little or no perfuming value and it is then advantageous to shorten the time of distillation thus obtaining an oil of higher quality and reducing the cost of labour and fuel.

THEORY OF DISTILLATION

As already specified rose oil consists of the mixtures of volatile solids and liquids which vary considerably in volatility and boiling point. Any susbstance evolves a vapour which exerts a definite pressure at a given temperatures in exactly the same way as the atmosphere does. This pressure is known as the vapour pressure -of the substance and varies with temperature. Vapour pressures are usually measured in mm of Hg. Different substances have different vapour pressure and different rate of variation of vapour pressure of a liquid is increased by heating until it equals the pressure of the atmosphere. The liquid boils if the atmospheric pressure is reduced it follows that the temperature at which the liquid boils will also be reduced.

Distillation can be used to separate two liquids of different vapour pressure.

DISTILLATION OF HOMOGENOUS LIQUIDS:

When the constitutents of a mixture of liquids are all soluble in each other they form a single homogenous liquid and its vapour is a mixture of the vapours of all the constitutents in the proportions in which they are present in the liquid. Its vapour pressure is therefore dependent on the composition of the liquid. An essential oil is a homogenous mixture of those type and in distillation the lower boiling constitutents distill off first, the boiling point gradually rising to that of the highest boiling constitutents. This type of distillation is used in the purification and fractionisation of essential oil and these operations are rarely carried out by the primary producer.

DISTILLATION OF HETROGENOUS LIQUIDS:

A hetrogenous liquid is a mixture of two liquids which are not soluble in each other and which therefore form separate layers when left undisturbed. In such a case each liquid continues to exert the same vapour pressure as it would if present above. The total vapour pressure of the mixture is therefore equal to the sum of the vapour pressure of the individual constitutents of the mixture (provided they do not react chemically) and is not affected by the actual or relative amounts of the constitutents present in the mixture. It follows from this rule that the boiling point of the mixture will be lower than that of any are constituent when heated above. It is for this reason that the boiling point of the mixture will be lower than that a single constituent.

The vapour contains all the constituents of the mixture in volumes proportional to their vapour pressure at the boiling temperatures. This temperature will rise a little as each volatile constitutent is completely removed. But not until the whole of the essential oils has distilled over will it reach that of the means liquid left in the still overheating of the essential oil in this avoided.

METHOD OF DISTILLATION:

Most of the industrial stills employed today are directly fired and are of 1000 to 2000 litres capacity requiring no steam generator. They offer the advantage of low initial capital investment and simplicity of operation important features in the primitive valley of roses. The stills are made of copper or aluminium and are of cylinderical shape insulated with bricks or some other suitable material permits even distribution and retention of heat inside of retort. The still top is provided with man hole through which the flowers can be charged. A grid, a few inches above the bottom of the retort to prevents contact of the with the directly fired bottom. On the side, and level with the grid is another manhole through which the exhausted flowers and the residual water can be quickly discharged after the distillation is over. The still is also equipped with a pipe and valve beneath the grid which permits drawing off the residual water when the still is used for cohobation.

Generally the retorts are charged with flower upto about 10" below the still head. The quantity of roses charged depends upon their condition, fresh flower taking up much more space then those stored in the distillery for a few hours. Retorts of 1200 mto 1500 litres capacity -the most popular of the type are charged with 250 to 300 kg of rose petal and 1200 litres of water are added. The whole mass is stirred thoroughly.

Then the manhole in the still is closed and the fire started. After about 1.5 hour actual distillation starts this last another 1.5 hour. The entire operation thus requiring 3 hours.

At the begining great care must be exce rised to keep the fire low, so that tha actual distillation starts slowly. Otherwise the warm expanding air will blow through the condensers with great velocity carry along the most volatile material along with it. During the operation the inlet for the cooling water in the condensers must be regulated so that the condensate flows at a temperature of 35° to 40°c. At lower temperatures the oil which contain a good deal stearoptene will solidify in the condenser tubes and no oil will appear in the florentine flask (oil separator)

Distillation of the flowers after a slow start should proceed at a lively pace is completed when about 140 litres of water per 250 kg. of flower charged have distilled over. The very small quantity of greenish oil separating with oil separator is called the direct oil. This is drawn off with a pipette and poured in a glass bottle when the oil has been decanted the 140 litres of distillation water are pumped into a storage tank and bucked with first waters, freed from the separated oil of other operations. As soon as first water accumulated they are redistilled as explained below. The exhausted flavour together with the water in the retort are thrown away.

The yield of direct oil obtained by the distillation of flower is very low since much of the oil might have dissolved in the first water. To isolate the dissolved oil the first water has to be redistilled again. For this purpose 1200 litres are pumped into a retort of 1800 litres capacity and 140 litres are slowly and carefully distilled off for 2.5 hours. The water oil is drawn off with a pipette and added to the direct oil. Combined the above two will constitute the rose oil. The oil thus obtained is poured and kept in glass container in Sun light for several hours. This helps the impurities to precipitate and water to separate . The clear oil is then carefully decanted and filtered and stored in tinned copper containers. The oil thus obtained will consist of 25 % direct oil and 75 % water oil. The water in the retort left after this distillation of 140 litres of water is used as the water for first distillation.

1 Kg Rose oil is yielded from 4000 Kgs of pink rosa damascena (rose) flower.

PROCESS FLOW SHEET

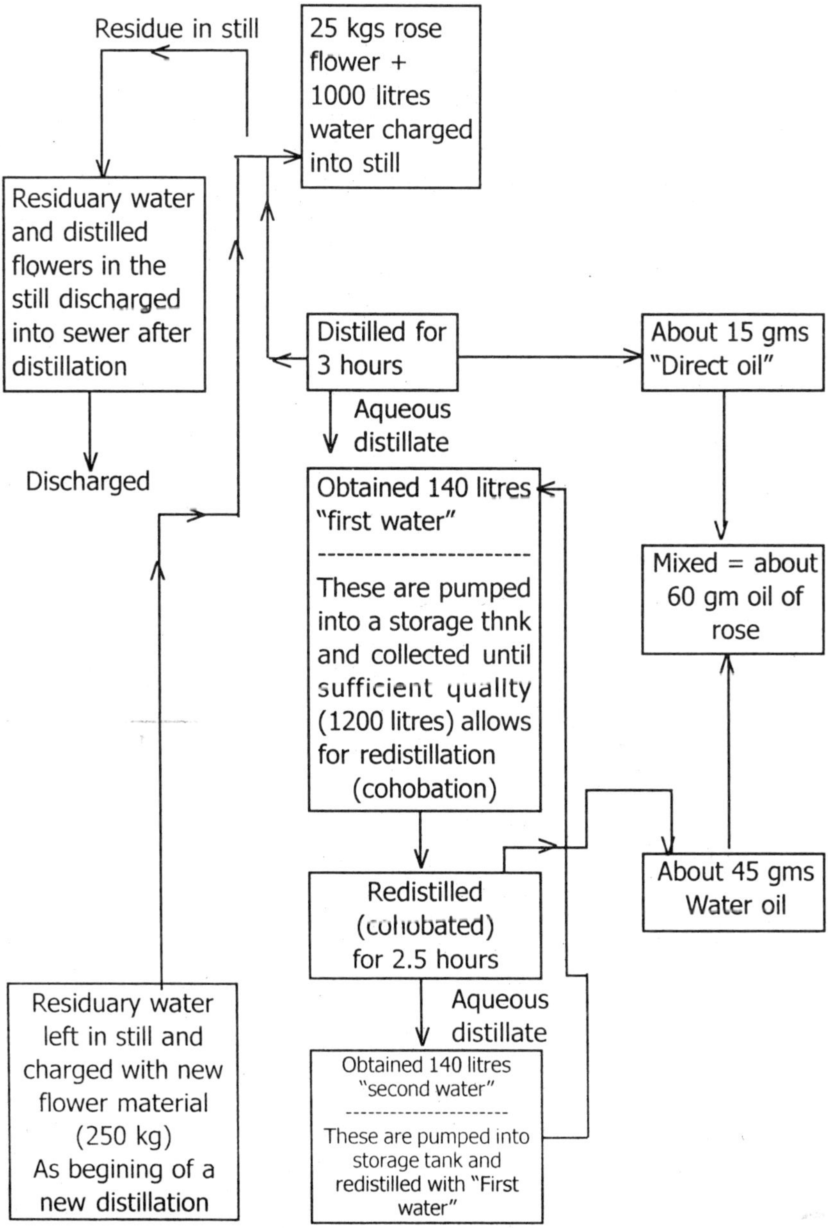

PLANT ECONOMICS OF Rose Plantation&Rose oil Extraction

Rated Plant Capacity = 400.00 ML/Day

LAND & BUILDING

Land 11 acres (10 acre for cultivation, 1 acre for processing)

Rs. 5,50,000.00

PLANT & MACHINERY

1. Tin lined copper vessel (cylindrical) with accessories.
2. Coal fired oven of clay brick.
3. Condenser S.S.lined.
4. Water circulation pump.
5. Cylindrical S.S. collecting vessel
6. Laboratory equipment.
7. Water storage tank
8. Tube well pumps
9. Pipes & fittings, pumps, storage, stainer.

FIXED CAPITAL

1.	LAND & BUILDING	Rs.	10,72,500.00
2.	PLANT & MACHINERY	Rs.	7,60,000.00
3.	OTHER FIXED ASSETS	Rs.	5,95,000.00
	TOTAL	Rs.	24,27,500.00

RAW MATERIALS

1. Manures, pesticides, chemicals.
2. Rose flower from outer sources
3. Packaging bottles, caps, cartons etc.

TOTAL CAPITAL INVESTMENT

TOTAL FIXED CAPITAL	Rs.	24,27,500.00
TOTAL WORKING CAPITAL	Rs.	3,83,125.00
TOTAL	Rs.	28,10,625.00

TURN OVER/ANNUM

1. By sale of 18 Kgs of rose oil
2. By sale of rose water 10000 litres

TOTAL	Rs.	27,20,000.00

PROFIT SALES RATIO = Profit / Sales x 100 = 22.95 %

RATE OF RETURN = Operating profit / T.C.I x 100 =22.21 %

BREAK EVEN POINT (B.E.P) = 52.15 %

Chapter-33

SPICE OILS OR OLEORESINS

EXTRACTION OF ESSENTIAL OIL (CARDAMON, JEERA, AJOWAN, GINGER OIL & OTHER SPICE)

MANUFACTURING PROCESS

The Oil is obtained by the steam distillation of the dried raw material. The best raw material is African ginger. It is not only lower priced than other qualities but also gives a higher yield of oil. In general the yield varies from 1.5 to 3 percent of volatile oil. averaging 2%. Prior to distillation the dry material should be comminuted, then charged into the stills immediately. Care must be taken to distribute the mass evenly on several trays. Within the still Distillation is Carried out with direct steam depending upon the charge in the still and the steam depending upon the charge in the still and the steam pressure Applied, distillation of one charge may require up to 20 hour. The distillation water may require cohobation.

Peeling and shaving of the rhizomes constitute an excellent material for distillation, giving a good yield of oil, provided distillation is carried out immediately after peeling.

PRACTICE OF DISTILLATION

STEAM DISTILLATION

Let us now consider some practical Aspects of steam distillation a method which in recent years has become quite popular among small producers using portable distillation equipment that can be moved from field to field. The smaller units are heated by direct fire, the larger ones by a steam Jacket, a closed steam coil or in rare cases by open steam coils. When using direct fire, precaution must be taken to ensure that only the bottom of the still, the section. Containing water below the grid which carries the plant charge is heated. If the upper part of the still were exposed to direct fire, the plant material might be dangerously overheated. It is advisable, therefore, to use indirect steam as a source of heat, but not direct fire. In the steam distillation, steam alone contacts the charge, the steam either being generated from or passing through water in the still. Thus overheating or drying of the charge is avoided because the temperature can not rise above that of saturated steam at the pressure prevailing in the still (at atmospheric temp never above 100°C) Steam distillation therefore represents a typical case of distillation with saturated low pressure steam.

Preparation of the plant material is much more important in this method of distillation than in water distillation. Since the steam contacts the material only by rising through it, the plant charge must be so disposed that all parts of it are uniformly contacted if high yield of oil are to be maintained this requires that the charge be homogenous as to size and further more, that the average size of individual pieces be controlled within rather narrow limits. If for example, the material is finally ground, it will tend to pack and offer strong resistance to the passage of steam. This in turn may develop steam pressure beneath the charge until such pressure is sufficient to penetrate it, such penetration, However will take, place only at few places, releasing the pressure and permitting the steam to escape through only a few passage or channels sometimes called "ratholes", Obviously, under these circumstances most of the plant material is never contacted by the steam and the recovery of oil is incomplete. If, on the otherhand, a charge consist of a say, whole stalks, leaves and flowers, there obviously will be fair large passage through the charge which offer little or no resistance to the passage of steam.

Steam will then escape through there and again permit most of the charge to remain unaffected by it. Therefore, in steam distillation, the plant material should not be too finally ground nor should it contain excessive long stalks or large roots or piece of bark. Granulation usually gives the best results. Experience along can determine the optimum size to which the material should be reduced and this will vary from plant. At any rate, the preparation of charge for steam distillation must always be given most care ful attention.

Another problem to be considered in steam distillation arises from the fact that the charge is cold at the start and that the first steam to enter it will condense thus wetting the plant material. This wetting will continue until the entire charge reaches the boiling temperature of water at the operating temperatures. To avoid the continuation of wetting due to loss of heat by radiation from the walls of the still, the the upper part of the retort in other works, the section housing the charge should be insulated.

The rate of distillation in the case of steam distillation is not as important as in the case of water distillation. It effects only the rate of production but not always the quality or yield of oil. A lively pace of distillation recommends itself, however in order to prevent excessive wetting of the plant charge and in order to increase the production rate. Regarding oil production per hour steam distillation is less efficient than other. When using steam distillation, it is always possible after the initial period during, which the charge in the retort is warning up and condensation taking place, the steam may be slightly superheated.

END OF DISTILLATION

As the distillation proceeds and as the oil content of the charge decreases correspondingly, the ratio of water to oil in the condensate will increase, because the steam can no longer contact the oil in the charge efficiently, regardless of rate of distillation, and also because the remaining constituents are mostly high boiling. The operator must then decide at what point it is no longer economical to continue the distillation. From the knowledge of size of charge of distillation and from experience or trial distillations in a pilot plant, it can quickly be determined whether or not the charge has been nearly exhausted.

TREATMENT OF THE VOLATILE OIL

The handling of the condensed oil is worthy of brief comment since its quality may deteriorate, particularly if the oil must be stored for some time, Just as the condensed water (distillation water) is always saturate with oil so the condensed oil will always be saturated with water. There remains also the probability of slow reaction between the oil and water, unless latter is almost completely removed. The oil can be brightened by filtering through Kieselguhr or magnesium carbonate on filter paper. This procedure removes all small droplets of water which causes the cloudiness, but it does not completely dry the oil. Larger quality of the oil may be filtered through mechanical filter, filterpresses or seen through high speed speed centrifuges.

TREATMENT OF THE DISTILLATION WATER

The distillation water flowing off the oil separator contains some of the volatlle oil in solution or suspension, the quantity depending upon the solubility and specific gravity of the various oil constituents considering the distillate presents a mixture of condensed steam and oil vapors-it is evident that condensed steam and oil vapours- it is evident that the water phase of the distillate actually presents an aqueous solution of oil, completely saturated at the prevailing temperature. Those oil constituent which are some what soluble in water will be partly dissolved in the distillation water, and the dissolved portlon of this oil will be different in composition from that of oil separated in the florentine flask. The latter is usually called main or direct oil, the former water oil. The water soluble constituents consist mostly of oxygenated compounds and since these compounds possesses higher specific gravity than non-oxygenated compounds the water oil usually has a higher sp. gravity than the main oil. This difference, however is not always pronounced, because the distillation water contains not only oil in actual solution but also in suspended and emulsified form. A more or less appearance of distillation water thus indicates the presence of the oil.

Such distillation water can not be discarded, must be submitted to further treatment to prevent loss of oil. In case of water and steam distillation, It may be automatically returned into the retort during distillation. In case of steam distillation (with live steam from a separate steam boiler) the distillatiion water should not be returned into the retort, as too much liquid would condense and accumulate within it and wet the plant charge the distillation water therefore is pumped or injected into a separate still for redistillation. The process of recovery the oil from the water by redistillation is commonly called cohobation, the still, serving this purpose being known as cohobation stcohobation implies that distillation water is used over and over for the distillation of a new plant charge but to day cohobation simply means redistillation of the distillation water. The distillation waters are redistilled most efficiently in round stills provided with a steam jacket or a closed steam coil. Indirect heating is preferable because the injection of live steam into the retort would cause too much water to accumulate within the retort and hinder the vaporization of oil from water. In case of many distillation water only 10 to 15 % need be distilled of recover most of the oil dissolved or suspended there in the residual water may be discarded.

To shorten the cohobation and increase the quantity of oil in the condensate, the water in the cohobation still is saturated with common salt (Nacls). This decreases the solubility of the volatile oil in the water. The oil distills over more quickly, and with a smaller quantity of water. This procedure is recommended where the distillation water contains slightly water soluble constituents of high boiling point, which can not be recovered by mere steam distillation.

The separation of oil and water is based upon the simple principle that a mixture of oil vapours and steam possesses a slightly lower boiling point than pure water vapours (steam), and that the vapour mixture arising contains more oil than the liquid phase. By reduction of the speed of cohobation, the oil content of the distillate may be increased because the rising steam will be more thoroughly saturated with oil vapours.

An other method of recovering the Oil dissolved or suspended in the distillation water consists in saturating latter first with salt and then extracting the solution with volatile solvents - as highly purified petroleum there or benzene. This is usually done twice. The drawn off and united solvent solutions are there concentrated in still by driving off the solvent first at atmospheric pressure and later in vacuo, until every trace of solvent is eliminated from the Oil.

PROCESS OF MANUFACTURE

The process of extraction oil involves the following major steps.

1. Drying the items
2. Cutting the item into small pieces/pulverising
3. Solvent extraction & distillation
4. Bottling the oil
5. Disposing the cake

DRYING

The item whose oil is to be extracted is dried. This process is proposed to be carried out in sun, for economic reasons. The place where these items are kept for drying in sun should be detected such that the dust and dirt water or any other foreign matter shouldn't get contaminated during drying. One most suitable place is the roof of the working shed. The side walls of the roof should be of sufficient height.

CUTTING INTO PIECES

The items like cardamom, cumin seeds and King's cumin are not need to be cut into pieces for they are naturally present in small size. But for Ginger, it is need to be cut into small pieces.

PROCESS FLOW DIAGRAM

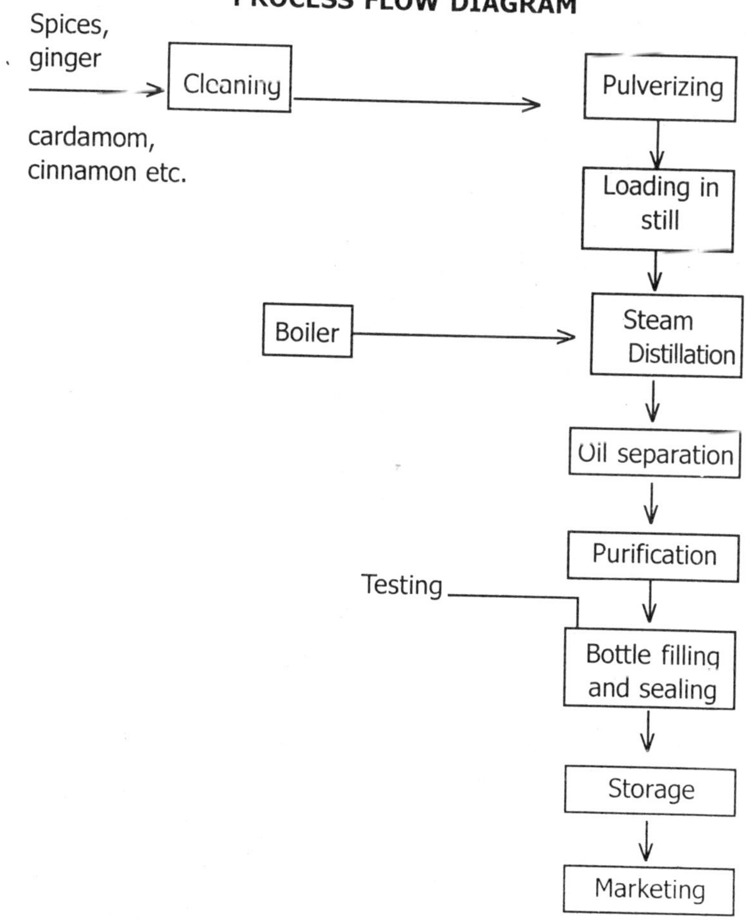

PREPARATION OF SESQUI TERPENELESS SWEET ORANGE OIL

To obtain sesqui terpeneless orange oil. Nichools suggests preparing first a ten times concentrated oil by vacuum distillation and transferring this concentrated oil to gas-heated still fitted with an efficient fractionation column, and with joints well sealed, to obtain the highest possible vacuum. If the pressure in the still exceeds 1 mm, the resulting oil is likely to be "burned" and of inferior quality. The contents of the still are the then slowly distilled, collecting about twenty equal fractions, using some modification of the Perkin triangle to maintain the vacuum in the still while the receiver is being changed. The various fractions are numbered and tested for solubility in 80 per cent alcohol. Those fractions, which shows a soluability at 20^0 of one part of oil in 9 volumes of alcohol, are bulked together and form the sesquiterpeneless oil.

The preparation of this sesquiterpeneless oil is in accordance with the tendency in recent years to utilize better and finer raw materials in the manufacture of flavuoring extracts. It uses in the preparation of fruit squashes prevents the formation of the objectionable "ring" found on the necks of bottles containing inferior products and gives the squash a fresher and purer flavour. Laboratory product, and the task should be tackled with understanding of the varability within limits of the oil from natural sources.

Sweet orange oil consists largely of terpenes (more than 90 per cent) and about 2 per cent of resinous and colouring matter. The mixture of oxygenated bodies which constitute terpeneless orange oil can be obtained by careful distillation (in vacuum) with a yield varying from 1.2 per cent to 1.5 per cent.

Specific Gravity at 15.5^0..................0.8926 to 0.9094
Optical Rotation at 15.5^0.................+27^{0}0' to +33^0 0'
Aldehyde Content, Calculated as Decyl
Aldehyde (Hydroxylamine Hydrochloride Mryho) .... 29.50 to 36.65%
Free Alcohol Content ....37.0 to 44.9%
Ester Content ....8.0 to 12.0%

The free alcohols are chief d-linalool and d-terpineol

PROCESS FLOW CHART

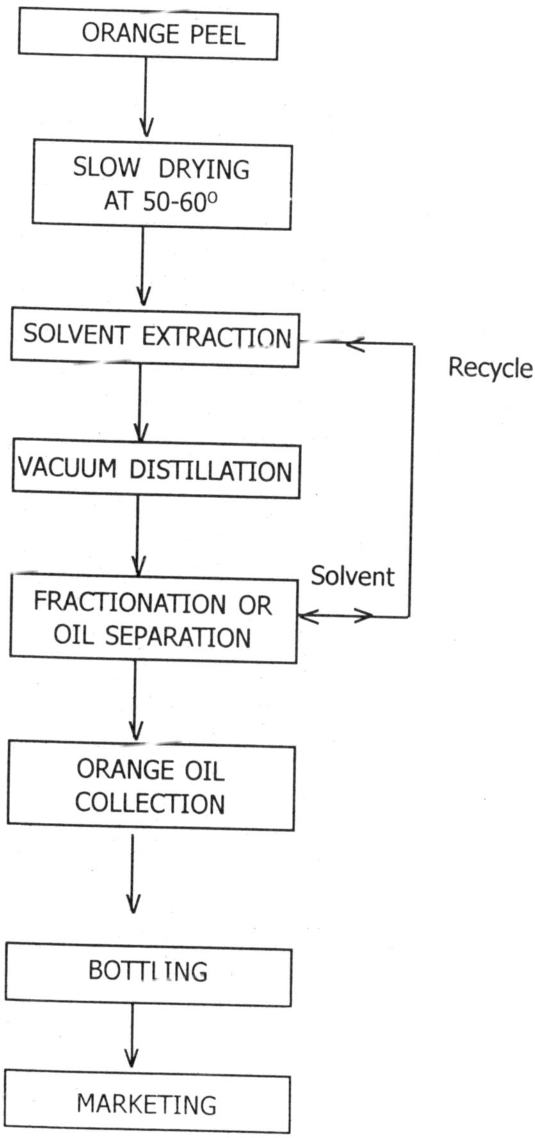

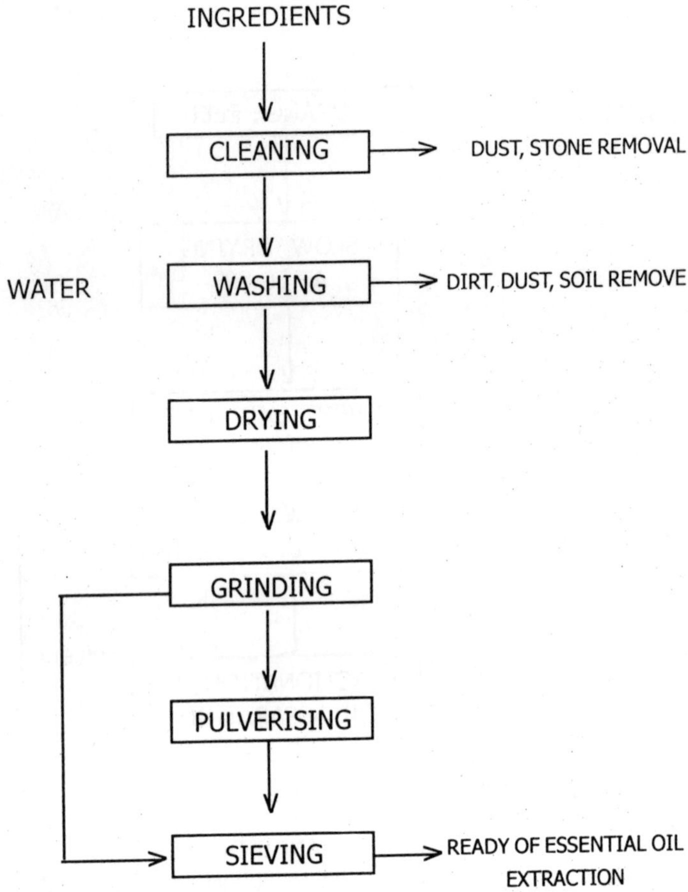

PREPARATION OF RAW MATERIALS

PLANT ECONOMICS OF ESSENTIAL OILS FROM SPICES

Rated Plant Capacity = 12.50 Kgs/Day

LAND & BUILDING

1.	Land required 350 sq. mts.	Rs.	7,35,000.00

PLANT & MACHINERY

1. Automatic washing machine
2. Cabinet dryer electric operated
3. Disintegrator complete with motor
4. Micropulveriser with cyclone separator
5. Automatic sieving machine
6. Small pulveriser
7. Solvent Extraction system with complete accessories and heating system
8. Vacuum distillation system with condensor
9. Centrifugal separator
10. Laboratory testing equipments
11. Bottle filling and sealing machine
12. Baby Boiler
13. Miscellaneous machines as pipes fittings, pumps, valves, solvent storage tanks, oil storage tanks.
14. Semi automatic carton sealing machine.

FIXED CAPITAL

1.	LAND & BUILDING	Rs.	7,35,000.00
2.	PLANT & MACHINERY	Rs.	15,20,000.00
3.	OTHER FIXED ASSETS	Rs.	4,50,000.00
	TOTAL	Rs.	27,05,000.00

RAW MATERIALS

1. Cardamom
2. Cumin (Jeera) seeds
3. Ajowan (Bishop seed)

4. Ginger dried (saunth)
5. Orange Peels (dried)
6. Solvents

TOTAL CAPITAL INVESTMENT

TOTAL FIXED CAPITAL		Rs.	27,05,000.00
TOTAL WORKING CAPITAL		Rs.	16,86,750.00
	TOTAL	Rs.	43,91,750.00

TURN OVER/ANNUM

1. By sale of 680 kgs Cardamom
2. By sale of 910 kgs Cumin seed (Jeera) oil.
3. By sale of 300 kgs Ajowan oil
4. By sale of Ginger oil 360 kgs.
5. By sale of 1500 kgs Orange Peel Oil Rs. 97,02,000.00

PROFIT SALES RATIO = Profit / Sales x 100 = 17.75 %
RATE OF RETURN = Operating profit / T.C.I x 100 = 39.21 %
BREAK EVEN POINT (B.E.P) = 49.84 %

Chapter-34

INTERNATIONAL IMPORTERS & EXPORTERS

Aff Aromatics Pvt. (Registered Office)
17, Ezra Street
Calcutta- 700001 (W.B.)
Ph. : 033-2215790
Fax : 91-33-2215796
(Manufacturer of :
Natural Fragrances)

Al Khair Trading Co.
P.O. Box-5293, Abu Dhabi, U.A.E.
Ph. : 9712-787898
Fax : 9712-784407
(Ayurvedic Medicines)

Aerofarm
Russia, Moscow,
Staropansky per, 5
Ph./Fax : 095-9250784
(Pharmaceuticals, Perfumery, Healthcare products)

Al Ahram
P.O. No. - 17688 Alian U.A.E.
Ph. : 9713-514788
Fax : 9713-514799
(Veterinary Equipments, Veterinary Pharmaceuticals)

Adam & Eve Trd Est.
P.O. Box-712
Abu Dhabi, U.A.E.
Ph. : 9712-657777
Fax : 9712-660500
(Essential Oil)

Al- Badri Trading Est.
P.O. Box - 15922, Abu Dhabi, U.A.E.
Ph. : 9713-215655
Fax : 9713-213031 (Chemicals)

Benzen Trading
483, Lavezares street
Binondo, Manila - 1006
Ph. : 00632-2424310, 2431924
Fax : 00632 2424307
(Menthol crystal)

Belimex Moscow
Ph. : 0959037766
Fax : 9037777
(Pharmaceutical Substances)

Bhandya Narshimha Vaman Pai
190/V, High School Road, PB 26
Kundapura Tel. : 20621
(Aroma chemicals & essential oils)

Bharat Bottle Stores
Afzal Gunj, Hyderabad- 500012
Ph. : 4619064, 636612
(Perfumery compounds and Natural essential oils)

Cure Chem Overseas Pvt. Ltd.
The Colonnade Msasa
P.O. Box-GD 943 Greendale Harare Zimbabwe
Ph. : (263-4) 486461, 490500
Fax : (263-4) 486817, 481204
(Merchant & Exporter of : Menthol crystals, Essential Oils & Other Chemicals)

Chunilal Dayaldas Batliwala
15-5-97, Afzal Gunj
Hyderabad - 500012
Ph. : 524998, 557001
(Aromatic chemicals, perfumery compounds flavours, essential oils and resinoids)

Decan Chemical and Essence Mart
15-9-382/5, Maharani Jhansi Road, Afzalgunj, Hyderabad-500012
Ph. : 500970
(Aromatic chemicals, perfumery compounds essential oils and resinoids)

Dhabian Trading Agencies Est.
P.O. Box-25623, Abu Dhabi, U.A.E.
Ph. : 9712-332844
Fax : 9712-335199
(Oilfield Chemicals)

Eqidbiomed Moscow
Oruzheiny per. 25/1
Ph. : 095-9783235
Fax : 2519725
(Pharmaceutical . " BETALEIKIN")

Gelean Incorporated
No.1, St. Francis Metro Manila
Ph. : 00632-6461297
Fax : 00632-9320232
(Pharmaceutical Chemicals)

Hercules Agro-Industrial Corp.
P.O. Box - 2790, MCPO
Metro Manila
Ph. : 0632-8932724, 8932773, 2932684
Fax : 0632-8160337
(Phermaceutical raw materials)

House of Perfumes
P.O. Box-297, Dubai, U.A.E.
Ph. : 9714-686900
Fax : 9714-686755 (Chemicals)

Hitesh Aromatic
Nalsar, P.O. Baggi-175027
Distt. Mandi (H.P.)
Ph. : 45288, 45023
Fax : 1905-45141
E-mail: hitesh1@ nde.vsnl.net.in
(Manufacturer & Exporter of : Essential oils of Himalayan Range)

International Technical & Trading Co.
P.O. No. 71871, Abu Dhabi
Ph. : 9712-543700
Fax : 9712-543702
(Chemicals Products)

Liwa Chem,
P.O. Box-29861; Abu Dhabi, U.A.E.
Ph. : 9712-334446
Fax : 9712-334436
(Oilfield Chemicals)

Liwa Chem
P.O. Box- 29861 Abu Dhabi, U.A.E.
Ph. : 9712-334446
Fax : 9712-334436
(Oiffield chemicals)

Laser Creation & Marketing
P.O. No. 26926, Abu Dhabi, U.A.E.
Ph. : 9712-661160
Fax : 9712-665354
(Aluminlum foil, Pesticides, Perfumes, Artificial flowers, Dry fruits)

Multipharma Moscow
Ph. : 7213050 Fax : 7213051
(Pharmaceuticals)

Maienfelser Naturkosmetik
Galerie der Dufe, H.P. Linderman
71543, Wustenrot Maienfels, Germany Ph. : 07945-2582
Fax : 0049-5231, 35183
(Essential Oil Since organic)

Mahendra Peppermint Udyog
Off. RJT-405, Rajindra Jain Tower
18, Comm. Centre
Wazirpur Industrial Area
New Delhi-110052 (India)
Ph. : 7403445, 7215354
Fax : 11-7223936
(Manufacturer & Supplier of : Natural Mentha oil, Bold Crystals, D.M.O. & Other Essential Oils)

Novya Zarya
Moscow ul. Pavla Andreeva-23
Ph. : 095-2366584
Fax : 095-2378478
(Ayurvedic cosmetic products)

North Indies Trading & Leading Co.
263, Prudencio Street,
Sump, Manila
Ph./Fax : 00632-7150269
(Ayurvedic Herbal Products)

Nova-Interholod
Moscow, ul. Varvarka-14
Ph./Fax : 095-2985940
(Tabacco)

Oases Chemicals Co. LLC
P.O. Box-29861, Abu Dhabi, U.A.E.
Ph. : 9712-795439
Fax : 9712-794586 (Chemicals)

Pharmasan Inc.
6, Agatha Street, STA
Teresita Village, Marikina City, Metro Manila
Tel./Fax : 00632-6463532
(Pharmaceutical Raw Material & Chemicals)

Pentachem Inc.
301, Bel Air Apts Building
1020 Roxas Blvd, Ermita
Manila, PHilippines
Ph. : 00632-2933844
Fax : 00632-2921686, 2920639
(Various oilmeals & compound feed)

Pharmalines
P.O. Box-29899, Abu Dhabi, U.A.E.
Ph. : 9712-788161

Fax : 9712-795532 (Perfumes)

Rasai perfumes Industry
P.O. Box - 16878, Abu Dhabi, U.A.E.
Ph. : 9714-816655
Fax : 9714-816429
(Perfume & Cosmetics)

Ros Tok Corporation Too
6, Bobrov Per, 101000 Moscow
Ph. : 9256957 Fax : 9254786
Pharmaceuticals (At present specialises in Japanese ph armaproducts distribution)

Radhika Containers Pvt. Ltd.
UG-7&8, Padma Tower-II, 22, Rajindra Place
New Delhi- 110008 (India)
Ph. : 5753877/78, 5761074/75
Fax : 011-5758817
(Manufacturer of: Fibre Drums, Textile Paper Tubes, Composite Cans & Paper Cores)

Turgen International Technical Services
P.O. Box-45809 Abu Dhabi, U.A.E.
Ph. : 9712-777960
Fax : 9712-778330
(Tabacco processing plant)

United Eastern for Companies representation
P.O. Box-7615, Abu Dhabi, U.A.E.
Ph. : 9712-272737
Fax : 9712-270048
(Bulk Pharmaceuticals, Raw Materials)

United Chemical & Perfumes
Off. No. 1, 1st cross Manvarth peth
K.V.Temple Street cross
Banglore-560053 Ph. : 2876036
Fax : 080-2287863
(Deals in : Aromatic Chemicals, Perfumery Compounds, Essential oils & Resinoids)

Yugas
Russia, Moscow, 1 Zachatievsky per.6 Ph. : 095-2035092
Tel./Fax : 2033897 (Tobacco)

Chapter-35

PLANT & EQUIPMENTS SUPPLIERS

Ashok Kumar Jha
194, Suraj Apartment,
Suraj Kund Road Pul Prahlad Pur,
New Delhi- 110 044
Ph. : 6418421 Fax : 011-6819209
Menthol Essential Oil & Aromatic Consultants at your Service, 17 Years Experience in this Field will help you with all your problems of Project, Quality Control Manufacturing Formulation.

Bhagsons Engineers & Consultant P. Ltd.
9, Amar Park, Rohtak Road,
Delhi - 110 035 Ph. : 5412707
Fax : 5110211
E-mail : bhagsons@bol.net.in.
Manufacturer of : Reactor & Pressure Vessels, heat Exchanger, Rotary Vacuum Extractor, Distillation Unit, Mixers-Planetary, Ribbon, Kneader Ball Mills, Filters, Tanks, Coating Pans Etc.

Brintex Sales Corporation
ED - 55, Tagore Garden,
New Delhi - 110 027
Ph. : 5460255
Manufacturer of : Elmach, Blister, Subnil Tube, Filling Alliance, Fluid Bed Dryer, Komal DM/RO Plants, Magumps/Monita, Pharma M/Cs. Bifriends Vacuum Dryer, Flakers, Filters. EM Boiler, Thermic Heaters, Intech Lequid, Injectable M/cs.

Blue Star Limited
Blue Star house, 9a Ghatkopar Link Road Sakinaka, Mumbai - 400 072
Ph. : 91-22-8523600
Fax : 91-22-8522988
Website : www.bluestarindia.com
(Cooler/Freezer, Deep Freezers)

Danfoss Industries Pvt. Ltd.
Regd. Office: 296 Old Mahabalipuram Road, , Sholinganallur,
Chennnai 600 119,
Ph. : 91-44-4963511-17
Fax : 91-11-6817668

Delhi: F-89/13 Okhla Industrial Area Phase I, New Delhi 110 020
Ph. : 91-11-6813692-96,
Fax : 91-11-6817668,
Mumbai : Unit No. II, Ground Floor, Corporate Park, Sion-Trombay Road, Chembur, Mumbai - 400 071.
Ph. : 91-22-5289091-95,
Fax : 91-22-5289098
Manufacturer of : Refrigeration Controls, Compressors for Refrigerators & Freezers, Commercial Compressors & Condensing units, Thermostats, Industrial Control

Hckl Barrel Container Works
11-A, Najafgarh Road, Shivaji Marg (Moti Nagar), New Delhi - 110 015
Ph. : 5423803, 5937270
Fax : 91-11-5423803
Manufacturer of G.p., Double Liner, Open Top Grease, Lube Expoxy Coated, PU Insolated Tanks, Hot Dipped Galvanised Heavy Barrels

Jitendrea Cooling Tower (Engs.)
Head Off. A-81, Jagatpuri, Mandoli Road, Delhi- 110093
Ph. : 011-91-2283158, 2126592
Fax : 011-91-2283158, 2128056, 2124844
Manufacturer of Cooling Towers :- Applications : D.G. Set, Solvent Plant, Induction Furnace, Compressors, Injection Moulding, Menthol - Essential Oils Plant

K.G. Scientific Engineering Works
Bawana Road, Near Rajdhani Properties, Prahladpur, Delhi
Ph. : 7894294, 7898001,
Fax : 011-7294598
A Name of Latest Technology Pharma, Chemicals & Mentha Peppermint industry Distillation Plants, High Grade Flake & Crystal Machines, Melting Tanks, Filtration Unit, Crystal Drying Machines, Storage Container, Aluminium Can, etc.

Kemitek Links India (Pvt.) Ltd.
C-33, New Multan Nagar, Rohtak Road, New Delhi - 110 056
Ph. : 0091-11-5587989, 5583128
Fax : 0091-11-5675679
(High Fractional Distillation Units, Reaction Units in Glass & Stainless Steel, Laboratory Equiqments for R & D Units)

Kemitek Links India (P) Ltd.
C-33, New Multan Nagar,
New Delhi- 110 056
Ph. : 0091-11-5587989, 5583128
Fax : 0091-11-5675679
Manufacturers of : Fabricator Designers of Glass Units for Essential Oils & Menthol Industries

Metal Plants
17, Anupam Industrial, Estate No.2
Off. Pt. M.M. Malaviya Marg
Mulund West. Mumbai 400 080
Telefax : 5610628/5654607
E-mail : koppa@bol.net.in
(Distillation plant for Geranium, Citronella & Lemon Grass Oil, PLC Controlled automated Batching/

Blending systems, MS-3 Emulsifiers, Contra Rotary Mixers, Process Equipments : Reactors, Heat Exchangers, Columns, etc.)

Premier Refrigeration Limited
Unit 1-2, Akurli Indl. Estate Akurli Road, Kandivli (E) Mumbai - 400 001
Ph. : 91-22-8870304/8870305
Fax : 91-22-8841275
E-mail : premierchiller@vsnl.com
(Cooler/freezer Etc.)

Prestair Systems P.I.C
H-43, Sector - 9, Nolda 20301
Ph. : 91-914-4538824/4526777
Fax : 91-914-4526777
E-mail : 777@mantraonline.com
(Water Collers, Deep Freezers, Display Trays)

Pooja Steel & Alloys
11, Ardeshir Dady Cross Lane
Pathak Bldg. Office No. 20 Nr. C.P. Tank, Mumbai - 400 004
Ph. : 91-22-3872562/3829630
Fax : 91-22-3829630
E-mail : jayantilal@vsnl.net
(Distillation Plants,
Deep Freezers, etc.)

Kesar Steel Udyog
C-91/9, Wazirpur Industrial Area, Delhi - 110052
Ph. : 7231285, 7131470, 7231287
Fax : (011) 7249960
Manufacturer of : All Sizes Alluminium & Stainless Steel Containers for flex & Bold Crystals

Radhika Containers Pvt. Ltd.
UG-7&8, Padma Tower - II,
22, Rajindra Place,
New Delhi- 110 008
Ph. : 5753877/78,
5761074-75, 5772131
Fax : 011-5758817
Factory : 5476858
(Fibre Drums)

Ruchi Sales Pvt. Ltd.
4233/1 Ansari Road, Darya Ganj,
New Delhi - 110 002
Ph. : 3272757 Fax : 3273173
E-mail: ruchisal@mantraonline.com
Refrigeration & Air Conditioning Spares & Accessories

Swaraj Herbal Exports
Faizabad Road, Barabanki-1 (U.P.)
http://www.swaranjindia.com,
lucknowonline.com/swarajindia
E-mail : herbal@swarajindia.com
Ph. : +91-5248-22792, 23142
Fax : +91-5248-24444, 22569
Specialities in Manufacturing : Hydro and Steam Distillation Unit for Essential Oils, Extraction Unit for Herbal and Medicinal Plants. Solvent Extraction Plant, Agitated Reaction Vessel, Vacuum Concentrator, Fractionating Column, Water Treatment Plant, Stainless Steel Storage Tank.

Sangeeta
Scientific Instruments
2847-B, Sant Nagar, Rani Bagh,
New Delhi - 110034
Ph. : Off : 7016197
Manufacturer of : Distillation Colm. for Mint Products, Essential Oil,

Aromatic Chemicals, Vacuum Stainless Steel Pump, Reaction Vessel, Coloumn Packing Stainless Steel, Storage Tank, Heating Mentles Labs, Heat Exchanger.

Swaraj Fabricators
Faizabad Road
Barabanki - 225001 (U.P.)
Ph. : 22792, 24444, 23142
Fax : +91-5248-24444, 22569
E-mail : swarajindia@yahoo.com
Manufacturer of : Distillation and Extraction Plant, Dairy Equipment, Water Treatment & Solvent Extraction Plant)

Shiva Udyog
Shiv Vihar, Sonepat Road, Sampla
Distt. Rohtak - 124501
Ph. : 01262-63605, 63305
Fax : 01262-63180
(Mfrs. of : Steel Barrels & Cantainers)

Toshiba India
2/2, DsIdc Community
Works Centre -Block Shakurpur,
Delhi - 110 034
Ph. : 7108890, 7184490
Fax : 011-7108890
E-mail : toshiba@del3.vsnl.net.in
Manufacturer of : Refractometer, Moisture Meter, Hardness Tester, Autoclave, Incubator, Oven, Deep Freezer, Cabinet, Etc.

U.S. Enterprises
487/108, Peeragarhi Indl.Area,
Rohtak Road, Delhi- 110 041
Ph. : 5587989, 5583128
Manufacturer of : Menthol Plants, Menthol Essential Plants

Chapter-36

MANUFACTURERS & EXPORTERS OF ESSENTIAL OILS & AROMATIC CHEMICALS

Arovision Industries
B-13, Industrial Estate, Salarpur,
Budaun - 243601
Ph. : (05832) 27696
Fax : (05832) 24746
(Pipper Mint Oil, Terpenes, Menthone, Linalool, Anthole, M. Chavicol etc.)

Aerofarm
Russia, Moscow Staropansky per, 5
Ph./Fax : 095-9250784
(Pharmaceuticals, Perfumery, healthcare Products)

A. T. F. Chem Oils
Near Dharam Kanta Joya Road
Amroha-244221
Distt. J.P. Nagar (U.P.)
C.P. : Mr. Abhinay (Sonu)
Ph. : (O) 51206, 62486
(R) 62386 Fax : 62197
Mobile : 98370 78005
Mfrs. & Supplier of:
Menthol & Flakes, Bold Crystals, D.M.O. & Other Essential Oils

Absolute Aromatics Limited
Regd. Off. ITI Road
Aligarh-202001 (India)
Tel. : 91-571-400995, 402215
Mfrs & Exporters of : Essential Oils & Mint Products, Aromatic Chemicals

Aroma Aromatics & Flavours
67-68-69, Industiral Area
Baddi - 173220 Distt.- Solan (HP)
Ph. : 91-1795-44431
Fax : 91-1795-44430
Offers Specialisty : Aromatics Chemicals for Flavours & Fragrance

Anamica Enterprises
Shanti Kunj Professor Colony
Budaun- 243601 (U.P.)
Ph. : (O) 24041, 25200
Manufacturer & Supplier of : Essential Oils, Aroma Chemicals, Mint Products

Ace Industries
L1, L2, Parasakehra, Indl. Estate
Bareilly - 243502 (U.P.)

Ph. : 480341
Mobile : 98370-30121
Manufacturer of : Mint Products, Peppermint oil (All grades) Aromatic Chemicals.

Ambica Chemicals
Subhash Road, Chandausi - 202412
Ph. : (O) 50606 (R) 51106
Manufacturer & Supplier : Natural Mentha Oil, Natural Menthol, Mentha Bold Crystals, De-Mentholised Oil, Natural Essential Oil.

Ambika Chemicals
Subhash Road
Chandausi - 202412 (U.P.)
Ph. : 50606, 51106
Manufacturer & Supplier of : Natural Menthol, Flakes, D.M.O., Bold Crystals, Basil oil & Essential oils.

Anil Garg S/O Narendra Garg
Moti Bazar, Haridwar - 249401
Distt. Dehradoon (U.P.)
Ph. : 423341,
Mobile : 98370-72295
Deals in : Mentha Oil, Menthol, Bold Crystals, D.M.O. & Other Essential Oils.

Anand Trading & Mfg. Co.
133/148, Block 'O' Kidwai Nagar
Kanpur - 208023 (U.P.)
Ph. : 319288, 273177 Fax : 270164
Manufacturer of : Sandalwood Oil, Nagar Mohta Oil, Rooh Khus, Essential Oil, Natural Indian Attars.

Aggarwal Exports
Bazar Ganj, Sambhal - 244302 (U.P.)
Ph. : 24123, 24321
Sipplier of : Mentha Oil, Menthol, Bold Crystals D.M.O. & Other Essential Oil.

Aroma Chemicals
Siddh Sadan Tabewell Colony
Moradabad - 244001
Ph. : 418960 Fax : 424408
Manufacturers Exporters of : Essential Oils & Menthol Bold Crystal

Aggarwal Exports
B-6, 7&8, Industrial Estate
Rampur - 244901 (U.P.)
Ph. ` : 350188, 351361, 6921919 (Delhi) Fax : 350031, 6921819
Manufacturer & Exporter of : Menthol Crystal IP/BP/USP, Menthol Fine Flkes, Peppermint oil, All Grades Thymol IP/BP/USP Mentha Piperita oil, Liquid Menthol & other Essential oils.

Bush Boake Allen (I) Ltd.
Floral Deck Plaza, 3rd Floor
"B"Wing Off. Midc Central Road
Andheri (East) Mumbai - 400 093
Ph. : 91-22-8236677
Fax : 91-22-8203834/3835
Manufacturer & Marketeers of : Fragrances & Flavours Food Colours & Specility Chemicals

B.D. Aromatics (P) Ltd.
35/A-7, Civil Lines, Chowki Chauraha, Bareilly - 243001 (U.P.)
Tel. : (O) 452596
(F) 475554, 822240
Manfacturere of: Menthol crystals (T.L.), Mint & Basil Isolates, Aromatic Chemicals & Natural Essential oils.

Benzen Trading
483, Lavezares street, Binondo

Manila - 1006
Ph. : 00632-242310, 2431924
Fax : 00632-242307
(Menthol crystal)

Balbir Ratta Sanjeev Kumar
Purani Painth, Bisauli Gate
Chandausi - 202412 (U.P.)
Distt. Moradabad
Ph. : 51706, 52615
Mobile : 9837154104
Broker of : Mentha oil, Flakes, Bold Crystals, D.M.O. & other Essential oils.

Balaji Chemicals & Aromatics
405-B, Kunwarpur
Opp. City Malgodam
Bareilly - 243003 (U.P.)
Ph. : (O) 475081, 576019
(F) 480421
Manufacturer of : Terpene Based, Aroma Chemicals, Essential oils, Mint Products.

Classic Crystals
Arya Samaj Road, Nai Sarai
Sambhal- 244302 (U.P.)
Ph. : 24273, 24275
Manufacturer & Supplier of : Natural Menthol, Bold Crystals & D.M.O.

Cure Chemindia
D-3/3582, Vasant Kunj, New Delhi-110070 (India)
Tel. : (91-11) 6898689
Fax : (91-11) 6139884, 6121756
E-mail : cci@mantraonline.com,rcg@vsnl.com
Manufecturer of : House of Natural Menthol & Essential Oils, Crystal Bold (Export quality) Mint Products For All your Chemical Requirement.

Dee Kay Exports
Shakuntala Bhawan
Malgodam Road, Budaun-243601 (U.P.) Ph. : (O) 24331, 24922, 24883, 24507 Fax : 25085
Manufacturer & Exporter of : Natural Essential Oil, Aromatic Chemicals, Menthol Crystals, D.M.O. & Peppermint Oil.

Durga Chemicals
Ramnaumi Streets
Chandausi - 202412 (U.P.)
Ph. : 50337
Manufacturer & Supplier of : Natural Menthol, Flakes, D.M.O. Bold Crystals & other Essential oils.

D.N. Mentha Products
Akbarpur Mandi
Sambhal - 244302 (U.P.)
Ph. : 24258, 24918
Manufacturer of : Menthol, Crystals, Mentha Oil, D.M.O.

Essence Aromatics
Off. 5-4-187/3&4, 3rd Floor
M.G. Road,
Secunderabad - 500 003 (A.P.)
Ph. : 7543658, 7544058, 7541729
E-mail : info@ea-menthol.com
Deals in : Natural Menthol, Bold Crystal, D.M.O. & other Essential Oils

En-Chem Products
Fact. : Kote East Sambhal (U.P.)
Ph. : 05923-24650
(Manufacturer & Exporter of Mentha Oil, Natural Menthol Bold Crystals)

Ever Green Aromatics Pvt. Ltd.
6-A, Industrial Estate, Roshan Bagh
Civil Lines, Rampur-244901 (U.P.)

Ph. : 350184, 350190
E-mail :
evergreen@del5.vsnl.net.in
Manufacturer of : Peppermint oil (All grades), Liquid Menthol, Mint Terpenes, Menthone, Linalool Menthyl Chavicole, M. Piperita, M. Citrata, Spearmint. Anethole, Cis-3 Hexenol, 3 Octonol.

Flotech
Government College Road
Pilibhit - 262001 (U.P.) Ph. : 42983
Fax : 05882-43309
Export in : Automation for Essential Oil Plant

Ghaziabad Aromatics
Devi Mandir Compound, Delhi Gate
Ghaziabad - 201001 (U.P.)
Ph. : 732377, 734967
Manufacturer of : Essential oils, Peppermint oil, Menthone, Thymol, Hexinol, Anithole, M. Chevicol Linalool.

Gupta Enterprises
Near State Bank of India
Main Branch, Civil Lines
Budaun-243601 (U.P.)
Supplier of Mentha Oil, Menthol Crystals, Peppermint Oil, Essential Oil, Basil Oil, Piperita Oil & Spearmint Oil

Glorious Perfumes Centre Pvt. Ltd.
608, 609, 6th floor,
"City Centre" 63/2
The Mall, Kanpur - 208001 (U.P.)
Ph. : 354528, 313483, 317343
Fax : 90-512-313977
Tix : 325-285 SKYP AL-OBAID IN
Gram : AL-OBAID
Manufacturer & Exporter, Importer of : Perfumes, Cosmetics

Indira Dinesh Chemicals
131, HSIC Industrial Estate
Kundli (Sonepat) Haryana - 131028
C.P. : Dinesh Sharma
Ph. : 01264-470123, 701131
Fax : 91-11-6830158
E-mail : idchem@vsnl.com
Webpage : http:/dinesh.vsnl.com/
menthol Manufacturer of : Menthol Oil 50%, Menthol Flakes I.P., Menthol Oil 50% Menthol Flakes I.P., Menthol Crystals I.P./B.P./U.S.P., Menthol Crystals Terpeneless, H Menthone, L-Menthol Spearmint Oil, Piperita Oil, Basil Oil, Aniseed Oil and other Aromatic Products & Essential Oils

Indian Herbs Extractions
Painth Parao, Behind S.B.I.
Ram Nagar - 244715
Distt. Nainital (U.P.)
Ph. : 51423, 51246
Fax : 05947-51456
Manufacturer & Exporter of : Natural Menthol, Menthol Flakes, Bold Crystals (Terpeneless) BP/USP/IP, Peppermint oil, Menthone, Thymol & other Essential oils.

Irving R. Boody & Co.
11 Penn Plaza, Suite 310
New York, NY 10001
Ph. : 212-947-3800
Facsimile : 212-947-8301/2
E-mail : info@body.com
Specializing in finished and unfinished fabrics, Natural Menthol/Essential Oils and Natural and Synthetic Fibers.

Jugal Kishor Rajeev Kishor
Kuncha Parameshwari Dass
Bara Bazar, Rampur - 244901 (U.P.)
Ph. : 340418
Broker of : Mentha oil, Flakes, Bold Crystals, D.M.O. & Other Essential Oils.

Jai Durga Chemicals
C-408, Rajendra Nagar,
Bareilly - 243122 (U.P.)
Ph. (O) (0581) 449214
Fact. : (05821) 74947
Mobile : 98370-43782
Manfacturer & Distiller of: Natural Essential Oils, Menthol Flakes, Bold-Crystals, De-Mentholised Oil

Jayant Shafts Pvt. Ltd.
B-136, Phase-II, Noida - 201301
Distt- Ghaziabad (U.P.)
Ph. : 91-568525
Manufacturer & Supplier of : Natural Menthol, Bold Crystals & Essential Oils

Kaizen Organics Pvt. Ltd.
G-6, Amber Tower, S.C. Road
Jaipur - 302001
Ph. : 91-141-375230, 379641
Fax : 91-141-383461
Mobile : 098290 13111
Manufacturer & Exporter of : Natural Menthol & Allied Products

Menthol & Allied Products
Fact. : F-26/1, B.S. Road, Indl. Area, Site - 1, Ghaziabad - 201009 (U.P.)
Ph. : (O) 0120-4700257, 4700442, 4701995
Fax : 0120-4700257
E-mail : menthol@satyam.net.in
Manufacturer of : Peppermint Oil (All Grades)
Menthone, L-Menthol, Anethole, Linalool & other Essential Oil

Malayagiri Sandal Wood Oil Distillery
105/696, Kalpi Road
(Bhannana Purwa)
Kanpur - 208003 (U.P.)
Ph. : 546579, 313680
(F) 295730, 297708
Fax : 319556
Manufacturer of : Sanadalwood Oils, Agmarked Quality & Other Essential Oils.

Mohit Chemicals
Jharna Essential Oils
Agarwal Enterprises Shakuntala Bhawan, Malgodam Road
Budaun-243601 (U.P.)
Ph. : (O) 24331, 24922, 24883, 24507 Fax : 25085
Manufacturer, Distiller & Exporter of: Peppermint Oil, Menthol Bold & Small, Crystals, D.M.O. Mentha Oil, M. Piperita Oil, Spearmint Oil, Anethole, Indian Basil Oil, Citrata Oil, Jamrosa

Menthol & Allied Products
F-26/1, B.S. Road
Industrial Area, Site 1
Ghaziabad - 201009 (U.P.)
Ph. : 700257 Fax : 700257
Manufacturer of : Peppermint Oil, Menthone, Thymol, Liquid Menthol, Anethole, Linalool, M.Chavicol & Other Essential Oils.

Mentha & Allied Products Ltd.
Rahe - Raza Road, Civil Lines
Rampur - 244901 (U.P.)

Ph. : 350855, 350404 Fax : 350046
Manufacturer & Exporter of : Natural Menthol, Bold Crystals (Terpenless) Mint Products, Essential oil & Aromatic Chemicals.

Mint Port
D-24-27, Harthala, Industrial Estate
Moradabad - 244001 (U.P.)
Ph. : (0591) 50754
350799, 351708
Fax : (0591) 350896, 351743
E-mail : quality@del2.vsnl.net.in

Mentha & Allied Products Ltd.
Munshi Niketan 1/10, Asaf Ali Road,
New Delhi - 110 002
Ph. : (91-11) 323-1614, 1655
8356, 8993
Fax : (91-11) 323 1189
E-mail : mentha@del2.vsnl.net.in
Website : www.mentha.com
(Menthol, Pepper mint
Oil, Menthones)

Narain Terpene & Allied Chemicals
Gajraula - Chandpur Road,
Mandi Dhanaura - 244231
Distt. Jyotiba Phule Nagar (U.P.)
Tel.: (O) 73095, 73241, 73328
(R) 73090, 73251
Fax : 73328

Ninniku Exports Pvt. Ltd.
56, Industrial Estate,
Mandsaur - 458001 (M.P.)
Ph. : Deals in : Garlic Flakes & Powder, Withania Somnifera Root Dry Extract. Soya Dry Extract, Trigonella Foenum Graecum, Garlic Oil & Garlic Oleoresin

Naini Essential Oils & Chemicals
Main Bazar, Shastri Nagar
P.O. Bazpur- 262401
Distt.- Udham Singh Nagar (U.P.)
Ph. : (O) 88465,88359
Fax : 88135
Manufacturer & Supplier of : Natural Essential oil, Mint Products, Aromatic Chemicals.

Nova - Interholod
Moscow, ul. Varvarka- 14
Abu Dhabi, U.A.E.
Ph./Fax : 095-2985940 (Tabacoo)

Neeru Enterprises
6, Saleem Manzil, Civil Lines
Rampur - 244901 (U.P.)
Ph. : 350829 Fax : 350023
Manufacturer & Exporters of : Mentha Oil, Menthol, Flakes, Bold Crystals, D.M.O., Peppermint Oil, Spearmint Oil, Basil Oil, Davana Oil & Other Essential Oils.

Orissa Fragrances
74, Saraswati Nagar, University Road, Gwalior - 474011 (MP)
Ph. : 0751-340381, 60289
Leading Manufacturers of : Keora Gulab Shamama & All kind of Indian Natural Flower Perfumes, Natural Menthol, Bold Crystal (Terpineless)

Prince Enterprises
Admn. Off.: 38, A.C. Basement
Anand Cloth Market
Sarangpur Bridge
Ahmedabad- 380 002
Ph.: (R) 7506458, 6425430
(O) 2140829
Fax : 079-7508642

Deals in : Menthol, Thymol, Bras kappur, Pippermint Oil, Camphor, D.M.O., Mercury, Noshadar, Rosin, Spearmint, Pipereta, Anethole, Liquid Menthol, Eucalyptus Oil, Methyl saliclicate, Herbs & Sherbs, Paraffin Wax & all type of Menthol Products & Essential.

Progressive Enterprises
Shastri Nagar, Main Bazar
P.O. Bazpur-262401
Distt. - Udham Singh Nagar (U.P.)
Ph. : 88489, 88030 Fax : 88465
Mobile : 098370 36504
098370 47647
Manufacturer & Supplier of : Mint Products, Essential Oils & Aromatic Chemicals, Bold Crystals

Pragati Aroma Oil Distillers (P) Ltd.
Hargovind Das & Sons, 2/6, Anand Bhawan, 17, Babu Genu Road
Princes Street, Mumbai - 400 002
Ph. : 8911088, 2016509
Fax : 8903260, 2072599
E-mail : hindoil@bom3.vsnl.net.in
Manufacturer & Exporter of : Indian Attars Distillers of Sandal Wood Oil And Other Essential Oils

Quality Aromatic Pvt. Ltd.
40, Court Road, Civil Lines
Rampur - 244901 (U.P.)
Ph. : 350869, 350543
Manufacturer & Exporter of : Natural Essential oils & Aromatic Chemicals.
Rati Enterprises
C-3 & 4, Roshan Bagh

Industrial Estate
Rampur - 244901 (U.P.)
Ph. : 350188, 351361
Fax : (0595) 350031
Manufacturer & Exporter of : Menthol Crystal (IP/BP/USP), Menthol Fine Flakes, Peppermint Oil (All Grades), Tymol IP.BP.USP., M. Piperita Oil, Liquid Menthol & other Essential Oils.

Rakesh Kumar Jain
Shahukara, Near Jain Dharmshala
Ujhani - 243639, Distt-Budaun (U.P.)
Ph. : 62343
Deals in : Menthol, Essential Oils

Rakesh Kumar Pradeep Kumar
Miston Ganj, Rampur - 244901 (U.P.)
Ph. : 340389
Broker of : Mentha oil, Flakes, Bold Crystals, D.M.O. & other Essential oils.

Shri Nath Chemicals
Kantth Road, Amroha - 244221
Distt. J.P. Nagar (U.P.)
C.P. Mr. Sanjay Agrawal
Ph. (O) 63326, 63272
Mfrs. & Supplier of : Natural Menthol, Bold Crystal, D.M.O. & Essential Oils

Sarman Industries
A-37, Gandhi Nagar
Moradabad-244001 (U.P.)
Ph. : (0591) 493544, 492544
Fax : (0591) 492187
E-mail : sarman@nde.vsnl.net.in
Manufacturer & Exporter of : Menthol, Peppermint Oil, Essential Oils

Shree Nathji Mentha Commission Agent
Dispensary Road
Chandausi - 202412 (U.P.)
Ph.: 51566, 51606

Mobile : 98370-09056, 98370-56750
Manufacturers, Supplier Comm. Agent : Mentha Oil, Menthol, Bold Crystals, D.M.O. & other Essential Oils

Sanjeev Kumar Vikas Kumar
Peer Mohalla, Purani, Painth
Chandausi - 202412 (U.P.)
Distt. Moradabad
Ph. : 51000, 50808
Broker of: Mentha oil, Flakes, Bold Crystals & D.M.O.

Shree Krishna Aashirwad
45, Saubhavya Apartment
Plot # 19/11, Sector-9, Rohini
New Delhi - 110085
Ph. : 91-11-7052975
Fax : 91-11-7040716
E-mail : radhika1@del3.vsnl.net.in

Snow Stic (India)
B-140, Sector-2, Noida
Ph. : 91-45550421
Manufacturers of : Terpeneless Menthol, Bold Crystals

Som Extracts
Som Shanti House 152, Patpar Ganj Industrial Estate, Delhi - 110 092
Ph. : 2148207, 2143195
Fax : 2143066,
E-mail : som@ndb.vsnl.net.in
(Essential oils, Aroma Chemical, Resinoids, Carrier Oils)

Suneel Kumar Goel
Off : Kaith Wali Maszid
Rampur - 244901 (U.P.)
Ph. : 310089, 326168
Deals in : Mentha Oil, Menthol, Flakes, Bold Crystals, D.M.O. & other Essential Oils

Surendra Traders
(Fact.& Off.) Ganj Road
Sambhal - 244302
Distt. - Moradabad (U.P.)
Ph. : 24919, 24336
Fax : 05923-24826, 24455
Manufacturer & Supplier of : Mentha Oil, Menthol, Bold Crystals, D.M.O. & Other Essential Oils

Shail Herbal & Alied Products
Fact. : 44 Km. Bareilly Road
P.O. Modipur, Rampur - 244926
Ph. : 353932
Fax : (0595) 352314, 352331
Manufacturers of : L. Menthol (Any grade), Menthone (95%+, 98%+), Cis-3 Hexenol, Mint Terpenes & other Essential Oils, PP Oil (All grade)

Tarun Chemical Company
266, Katra Peran, Tilak Bazar
Delhi - 110006
Ph. : 3963211m 3910169
Fax : 3963211
Deals in : Caustic Soda, Flakes, Sodium Sulphate,
Distributor of : Grasim Inds Ltd. for Annhydrous Sodium Sulphate & Coustic Soda Flakes

United Chemicals
44, Budaun Road (Near Petrol Pump)
Chandausi - 202412 (U.P.)
Ph. : 50786, 51786, 50656
Mobile : 9837040764, 98370 41999
Manufacturer & Supplier of : Natural

Menthol, Menthol Flakes, Bold Crystals, D.M.O. & Essential oils.

Vishal Essential Oils & Chemicals

H.O : C-44A, West Jyoti Nagar
(Near Gopal Nurshing Home)
Shahdara, Delhi - 110094
Ph. : 2280185 Fax : 2111441

Our Manufacturing Products : Peppermint oil, Thymol, Anethole 99.6%, Cedar Wood Oil, Linalool, Menthol (Crystal), Clove (Rect.), Spearmint Oil, M. Chavicol, Menthyl Acctate, Terpenyl Acetate, Phenyl Acetic Acid, Essential Oils & Aromatic Chemicals

Vishal Essential Oils & Chemicals

B.O. : 316, Swadeshi Market Bldg.
2nd Floor, Room No. 195
Kalbadevi Road, Mumbai - 400 002
Ph. : 2054011

Manufacturing Products : Peppermint Oil, Thymol, Anethole 99.6%, Cedar Wood Oil, Linalool, Menthol (Crystal), Clove (Rect.), Spearmint Oil, M. Chavicol, Menthyl Acetate, Terpenyl Acetate, Phenyl Acetic Acid, Essential Oils & Aromatic Chemicals